The
EVERYTHING®
Understanding Islam Book

Dear Reader:

For the past several years, I've hosted an Internet community where people learn about Islam, ask questions, and make friends. Millions have turned to this Web site, located at *http://islam.about.com;* some visit because they are seeking information, others want to voice their opinions, and yet others are there to vent their anger.

I've heard just about every opinion, idea, and question there is about Islam, from matters of daily living to complex political ideologies. What I've found is that most people, even the angry ones, want to understand. Deep down they realize that Islam, indeed any religion, could never preach hatred and violence. This book comprises my honest answers, based on my experience and understanding, about what Islam is and what Muslims feel is important about their faith.

My hope is that you will come away with a better understanding of what Islam means to the people who actually practice the faith. May this book be a beginning, not an end, to your search for understanding.

Christine Huda Dodge

The EVERYTHING® Series

Editorial

Publishing Director	Gary M. Krebs
Managing Editor	Kate McBride
Copy Chief	Laura MacLaughlin
Acquisitions Editor	Bethany Brown
Development Editor	Julie Gutin
Production Editor	Khrysti Nazzaro

Production

Production Director	Susan Beale
Production Manager	Michelle Roy Kelly
Series Designers	Daria Perreault
	Colleen Cunningham
Cover Design	Paul Beatrice
	Frank Rivera
Layout and Graphics	Colleen Cunningham
	Rachael Eiben
	Michelle Roy Kelly
	Daria Perreault
	Erin Ring
Series Cover Artist	Barry Littmann
Interior Photographs	©2001 Brand X Pictures

Visit the entire Everything® Series at everything.com

THE
EVERYTHING®
UNDERSTANDING
ISLAM BOOK

A complete and easy-to-read
guide to Muslim beliefs, practices,
traditions, and culture

Christine Huda Dodge

Adams Media Corporation
Avon, Massachusetts

An Everything® Series Book.
Everything® and everything.com® are registered trademarks of F+W Publications, Inc.

Published by Adams Media, an F+W Publications Company
57 Littlefield Street, Avon, MA 02322 U.S.A.
www.adamsmedia.com

ISBN 13: 978-1-58062-783-2
ISBN 10: 1-58062-783-8
Printed in the United States of America.

J   I   H   G   F   E   D

Library of Congress Cataloging-in-Publication Data
Dodge, Christine Huda.
The everything understanding Islam book / by Christine Huda Dodge.
p.   cm.   -- (An everything® series book)
Includes index.
ISBN 1-58062-783-8
1. Islam. 2. Islam–Doctrines. 3. Islam–Essence, genius, nature.
I. Title. II. Series. Everything series.
BP161.2 .D63   2003
297–dc21   2002014685

This publication is designed to provide accurate and authoritative information with
regard to the subject matter covered. It is sold with the understanding that the pub-
lisher is not engaged in rendering legal, accounting, or other professional advice.
If legal advice or other expert assistance is required, the services of a competent
professional person should be sought.
        —From a *Declaration of Principles* jointly adopted by a Committee of the
American Bar Association and a Committee of Publishers and Associations

Many of the designations used by manufacturers and sellers to distinguish their
products are claimed as trademarks. Where those designations appear in this book
and Adams Media was aware of a trademark claim, the designations have been
printed with initial capital letters.

This book is available at quantity discounts for bulk purchases.
For information, call 1-800-289-0963.

Contents

Acknowledgments

This book would not have been possible without the wisdom and assistance of brother Mohammed Siala, and the support and sacrifice of my husband, Faris.

Top Ten Interesting Facts about Islam

1. The first (and most important) of the six articles of Islamic faith is the faith in the One Almighty God.

2. Allah ("God" in Arabic) is the formal way of addressing God.

3. The holiest site in Islam is Mecca (in present-day Saudi Arabia).

4. Islam does not advocate forced conversion; the term jihad (holy struggle) may represent an inner spiritual conflict.

5. Five pillars of Islamic practice are the declaration of faith, daily prayer, the fast of Ramadan, giving alms, and a pilgrimage to Mecca.

6. According to Islam, Jesus Christ was a prophet of God and a man to be revered.

7. Moslems believe that after death each soul will be judged according to its deeds and will receive the award of eternal paradise or the punishment of Hellfire.

8. Islam does not advocate subjugation of women; men and women are equal in the eyes of God.

9. Moslems do not eat pork and cannot drink alcohol.

10. Because of strict laws against idolatry, traditional Islamic art avoided images of humans or animals.

Introduction

▶WHEN EXPLORING ANY FAITH, it's important to look at the totality of its teachings: its holy texts, its prophets, the history of its early faith community, and the interpretations of its modern scholars. And to do so, you need to understand what the basic terms of that faith actually are.

The word "Islam," at its core, means "peaceful worship of and submission to One Almighty God." Those who believe in and practice Islam are known as Muslims, or "those who find peace through trusting submission to and worship of God Alone." Muslims share their belief in one God with the other two monotheistic faiths, Judaism and Christianity. Today, one in five people on earth consider themselves Muslim.

From small and humble beginnings 1,400 years ago, the Muslim community expanded to cover three continents and some of the greatest empires of ancient history. As the foundation for one of the most advanced intellectual and cultural environments of all time, Islam was the embodiment of tolerance, scholarship, and justice. Indeed, it was Muslim leadership that helped to propel Europe out of the Dark Ages and into the modern era.

Today, however, Islam finds itself within its own Dark Ages. Muslims are often associated with extremism, violence, and intolerance; their beliefs are misunderstood and even despised. Lately, Islam has come under a lot of public scrutiny in the West. What do Muslims really believe, anyway? Does Allah want or need

Muslims to kill innocent people in His name? What is jihad all about? Do the Muslim perpetrators of terrorist acts have a justifiable understanding of the faith? How can anyone ever believe that mass murder is a "holy" undertaking?

It's easy to paint all Muslims with the same brush of mistrust, hatred, or pity. It's much more challenging to try to learn, understand, and come to appreciate the Muslim way of life. We must remember that criminals do not represent the worldwide community of Muslims, any more than Charles Manson represents the best that America has to offer. Most Muslims are not the rigid, fanatical followers of a false god they are sometimes portrayed to be. The Muslim world is as diverse as any, from Chinese rice farmers to Bosnian steelworkers, from Indonesian fishermen to Tuareg nomads. What unites all these diverse people in brotherhood is their common faith—faith in God, mercy, equity, and pious humility.

The Everything® *Understanding Islam Book* will help you learn about Islam and the people who practice this faith, and will surely answer the many questions you have about this religion. Whether you have a Muslim friend, neighbor, relative, or coworker, or simply want to better understand the issues of the day, this book is for you! Ⓔ

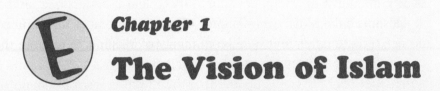

Chapter 1
The Vision of Islam

Islam is a faith based in peace and submission to God, in accordance with the teachings of His prophets. Central to the faith is a strict monotheism: a belief that there is One Almighty God, the Creator of all that is. The aim of the Islamic lifestyle is to live life in keeping with this belief.

What Islam Is All About

The word "Islam" is an Arabic word that means peace, security, and surrender—a person who believes in and follows Islam is called a Muslim, "one who peacefully surrenders to God." Muslims believe that by practicing their faith through submission to God alone, they can achieve peace and security in their lives.

Muslims believe that there is One Almighty God, who sends prophets through time to communicate His message to mankind. In fact, Muslims accept all of the biblical prophets of old, including Noah, Abraham, Moses, and Jesus. Muslims believe that their faith is a confirmation of the messages that these prophets brought: to believe in One Almighty God and to follow (submit to) His guidance. Muslims are commanded to say: "We believe in God, and the revelation given to us, and to Abraham, Ismail, Isaac, Jacob, and the Tribes, and that given to Moses and Jesus, and that given to all prophets from their Lord. We make no difference between one and another of them, and we submit to God" (2:136).

ALERT!

"Islam" is the name of the religion, and a person who practices it is known as a Muslim. The adjective "Islamic" usually refers to objects or places, not people. The term "Mohammedism" is an outdated, insulting name for the faith.

There are an estimated 1.2 billion Muslims in the world today—nearly one-fifth of the world's population—making Islam the second-largest faith community (Christianity being the world's largest). Muslims are to be found among virtually all ethnic groups, nationalities, and countries. Although often associated with the Arab world, fewer than 15 percent of Muslims are Arab.

The Essence of Islam

The essence of Islam can be summarized in the following words of God, which were reported to us by Muhammad.

O My servants, I have forbidden oppression for Myself and have made it forbidden amongst you, so do not oppress one another.

O My servants, all of you are astray except those I have guided, so seek guidance of Me and I shall guide you.

O My servants, all of you are hungry except for those I have fed, so seek food of Me and I shall feed you.

O My servants, all of you are naked except for those I have clothed, so seek clothing of Me and I shall clothe you.

O My servants, you sin by night and by day, and I forgive all sins, so seek forgiveness of Me and I shall forgive you.

O My servants, you will not attain harming Me so as to harm Me, and will not attain benefiting Me as to benefit Me.

O My servants, were the first of you and the last of you, the human of you and the jinn of you, to be as pious as the most pious heart of any one of you, that would not increase my Kingdom in anything.

O My servants, were the first of you and the last of you, the human of you and the jinn of you, to be as wicked as the most wicked heart of any one of you, that would not decrease my Kingdom in anything.

O My servants, were the first of you and the last of you, the human of you and the jinn of you, to rise up in one place and make a request of Me, and were I to give everyone what he requested, that would not decrease what I have, any more than a needle decreases the sea if put into it.

O My servants, it is but your deeds that I reckon up for you and then recompense you for. So let him who finds good, praise God; and let him who finds other than that, blame no one but himself.

Core Islamic Beliefs

Despite the diversity of the Muslim world, there are central tenets of the faith that all believers uphold. The cornerstone of Islam is an absolute faith in One Almighty God, and the fierce rejection of false gods and idols. Stemming from this faith is a commitment to the unity of mankind, and recognition of the unified message revealed by God's prophets throughout time.

Oneness of God

It is hard to overemphasize the Muslim devotion to the One Almighty God, Who created and sustains all that is in the heavens and on earth. Islam represents the total commitment to God—Muslims worship only Him, and believe that He alone is the Lord. Muslims reject any notion that God shares divinity with any other thing.

Muslims prefer not to use the word "God," since it is not considered a unique name—it can be changed to "gods," "goddesses," "god-awful," and so on. Instead, Muslims use the name Allah, which they believe to be the unique name of the One Almighty God. For the purposes of this book, the terms Allah and God will be used interchangeably.

In Islam, God is believed to be Merciful, Forgiving, Just, and Fair. Nobody has ever seen Him, but He can see and hear everything. He has power over all things, and there is no intermediary needed to become close to Him.

Oneness of Mankind

Muslims believe in the absolute wisdom of God, and His power over all creation. Thus, Muslims are not in a position to question God about the diversity in the world, or to arrogantly claim that they are better than other people. Islam makes it very clear that all people are created equal in the sight of God, and that individuals are not to be judged on factors that they had no control over. The Prophet Muhammad once said, "You are all from Adam, and Adam was created from dust. No individual is superior to another, except in faith and piety." In Islam, human diversity is a sign of the magnificence of God's creation.

The equality of all people extends to all aspects of spiritual life. In Islam, there is no priesthood, nor does any one person or class have special "access" to God. All stand equal before God, able to receive His guidance, mercy, and blessings.

Oneness of the Message

Muslims believe that God is unique and unchanging. His laws and guidance have been the same throughout time. Islam teaches that God sent prophets to communities all over the world, to repeat the eternal message: Believe in God, and follow His guidance. Thus, Muslims believe that Islam (peaceful submission to God) is the original teaching that God gave to all nations.

Muslims also recognize that throughout history, there have been those who followed the message, and those who rejected it. Islam acknowledges an individual's right to choose faith or not. Nobody must ever be forced to follow the message.

ALERT!

Islam is often portrayed as a forceful religion: Accept Islam or die. This is both historically inaccurate, and fundamentally contrary to the faith's teachings. The Qur'an, the holy Islamic text that contains Allah's revelation to the Prophet Muhammad, states very clearly: "Let there be no compulsion in religion" (2:256).

Who Is Allah?

According to Islam, God was the initiator of all Creation, the God of all time and all places. God has no partners or intermediaries, and nobody shares in His power. In Islam, this Almighty deity is referred to by His proper name, Allah.

Attributes of God

In Islam, God is understood by His characteristics and attributes. According to Islamic tradition, there are over ninety-nine such attributes that are used to describe God. For instance, God is:

- Al-Khaliq, the Creator
- Al-Rahman, the Merciful
- Al-Qudoos, the Holy One
- As-Salaam, the Source of Peace
- Al-Aziz, the Mighty, Strong
- Al-Razzaaq, the Sustainer, Provider
- Al-Aleem, the All-Knowing
- Al-Ghafoor, the All-Forgiving
- Al-Wadood, the Loving

These and other attributes of God help a Muslim to better understand his or her Creator, to know Him, and to approach Him in love and humility.

Up Close and Personal

Muslims believe that God is close to us; He knows our innermost thoughts, feelings, and fears. God is described as being closer to us than our "jugular vein" (Qur'an 50:16). He hears our prayers: "When My servants ask you concerning Me, I am indeed close (to them). I respond to the prayer of every supplicant when he calls on Me. Let them also, with a will, Listen to My call, and believe in Me, that they may walk in the right way" (Qur'an 2:186). He accepts our repentance and grants forgiveness: "But without a doubt, I am He that forgives again and again, to those who repent, believe, and do right. Those who, in truth, are on true guidance" (Qur'an 20:82).

Muhammad once related that God said: "When I love him, I am his hearing with which he hears, his seeing with which he sees, his hand with which he strikes and his foot with which he walks. Were he to ask something of Me, I would surely give it to him, and were he to ask Me for refuge, I would surely grant him it."

While God is close to us, Muslims approach God with reverence and respect, not as a "buddy." God is Merciful and Loving, but we also have a duty toward Him. If we are neglectful of our duty, or reject faith in Him, we have much to be concerned about. God is Merciful, but also Just. Muslims speak of God with awe and respect, and do not joke around about matters of faith.

The Islamic Lifestyle

In Islam, religion is a complete way of life, not just a spiritual yearning. When a person believes that God has created the world and has sent guidance to human beings, it naturally follows that a believer should follow His guidance. Islam provides an entire spiritual and social structure that regulates believers in every aspect of their lives: whom they marry, how they conduct business relations, what they say when praying, how they relate to their neighbors, and so on.

Muslims do not describe Islam as a religion. Rather, it is a *deen*, which comes from the Arabic for "way of life," "conviction," or "creed." Muslims contend that Islam is more than a religious belief—it is a way of living in accordance with one's religious faith.

Muslims believe that God's guidance in all matters, spiritual and physical, is a blessing so that life on earth will be harmonious and peaceful. After all, the One who created us knows what is best for us.

Focus on Faith

If you get to know an average Muslim family or individuals, you will probably find them to be humble and spiritual people. They help their neighbors and the poor, they work hard to take care of their families, and they turn to God for guidance and mercy throughout the day. Muslims pray five times each and every day, as a way of taking a break from the daily grind of life and to refocus. Prayer is the first thing they do upon rising, and the last thing they do before retiring for the night. Words of prayer and praise fall readily off a Muslim's lips, even during mundane conversation. Muslims try to be ever mindful of God's blessings, His mercy, and our obligations to Him as believers.

Focus on Family

After God, Muslims turn their attention to their families. Muslims believe in a strong family unit, which often extends beyond the nuclear family to include other relatives. Muslims are dutiful to their parents, lovingly discipline their children, and care for the ill and the elderly. In Islam, the emphasis is on community and family harmony.

Muslims also count among their family members their "brothers and sisters" in faith. The bonds of brotherhood/sisterhood are very strong in the Muslim community, so much so that every adult woman is an "auntie" and every adult male is an "uncle" to the community's children. The Muslim community forms a nation that Muhammad describes as "one body"—if one part of the body falls ill, the rest pitches in to compensate. He also described the community as bricks in a building, supporting each other as they work together cooperatively toward a common goal.

A Lifestyle of Moderation

Islam teaches people to be moderate in their lives, not falling into one extreme or another. Muslims pray and seek guidance from God, but also tend to mundane matters of life. They pray during the night, but also have time to sleep and get a good night's rest. Muslims spend time in fasting, but also eat. There is no monasticism in Islam; balance and moderation are key.

Islam discourages extremism in either direction. Muhammad once said, "Religion is very easy, and whoever overburdens himself in his religion will not be able to continue in that way. So you should not be extremists. Rather, try to be near to perfection, and receive good tidings that you will be rewarded."

Islamic View of the World

Muslims believe that God is the Creator of all that is in the heavens and on earth. In this Creation, God set up systems and laws that must be obeyed in order for all life to continue in harmony. The rain and water cycle, the phases of the moon, the gravitational pull—everything that one might consider to be "natural laws" of the world—is ordained by God.

The teachings of Islam emphasize the harmony of the natural world, and call upon people to reflect on the source of natural law. Everything has been put in order, down to the minutest detail. Muslims see evidence of God in all things, from the complex human brain to the intricate order of the galaxies; to Muslims, the complexity of the natural world is evidence of the existence of an All-Knowing Creator. Muslims believe that because God created the universe in His wisdom, the balance of His Creation must not be disrupted.

Muslims believe that everything on earth that follows God's natural law is "muslim," in the sense that it obeys God's will. The air, the wind, the trees, the animals, and all other things obey not by choice, but by their nature or instinct. Human beings are different in that they may *choose* to obey.

Islam teaches that human beings have a special responsibility toward the earth and all things on it. We have a duty to preserve the order that God has created, to be His "vicegerents on earth" (Qur'an 2:30). It is a sad fact that most human beings, as the Qur'an remarks, "transgress beyond all bounds" (96:6).

Islam and Other Faiths

Muslims may seem strange or foreign to the average Westerner, whose religious faith is probably not a part of his or her daily life. However, Muslims themselves feel that their faith is part of the same monotheistic tradition as Christianity and Judaism. The three Abrahamic faiths share many of the same prophets, beliefs, and historical accounts. Muslims generally try to focus on the similarities, and engage in respectful dialogue with believers of other monotheistic religions.

Father Abraham

Islam recognizes Abraham as "a man of truth, a prophet" (Qur'an 19:41). Muslims respect his legacy, and believe that they are following in his footsteps of faith. Abraham rejected all types of polytheism, and called upon the people to worship God Alone. Muslims believe that he, and other prophets, preached the message of Islam.

FACT

Muslims point out that Abraham lived before there was any such thing as Judaism or Christianity. They claim that Abraham, like all other prophets, submitted his will to God, believed in Him, and followed His guidance, actions that are the essence of Islam.

Some people mistakenly assume that Islam came into existence in the seventh century of the Common Era (C.E.), inspired by the message of the Prophet Muhammad. But Muslims believe that Islam—peaceful submission to God—was the message of Abraham, and all other prophets, including Muhammad, sent to guide mankind. Islam calls upon Muslims to do the following: "Say: 'Verily, my Lord has guided me to a way that is straight, a religion of right, the path trod by Abraham, the true in faith. And he certainly did not join other gods with God'" (Qur'an 6:161).

Muslims, Christians, Jews

Islam teaches that those of the Jewish or Christian faith are "People of the Book," meaning those who have received previous prophets and scriptures. Muslims respect the prophets of Judaism and Christianity, and believe that the faiths share the same original teachings.

Muslims are to speak to Jewish and Christian believers with words of respectful advice, and try to find common ground. Islam teaches that Muslims should say, "Oh People of the Book! Come to common terms between us and you: That we worship none but God, that we associate no partners with Him, that we do not erect, from among ourselves, Lords and patrons other than God . . ." (Qur'an 3:64). Islam calls upon all people to engage in respectful dialogue, seek the signs of God in the natural world, and reflect on His message throughout time.

QUESTION?

Do Muslims hate "unbelievers"?
No. Muslims recognize the truth in the messages of previous prophets, and respect them. They may disagree with a person's politics, behaviors, or beliefs, but Islam calls upon them to look at people as individuals, be tolerant, and engage in polite dialogue.

However, Islam teaches that followers of Christianity and Judaism have digressed from the teachings of God. While their origins were pure, their beliefs and practices today are corrupted forms of the faith that all prophets preached.

Chapter 2

The Diverse Muslim World

Muslims are found in all corners of the earth, and represent a wide variety of cultures and regions. Islam allows all of these diverse people to form one faith community that crosses all racial, ethnic, gender, linguistic, and political boundaries. Muslims are united solely by their faith, and fully embrace the diversity of their community.

The Muslim Community

The Muslim community of believers is called an *ummah,* a word that stems from the Arabic root word for "mother" and "nation." Muslims strongly believe that they are family to one another, and there is a strong brotherhood and sisterhood among the faithful. The Qur'an encourages Muslims to unite in faith: "Verily this ummah [community] of yours is a single ummah, and I am your Lord and Cherisher" (Qur'an 23:52).

Brotherhood of Believers

Muslims take their relationships with other Muslims very seriously. The brotherhood of Islam is a very deep concept based on faith, and it supersedes even strong blood and family relations. The Prophet Muhammad once told his followers that Muslims should be like one body; if one part of it falls ill, the rest of the body suffers along with it.

FACT

The Qur'an declares that "the believers are but a single brotherhood, so make peace and reconciliation between your two opposing brothers" (49:10). Traditionally, two Muslims who are at odds with each other are to make peace within three days, and not let disagreements fester.

It is often difficult for people to understand the strong sense of brotherhood felt within the Muslim community. It is not intended to be exclusionary, pitting "us" against "them." Rather, Muslims feel that they naturally have more in common with people who share their faith and outlook on the world. Most Muslims welcome friends and colleagues of all religions and viewpoints, and extend help and support to people in need, regardless of religious affiliation. However, when push comes to shove, Muslims tend to turn to each other for support and advice, knowing that their Muslim brothers and sisters share their values and religious teachings. Muslims feel a sense of duty to render assistance to all people, but especially to their brothers and sisters in faith.

Human Equality

In a compelling verse, the Qur'an makes clear that people are equal in worth, and that a person's wealth, color, or language does not make one better than another. "Oh mankind! We created you from a single pair of a male and a female, and made you into nations and tribes, so that you may know one another (not that you may despise one another). Verily, the most honored among you in the sight of God is the one who is the most righteous. And God is All-Knowing, All-Aware" (Qur'an 49:13).

In Islam, piety is the only distinguishing characteristic of any importance. Muhammad once said: "Surely God does not look at your faces or your bodies, but looks at your hearts and your deeds." Muslims are encouraged to look beyond outward appearances, and recognize a person's intrinsic worth.

ALERT!

Many of the first followers of Islam came from the lowest class of society: slaves, women, the poor, the ill, and the outcast. In Islam they came together as equals with wealthy merchants and societal leaders who later embraced the faith.

Diversity Is Beauty

Muslims consider the diversity of the world a sign of God's mercy, and an opportunity to rise above racism and conceit. "And among His signs is the creation of the heavens and the earth, and the variations in your languages and colors. Verily in that are signs for those who know" (Qur'an 30:22). Muslims feel strongly that since we are all created by God, we cannot say that one person is better than another, based on criteria that are not under our control.

During his life, Muhammad made several personal attempts to promote racial tolerance and respect among his followers. Shortly before his death, he gave a final sermon in which he advised his followers as follows: "All mankind is from Adam and Eve. An Arab has no superiority over a non-Arab, nor does a non-Arab have any superiority over an Arab. Also a white person has no superiority over a black person, nor does a black person have any superiority over a white person, except by piety and good action. Learn that every Muslim is a brother to every other Muslim, and that the Muslims constitute one brotherhood." This value has been practiced throughout Islamic history. Tolerance and equality among people have been central values that attract converts to the faith.

Around the World

Muslim individuals and communities are found virtually around the globe: in Africa, Asia, the Middle East, Europe, North America, South America, and Oceania. The largest concentrations of Muslims are found in Asia and Africa, with sizable minority communities all around the world.

There are an estimated 1.2 billion Muslims in the world today, approximately one-fifth of the world's population, making Islam the second-largest faith community after Christianity. Furthermore, due to birth and conversion rates, Islam is widely considered to be the fastest growing religion in the world today.

Muslim Countries

There are over fifty countries in the world that have a predominantly Muslim population. While Islam is often associated with the Arab world, fewer than 15 percent of the world's Muslims are in fact Arab. Indeed, in a 2001 survey of countries with the largest Muslim population, only one Arab nation (Egypt) can be found.

Countries with Largest Muslim Population*			
Country	Muslim population (in millions)	Country	Muslim population (in millions)
Indonesia	228.4	Egypt	69.5
Pakistan	144.6	Turkey	66.5
Bangladesh	131.3	Iran	66.1
India	123.6	Nigeria	63.3

*Information calculated from data found in the CIA World Factbook (2001).

These Muslim nations vary widely in their government, social practices, and geographic location. There are Muslim tropical islands such as Brunei and the Cocos Islands, and arid desert nations such as Mauritania and Saudi Arabia. Muslim countries are most often organized as republics, but democracies and monarchies exist as well. Predominantly Muslim nations of the former Soviet Union are just now coming out of decades of communist rule.

Beyond a shared faith, many Muslim populations have very little in common, and it's impossible to generalize about a "typical" Muslim country or people. In addition to predominantly Muslim countries, there are sizable Muslim minority communities to be found throughout Asia, Africa, Europe, and the Americas.

Islam in Europe

The Islamic empire at one time stretched into modern-day Europe, particularly in Spain and the Balkans. Today, there are an estimated twelve to twenty million Muslims in Europe, a population that has risen in recent years through immigration and conversion. European Muslims originate from a variety of places.

In France, Muslim immigrants have largely come from North African countries such as Morocco and Algeria. In Germany, immigrants from Turkey are more common. In Britain, most Muslim immigrants come from the Indian subcontinent. Most minority Muslim communities in Europe are made up of a diverse mix of first and second-generation immigrants, as well as native converts.

FACT

Ten percent of the population of Copenhagen, Denmark, is Muslim. In Sweden, Muslims account for 4 percent of the population. If present trends continue, Muslims will account for 10 percent of the entire population of Europe by the year 2020.

In southeastern Europe, Islam had arrived in the fourteenth century with the Ottoman Turks. Today, Albania is 70 percent Muslim, Bosnia-Herzegovina over 60 percent, and Bulgaria nearly 12 percent. This region has been plagued by ethnic and religious conflict, pitting the Muslim population against their Christian neighbors. In the former Yugoslavia, over 200,000 Bosnian Muslims were killed as part of a widespread ethnic-cleansing campaign in the mid-1990s.

Islam in Latin America

In Latin America, practicing Muslims began appearing in the mid-1800s, as a massive migration of Muslim Arabs came to Latin American soil, settling primarily in Argentina, Brazil, Venezuela, and Colombia. Later, these Muslims spread to other South American countries.

Today, over six million Muslims live in Latin America; this population includes Hispanics as well as recent emigrants from Muslim countries. The Islamic Organization of Latin America is headquartered in Argentina, home to 700,000 Muslims. The Cultural Islamic Center of Mexico, established in 1994, operates a small mosque and translates Islamic material into Spanish.

Islam in the United States

There are an estimated five to eight million Muslims living in the United States, who worship in over 1,200 American mosques. Many people do not realize that Muslims have been part of the cultural landscape of the Americas for the past two hundred years.

Early Exploration

Modern scholars generally agree that Christopher Columbus was not the first person to "discover" America. Citing evidence of ancient trade and ethnic diversity, scholars believe that explorers arrived on the North American continent several centuries before Columbus. Many of those first explorers were Muslims from West Africa. Historian Gaoussou Diawara has documented the story of one such explorer in his book, *The Saga of Abubakari II*. One of the first men to set sail to America from Africa (in 1312 C.E.), Abubakari was the brother of the famed Muslim king of Mali, Mansa Musa.

When Columbus made his historic voyage, he relied on the maps and geography studies done by the twelfth-century Arab scholar, Al-Idrisi. There are even reports that Columbus wrote in his diary about a mosquelike building on the top of a mountain near Gibara, Cuba.

Pre-Columbian ruins of mosques and inscriptions of Qur'anic verses have been discovered in Cuba, Mexico, Nevada, and Texas. Several noted archeologists and historians have reported on these findings, including Ivan Van Sertima (author of *They Came Before Columbus*) and the late Dr. Barry Fell (Harvard University ethnologist and author of *Saga America*).

In 1527, Estevanico, a Muslim explorer originally from Morocco, traveled to the Americas as the personal servant of Andrés de Dorantes on a mission from Muslim Spain. Estevanico acted as a guide on a land expedition from Florida to the Pacific Coast. After nine years of travels, his party reached Mexico City and told tales of their expeditions. He later performed early explorations of Arizona and New Mexico.

Slavery Years

The next wave of Muslims to arrive in North America were African slaves brought to the United States from what are now the West African countries of Nigeria, Senegal, Mali, and Gambia. A large number of these slaves were Muslims, and they struggled to maintain their Islamic practices even under the torment of slavery. Over time, many were forced to give up or hide their faith.

It was an interest in their ancestral roots that led many African-Americans to research and embrace Islam. The African-American movement known as the Nation of Islam was based in an attempt to reclaim the spiritual and cultural traditions of these noble Muslim ancestors.

While very little historical information has been preserved about these early African Muslim slaves, the stories of some have been passed along in historical records.

- Job ben Solomon ("Jallo") was a Fulani Muslim brought to Maryland as a slave between 1730 and 1733. He was a well-educated merchant from Senegal, the son of an imam who had memorized the entire Qur'an. The founder of Georgia, James Oglethorpe, helped Job ben Solomon gain his freedom; eventually, he was able to return home.
- Kunta Kinte, a Muslim from Gambia, strived to preserve his Islamic heritage by scratching verses of the Qur'an in the dirt while working in the fields. Alex Haley's book, *Roots,* was based on his search for this African ancestor.
- Abrahim Abd al-Rahman ibn Sori, "the Prince of Slaves," was a Muslim from Guinea who worked the cotton fields in Mississippi, and later became the overseer of the plantation. Abrahim was seen praying regularly and was respected by both black and white people for his dignity and piety.
- Yarrow Mamout was a slave from Virginia who lived to be over 100 years old. In 1819, American painter Charles Willson Peale went to Washington to do portraits of distinguished Americans. His portrait of Yarrow Mamout now hangs in the Georgetown Public Library.

Recent Immigration

Beginning in the late 1800s, the United States received an influx of refugees from Syria, Lebanon, and Palestine. Many were laborers who came to America to seek a better life, as did the many other immigrants who created the mosaic of American society. These early Arab immigrants established communities throughout America's heartland: in Iowa, North Dakota, Michigan, Pennsylvania, and Indiana.

FACT

There are approximately 1,200 mosques (Muslim houses of worship) in the United States today. The "Mother Mosque of America" was built in Cedar Rapids, Iowa, in 1934. It was the first building in the United States designed for use as a mosque, and is still used for worship today.

Today, the American Muslim community represents the full diversity of the faith. According to a 2001 survey by the Council on American-Islamic Relations, over 30 percent of all Muslims in the United States are African-Americans. About 33 percent are South-Central Asian, descending from Indian, Pakistani, or Afghani immigrants. Muslims of Arab descent make up about 25 percent, and immigrants from the African continent make up another 5 percent. There are also sizable groups of American Muslims of Iranian, Turkish, Southeast Asian, and European descent. Between 17 and 30 percent of American Muslims are converts to the faith; nearly two-thirds of these are African-Americans.

American Muslims are active and engaged in all aspects of American life, and work in all sectors of society—as physicians and university professors, taxi drivers and entrepreneurs. Several thousand Muslims serve in the U.S. Armed Forces. Over 60 percent of American Muslims are registered voters. Muslims in the United States value freedom and contribute to the cultural mosaic of the country.

QUESTION?

Do all Muslims speak Arabic?
The vast majority of Muslims do not speak Arabic as their native tongue. However, nearly all Muslims attempt to learn the basics of a language that is so central to their faith.

The Arabic Language

Muslims believe that God's final revelation to mankind, the Qur'an, was made known to us over 1,400 years ago in the Arabic language. In order to fully understand the words of their Lord in the original language of revelation, Muslims make every attempt to learn and understand the rich and poetic classical Arabic.

Arabic is a living language. As the mother tongue for over 200 million people, it ranks as the sixth major language of the world. Linguistically, Arabic is a Semitic language closely related to Hebrew and Aramaic. There are many local dialects, but Muslims attempt to hold onto the classical form of the language that is used in the Qur'an.

Muslims constantly use Arabic words and phrases in many aspects of daily life. When speaking of the future, Muslims say *Insha'Allah* (God willing). When admiring or praising someone, they say *Masha'Allah* (everything is from God). When beginning any action, they mention God's name with *Bismillah* (in God's name). When something is astonishing they often declare *Subhanallah!* (praise be to God).

The traditional Islamic greeting is *Assalaamu 'alaykum,* which means "Peace be with you," and the appropriate response is *Wa 'alaykum assalaam,* or "And peace also with you." More extensive greetings include wishes of peace, God's mercy, and God's blessings on the individual.

In their prayers, when reading the Qur'an, or even in simple conversations with each other, Arabic readily rolls off any Muslim's tongue. With the universal understanding of at least some basic Arabic, a Muslim always has a standard language to communicate and worship with other Muslims, no matter where in the world he or she may be.

The Alphabet

To the uninitiated, printed Arabic text may seem very complicated. However, the Arabic language is written with a standard phonetic alphabet that is rather straightforward. Once learned, the simple alphabet allows the non-native speaker to read and pronounce Arabic words with ease.

The Arabic alphabet is made up of twenty-eight letters and several vowel markings. Arabic was originally written without vowels, and even today, popular writing such as newspapers and magazines do not use them at all. (The Qur'anic text always includes the vowel markings, to aid the non-native readers in correct pronunciation.) Arabic is read from right to left, the opposite of English.

Unlike European languages, Arabic is based on a root word system. All Arabic words are constructed from three-letter "roots," each of which expresses a basic idea. For example, the root K-T-B conveys the idea of writing. By applying various prefix and suffix combinations, one can construct the words for "book," "scribe," "school," "library," "office," or "typewriter"—anything related to writing. To find a fundamental meaning of a word, one must look at the basic root construction and other related words.

The Arabic Alphabet

ث Thaa' (th)	ت Taa' (t)	ب Baa' (b)	أ 'Alif (a)
د Daal (d)	خ Khaa' (kh)	ح H'aa' (h)	ج Jiim (zh)
س Siin (s)	ز Zaay (z)	ر Raa' (r)	ذ Thaal (dh)
ط Taa' (t)	ض Daad (d)	ص Saad (s)	ش Shiin (sh)
ف Faa' (f)	غ Ghayn (gh)	ع 'Ayn (')	ظ Thaa' (z)
م Miim (m)	ل Laam (l)	ك Kaaf (k)	ق Qaaf (q)
ي Yaa' (y)	و Waaw (w)	ه Haa' (h)	ن Nuun (n)

The combination of letters S-L-M forms the root of the words "Islam" and "Muslim." This root implies peace, safety, security, protection, surrender, and submission. The word "Islam," therefore, means "a path of submission to God, wherein one finds peace and security."

Transliteration Issues

Writing Arabic words using the English alphabet can be confusing. There are several letters in the Arabic alphabet that do not have English equivalents. For example, the guttural "q" sound in the Arabic word "Qatar" does not exist in English. In addition, there are some letters in Arabic that represent sounds that, in English, are written with two separate letters. For example, the "sh" sound in "ship" would be written in Arabic with a single letter. English writers try to represent the sounds as best they can, using the limitations of the English alphabet.

When reading books or articles about Islam, you might encounter variant spellings of common words, depending simply on how they're transliterated. For example, the common phrase *Assalaamu 'alaykum* (peace be with you) may have any of the following variations in spelling:

Salaam alaykum
Assalamu alaikum
As-salamu'alaykum

Each author chooses the English spelling that he or she believes will best assist in the correct pronunciation of the word. Ⓔ

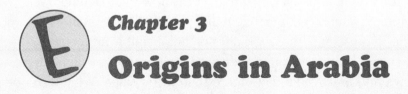

Chapter 3

Origins in Arabia

Before the coming of Islam, the Arabian Peninsula was steeped in ignorance. Although the people of Arabia did inherit the legacy of the Prophet Abraham, whose monotheistic teachings had once been preached in the land, their pure monotheistic faith had been lost. Suffering from tribal divisions and warfare, the people were ready for a uniting force.

Setting the Scene

When looking at any cultural or religious phenomenon, it's beneficial to go back to the origins, the context from which it sprang forth. Islam claims to have Divine revelation, which is timeless in its message and teachings. However, this revelation was given during a time and in an environment that had a direct impact on how the teachings were interpreted, embraced, practiced, and spread. The revelation did not occur in a vacuum; the book did not simply fall from the sky.

Thus it is important to understand the context in which Islam, as it's known and practiced today, entered the world stage. What were the main powers at work during that particular historical period, in that particular part of the world? How did the rise of Islam come about? What did this faith offer to the people of the time? How did it change and improve their lives? How did this new movement change the cultural landscape of the region? To answer these questions, one needs to look at the land and the people during the time leading up to the rise of Islam.

Regional Superpowers

In the centuries preceding the rise of Islam, several powerful civilizations emerged near the Arabian Peninsula. Among the more lasting were the Persian and Byzantine Empires, which dominated the area's cultural and economic development.

Persian Empire

The Persian Empire was established by the Sassanid kings, who had gained power in Persia in the third century C.E. It was located east of the Arabian Peninsula, in modern-day Iran and neighboring countries. Persians spoke Farsi, and they established Zoroastrianism as the state religion. Zoroastrianism is based on the belief that two cosmic forces rule the universe—one for good, and one for evil—and the existence of one god, who is known as Ahura Mazda. Zoroastrians believe Heaven is the reward for those that follow truth and goodness, while Hell is the punishment for those who choose falsehood and evil.

The Persian Empire was a strongly class-based society, in which the emperor and his family enjoyed a very luxurious lifestyle, thanks to his subjects, merchants, and farmers. Trade centers such as Esfahan and Shiraz attracted caravans from all over Asia to come to these cities to exchange their goods.

FACT

There are still approximately 150,000 Zoroastrians in the world today. They mainly live in Iran and India, although there are an estimated 5,000 Zoroastrians in North America as well.

Byzantine Empire

The Persian Sassanid Empire (226–651 C.E.) had long been in conflict with the other superpower of the region, the Byzantines, and these conflicts constantly realigned the borders of the two empires. The Byzantine Empire was the more dominant in the region, at one point stretching from southern Spain, across the Fertile Crescent (modern-day Syria and Lebanon), up to the borders of the Persian Empire in the east. The Byzantine Empire originated from the Eastern Roman Empire, and its official religion was Eastern Orthodox Christianity.

The Arabian Peninsula

The Arabian Peninsula is the largest peninsula in the world. It is surrounded on three sides by water: the Red Sea on the west, the Arabian Sea to the south, and the Persian Gulf to the east. More than a fourth of the land is sandy desert; there are no major lakes or rivers. While there are some areas of fertile vegetation and mountains, most of the peninsula is a harsh, barren landscape where the climate can reach the greatest extremes. During the summer months, temperatures can reach as high as 115 degrees Fahrenheit; in the cool winter evenings, it can dip below freezing. There is little transition between the seasons; the weather is usually either extremely hot or extremely cold.

The Arabian Peninsula is part of a larger region called the Middle East. "Middle East" is a geographic term that was coined in 1902 to describe the entire region where Africa, Asia, and Europe converge. The borders of the region, and the countries that are contained in it, are subject to some debate. Not all Middle Eastern countries are Arab; the main language groups include Arabic, Hebrew, Turkish, and Persian, among dozens of others. The world's three largest monotheistic faiths all began in this area.

The inhabitants of the Arabian Peninsula are a Semitic people called Arabs, who trace their origins to the Prophet Abraham, through his son Ishmael. The people of the Arabian Peninsula share many physical features: dark skin, coarse black hair, thin bodies, and dark, oval eyes. The language they speak is Arabic, which is a Semitic language related to Hebrew, Aramaic, and Syriac. While some variations are found in dialect and accent, the Arabic language unites a people with a long history and common ancestry. Today, Arabic is the native tongue of over 200 million people, in more than twenty predominately Arab countries.

ALERT!

The Prophet Abraham was known to have two sons: Isaac and Ishmael. Tradition holds that the Jewish people are the descendants of Isaac, and the Arabs are the descendants of Ishmael.

The Bedouin

Those Arabs who lead a nomadic lifestyle are known as the Bedouin. The Bedouin live in makeshift tents, and move from place to place according to the season, in search of water and vegetation for themselves and their cattle.

The Bedouin have historically lived a harsh and rugged lifestyle, prone to feuds and fighting among themselves and others. At the same time, they are a people known for their strong sense of honor, hospitality, loyalty, and bravery.

City Dwellers

Over time, many Bedouins settled in oases and villages, and established organized societies based on trade and agriculture. These villages grew into city-states led by local tribal leaders, who were prone to feuding. Merchants traveled throughout the region to establish trade relationships, while competing tribes conducted booty raids to disrupt those routes.

In the southern region of the Arabian Peninsula, more frequent rainfall and a more pleasant climate allowed the people to cultivate the land, develop irrigation systems, and build a prosperous civilization in Yemen. They established trade caravans and used ships to transfer goods between Africa and Asia.

In modern times, the discovery of oil has turned the Arabian Peninsula into a very developed region. Many of the greatest new economic and business centers are to be found there, including Riyadh and Dubai. However, the Bedouin values of hospitality, loyalty, and integrity are still very much a part of local culture.

Caravans and Trade

Trade with neighboring tribes and villages was always an important economic activity on the Arabian Peninsula. Trade cities served as important centers of commerce, as well as strongholds for the political and social establishment. The Arabs were also involved in the trade between Asia and the Mediterranean. Goods arrived by sea from India and were carried by trade caravans traveling north to Petra and Damascus, and south into Yemen. The most important trade route in the region ran parallel to the Red Sea. As naval battles rendered that area unsafe, an alternative inland route was made, right through the city of Mecca.

FACT

It was common for various tribes to forge treaties with others in order to protect their caravans from theft and looting. Tribes also allied themselves to protect each other from third-party warfare. However, these alliances were subject to change at whim, so that friends of today could easily become sworn enemies tomorrow.

Tribes and Social Structure

The people of Arabia were organized into tribes, where the dominating law was survival of the fittest. Each tribal leader, or sheikh, controlled all affairs of the tribe, in consultation with elders and other important leaders. In Mecca, the government was dominated by local pagan priests, due to the wealth they accumulated from offerings to the gods.

The Arab tribes held a general assembly near Mecca each year, in an event called *Souq Ukaz*. At this open-air community fair, poets and sportsmen held competitions, while merchants from all the different tribes watched folk dances, drank alcohol, and gambled on the outcomes of the competitions. Socially, the pre-Islamic Arabs (that is, those Arabs who lived before seventh century of the Common Era) formed a society of stark contrasts. While they were known for their generosity and hospitality, they were also prone to tribal violence and injustices toward women.

Women in Pre-Islamic Arabia

Before the coming of Islam, women were considered possessions to be bought and sold into marriage or slavery, or even inherited along with other "estate property." Men could marry as many women as they wished, as well as take an unlimited number of concubines and slaves. Female infanticide was commonplace, because families feared poverty and disgrace in raising young girls to adulthood.

Warfare and Violence

The people of Arabia took pride in being warriors. However, looting, murder, and slavery were rampant. Inter-tribal warfare, often instigated at the slightest provocation, resulted in blood feuds that lasted for generations.

The pre-Islamic period in Arabia is commonly called *Jahiliyyah*, which means "the days of ignorance." The Qur'an chastises the Arab people, who were "the worst in unbelief and hypocrisy, and most fitted to be in ignorance of the command which God has sent down to His messenger . . ." (9:97).

Tribes would get caught up in a vicious cycle of violence and revenge. In one example, a camel belonging to a certain tribe was found grazing on land belonging to a rival tribe. The offended men killed the camel, thereby insulting the camel's owners. They, in turn, killed the leader of the other tribe, and a war ensued. In another dispute, two men were engaged in a horse race, and one of the men died in the course of the race. This man's family, his tribe, and their allies attacked the tribe of the opponent in order to avenge his death. A war ensued that lasted forty years, resulting in the deaths of thousands of people.

Pre-Islamic Religions

Before Islam, the main religion of the Arabian Peninsula was pagan idolatry. Carved figures of wood, stone, and clay were worshipped either as gods, or as intermediaries between people and the gods. Some people worshipped the heavenly bodies, and it was not uncommon for children to be called such names as Abdel-Shams (sun worshipper) or Abdel-Uzza (worshipper of Uzza, an ancient pagan goddess).

In the city of Mecca, some people did understand the concept of monotheism, based on the local oral traditions of the Prophet Abraham. There were Jewish and Christian tribes in the local area, but the pagan leaders in Mecca did not welcome them. The economic foundation of the city had come to revolve around pagan business and religious practices, and the monotheistic faiths posed a threat to their economic prosperity. For this reason, the Jewish and Christian tribes remained in the outlying areas.

The City of Mecca

The city of Mecca has been an important commercial and social center for the people of the Arabian Peninsula for thousands of years. It is situated in an inland valley (the Valley of Abraham), surrounded by a rocky, rugged landscape.

ALERT!

In English, the word "mecca" is used to describe a center of activity, or a place that many people visit or hope to visit. For example, "Hawaii is a mecca for surfers" or "New York City is a mecca for tourists."

Mecca and the Prophet Abraham

In Arabic, "Mecca" means "the place of the drinking cup." This name comes from the story of the Prophet Abraham. According to the story, Abraham was unable to have children with his wife Sarah, and so he married an Egyptian woman named Hajar. After the birth of their son, Ishmael, God ordered Abraham to take his new family to a valley and leave them there. When Hajar saw Abraham leaving, she questioned him: "Did God give you a command to leave us here alone?" When he answered yes, she reportedly said, "Then God will not abandon us."

Hajar and her son struggled through hunger and thirst, and Hajar called upon God to help them. Muslims believe that it was then that the spring of Zamzam miraculously sprang forth, to nourish the child and his mother. From that time, the place became known as Mecca. Today, the spring of Zamzam still nourishes the city.

It is believed that Abraham later returned to visit Ishmael, and together they built a stone building dedicated to the worship of the One True God. This building is today known as the Ka'aba ("the cube"), a simple stone structure, a hollow cube with a small doorway on one side. However, later generations abandoned or modified the faith of Abraham. They desecrated Abraham's house of worship by erecting over 360 idols within the Ka'aba—a different god to worship each day of the year.

FACT

Mecca was once known as the city of Bakka. The Qur'an makes reference to the ancient name of the city. "The most important shrine established for people is the one in Bakka, a blessed beacon for all people. In it are clear signs—the station of Abraham. Anyone who enters it shall be granted safe passage . . ." (3:96). The name Bakka means "lacking water."

Pilgrimage

Mecca has long been a center of worship and pilgrimage, in honor of the Prophet Abraham. Generations after Abraham, however, his monotheistic teachings had become muddied by the addition of various pagan elements. The Bedouin peoples placed their idols inside the Ka'aba for safekeeping.

During the year, entire clans would come to worship and make offerings. They would clap their hands and dance in celebration of the gods. Because they felt it was not right to worship the gods in the same clothes they wore during their daily lives, they would remove them and dance around in the nude. Merchants would travel through for trade fairs and for pilgrimage celebrations to honor the idols.

The Year of the Elephant

Mecca's southern neighbor, Yemen, was under the rule of the Ethiopian governor, Abraha (aka Abramos, 530–570 C.E.), a Christian. Reportedly, Abraha was envious of the pilgrimage traffic that Mecca was attracting, and strived to build a rival place of pilgrimage in Yemen. He established a beautiful cathedral in Sana'a, and ordered people to go there instead. When no one came, Abraha set out to attack Mecca and destroy the Ka'aba.

Abraha's army marched on Mecca, supported by a "cavalry" of elephants, an animal that the Arabs had never seen before. As he approached Mecca, Abraha sent word that he did not want to hurt anyone; he wanted only to destroy the Ka'aba. If anyone resisted, however, they would be crushed. One of the leaders of Mecca, Abdul-Muttalib, was a monotheist who had not let his faith be corrupted by idolatry. He sent back the following response: "By God, we do not want to fight you. So far as this House is concerned, it is the House of God. If God wants to save His House, He will save it. And if He leaves it unprotected, no one can save it."

When Abraha's army moved on Mecca, Abdul-Muttalib told the Meccans to leave the city and seek refuge in the surrounding hills. He and a few other tribal elders remained in the precincts of the Ka'aba at first, prayed for God to protect His House, and then went to the hills to wait. As Abraha's army approached the Ka'aba to destroy it, Arab tradition holds that a flock of small birds flew over them, dropping small pebbles from their beaks and claws. The stones destroyed the army and injured Abraha himself; he died on his retreat back to Yemen. Abdul-Muttalib later helped negotiate a peace treaty between the two neighboring states.

It was shortly after this incident, which became known as the Year of the Elephant (570 C.E.), that Abdul-Muttalib's grandson was born, who was named Muhammad. At that time, it was still unknown that in the course of Muhammad's lifetime, the tribes and clans of Arabia would be united under one banner of faith, forever changing the landscape of Arabia and the world. Pagan influence would be eradicated from the Arabian Peninsula, and the Persians and Byzantines would soon give way to a new empire. Ⓔ

Chapter 4

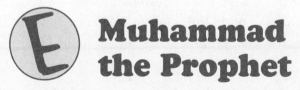

Muhammad the Prophet

Muhammad the Prophet is a central figure to the faith of Islam. Raised as an orphan, Muhammad grew up to become a respected merchant. He was a spiritual and reflective man, and went on to lead a faith community that impacted the entire world. The life of the Prophet Muhammad is a story of extraordinary hardships and achievements.

The Final Prophet

Muslims believe that God sent down messengers and prophets to every nation. Some are mentioned in the Qur'an by name, while others are not. These prophets and messengers brought the same message to each of their peoples: to worship One God alone, and to follow His guidance. Over time, those teachings were lost or corrupted, and new prophets and messengers were sent to confirm the previous teachings. Muslims believe that Muhammad was the final prophet to be sent to us by God.

FACT

Muslim tradition holds that there have been over 124,000 prophets sent to mankind through history, beginning with Adam and ending with Muhammad. Only twenty-five are mentioned by name in the Qur'an, and Muslims do not speculate about the identities of others.

Muslims believe that because Muhammad was the final prophet, he was sent to all of mankind. He re-established faith in the unity of God, and also delivered guidance in matters of worship and daily living, which are preserved in the Qur'an. During his lifetime, he also arbitrated in disputes, gave counsel to his followers, and set an example of piety and sacrifice. For this reason, Muslims educate themselves about his life, and how his personal example can be followed.

While Muslims look to Muhammad as an example to follow, they do not worship him or put him on a pedestal. Worship is for God alone, and the Qur'an makes it clear that "Muhammad was no more than a messenger; many were the messengers that passed away before him" (Qur'an 3:144).

Early Life in Mecca

Muhammad was born around 569–570 C.E. in Mecca, modern-day Saudi Arabia, into a respected tribe, the Quraish. His grandfather, Abdul-Muttalib, was a monotheistic believer who named his newborn grandson Muhammad, "the praised one," a name that was not common among the Arabs at that time.

As an infant, Muhammad was entrusted to the care of a Bedouin foster mother, as was the custom of the people of Mecca, so that young children could start out life in the healthy desert environment, away from the vices and bad habits of the city. Muhammad stayed with his foster mother until the age of three, when he returned to his mother, Aminah. His father, Abdullah, had died shortly before Muhammad's birth.

Shortly after returning to his mother's care, Muhammad traveled with her to the city of Yathrib to visit the grave of his father. On the journey back, Aminah fell ill and died. Muhammad was completely orphaned at six years of age. His affectionate grandfather took over his care, but died only two years later. At the age of eight, Muhammad was at last entrusted to the care of his paternal uncle, Abu Talib.

Abu Talib was a generous and gentle man, who offered Muhammad full protection and support. However, he was not a rich man, and young Muhammad had to earn his own livelihood. Muhammad served first as a shepherd to some neighbors, then as an assistant to his uncle's trade caravans and merchant activities.

Muhammad's Marriage to Khadijah

As Muhammad grew older, he became known in the community as a person of integrity and honesty. A wealthy businesswoman in Mecca, named Khadijah, heard about Muhammad's trade skills and mild manners, and was impressed. She often hired men to take goods to Syria and conduct business on her behalf, and she decided to consign some goods over to him to take to Syria by caravan.

When Muhammad returned, Khadijah was pleased with his hard work and dedication. Although she was a widow, several years his senior, the two decided to marry. Muhammad was twenty-five; Khadijah was forty.

The couple would remain happily married until Khadijah's death twenty-five years later. Muhammad and Khadijah had two sons who died in infancy, and four daughters: Zainab, Ruqaiyah, Um Kulthum, and Fatima.

ALERT!

During the prime of his life (age twenty-five to fifty), Muhammad was married only to Khadijah, and did not take on additional wives or concubines as other men of his rank often did. Throughout his life, he spoke very highly of her, and their relationship was a model for Muslim couples to follow. It was only after her death that he married again.

Good Reputation and Success

Muhammad's reputation in Mecca grew, and he became known as Al-Amin, the honest and trustworthy one. People would often come to him to arbitrate business or personal disputes. In one instance, several tribal leaders were arguing over who would have the honor of moving the special Black Stone back to its place, after some construction and repair had been done on the Ka'aba.

The argument almost degenerated into a blood feud, but at that moment Muhammad entered the area. The tribal chiefs agreed to let Muhammad arbitrate in their argument. In his wisdom, Muhammad found a solution that pleased them all. He laid a blanket over the ground, placed the Black Stone upon it, and allowed each of the tribal leaders to carry a corner of the blanket. Together, they moved the Black Stone back to its place. The tribal elders were satisfied, and Muhammad's reputation for trustworthy and effective mediation continued to grow.

The First Revelation

Muhammad would frequently go to the mountains during the month of Ramadan, to spend time in quiet solitude and prayer. He would often retire to a particular cave named Hira', located in the hills not far from Mecca, for worship and contemplation about the world. It was during one of these retreats, in the year 610 C.E., that Muhammad had an extraordinary experience. He was forty years old.

A Command to Read

One night toward the end of the month of Ramadan, the Angel Gabriel appeared to Muhammad and demanded, "Read!" Muhammad reportedly answered, "I cannot read," for he was illiterate. The angel repeated the request several times, and then relayed the beginnings of a revelation from God:

Read! In the name of your Lord and Cherisher, Who created:
Created man out of a leechlike clot.
Read! And your Lord is Most Bountiful.
He, Who taught the use of the pen,
Taught man that which he knew not. (Qur'an 96:1–5)

Shock and Waiting

Following this incredible experience, Muhammad rushed home and told Khadijah what had happened. She covered him with blankets, consoled him, and reminded him that he had always been a man of charity and honesty, that God would not lead him astray.

It is reported that Khadijah and Muhammad first approached Khadijah's cousin Waraqa ibn Nawfal for advice on the experience. Waraqa was a Christian convert and multilingual scholar. Waraqa reportedly told Muhammad that he had been chosen just as Moses was chosen, to receive revelation. He then predicted that Muhammad would be turned away and "met with enmity" for preaching the message of God.

After this first encounter, Muhammad experienced a brief pause in revelation. During this time of waiting, he devoted himself more to prayers and spiritual devotion. Then the revelations continued, with the command to "arise and warn" (74:2), "rehearse and proclaim . . . the bounty of God" (93:11), and to "admonish your nearest kinsmen" (26:214).

When Muhammad began to preach his mission, he spoke secretly with members of his own family. Then he shared the message with his closest friends and members of his own tribe. Several years after first receiving revelation, he finally reached the point where he was proclaiming God's message publicly in the city.

Preaching and Persecution

The leaders of Mecca were not pleased with Muhammad's message. He was commanding the people to reject the tribal idols that were the financial mainstay of the city. He encouraged people to be charitable and to free their slaves. He condemned the traditionally held beliefs and practices of the most powerful tribes in the city. He preached the Oneness of God in Mecca, the main center of idolatry.

Those who were firmly committed to their ancestral beliefs put up great resistance to Muhammad and his growing group of believers. The believers mostly belonged to the weakest members of society, those without tribal protection, who were attracted to the equality and justice of Muhammad's message. The more powerful groups persecuted and tortured them with impunity. Among other horrific acts of cruelty, the first Muslims were dragged through the streets by ropes, crushed with large stones, and tied up in the burning heat of the desert sun.

FACT

The first Muslim to be murdered for the faith was a woman, Sumaiyah bint Khabbab. She was stabbed to death by a powerful pagan leader, Abu Jahl, who was angered that she repeatedly refused to denounce her faith.

Flight to Abyssinia

After months of worsening abuse and murders, the Muslims began to look outside Mecca for refuge. Muhammad knew that the Christian king of Abyssinia (Ethiopia) was rumored to be a just and fair man. In the fifth year of the prophethood, Muhammad sent a small group of followers to the safety of Abyssinia.

In the subsequent months, a larger number of Muslims from Mecca migrated to Abyssinia. The Meccan leaders were outraged that the Muslims had found a safe haven. Two Meccan envoys were sent to the Abyssinian king to plead their case and demand extradition of the Muslims back to Mecca.

The Abyssinian king (Negus), being a just and fair man, heard their case. The Meccans explained that this group of people had abandoned the faith of their forefathers, and were preaching a faith as strange to them as to Negus himself. The king called for the Muslims to appear before him and respond.

The spokesperson of the Muslims, Ja'far (the Prophet Muhammad's cousin), spoke very eloquently about how their lives had been turned around and that they now followed teachings of faith, dignity, and truthfulness. At the king's request, Ja'far also recited some verses of the Qur'an, regarding the birth and piety of the Prophet Jesus. The king was moved to tears, and declared that the Muslims were "free to live and worship in my realm as they please." The Meccan envoys had to return empty-handed.

Muslims look kindly upon devout Christians. As the Qur'an reminds, ". . . nearest among them in love to the believers will you find those who say, 'We are Christians.' Because among these are men devoted to learning, and men who have renounced the world, and they are not arrogant" (5:82).

Those Muslims who did not emigrate faced the increased wrath of the Meccan opposition. The angry pagan leaders organized a boycott of the Muslims, forbidding all communication, commercial relations, and marriage contracts with them. This social boycott lasted three long years; during that time, the small Muslim community suffered from severe poverty and hunger.

The Year of Sadness

Shortly after the boycott was lifted, Muhammad suffered two deep personal losses. His protective uncle, Abu Talib, and his devoted wife, Khadijah, both passed away in what became known as the "year of sadness." However, it was during this time, when Muhammad's mission seemed to be at its weakest, that he was granted a beautiful sign from God.

Muslim tradition holds that during one night, Muhammad traveled to the far holy city of Jerusalem, and from there ascended up to the heavens. During the ascension, Muhammad was welcomed by the previous prophets, and was commanded by God to implement the five daily prayers. In Arabic, these two experiences are known as the *isra'* (the travel) and *mi'raj* (the ascension).

The Migration (Hijrah)

Meanwhile, the hostility of the pagan Meccans increased. They could no longer tolerate Muhammad's presence and his influence on the Meccan population. Without the protection of his uncle Abu Talib, Muhammad felt the pressure to leave. He tried to travel to Ta'if, but the people there threw stones at him and chased him out of town. Muhammad subsequently turned to other cities and tribes to find a place of shelter. He finally found a group of sympathetic people from the city of Yathrib, about 275 miles north of Mecca. They invited Muhammad and his followers to migrate to their city where the Muslims would be sheltered, protected, and treated as family.

A Murder Plot

After some preparation time and negotiations, small groups of Muslims began to secretly travel to Yathrib. As they left, the Meccan leaders confiscated their property. Soon whole quarters of the city were abandoned, and the only Muslims remaining in the city were Muhammad, his faithful friend Abu Bakr, and his son-in-law, Ali.

Seeing that the Muslims were escaping, the tribal leaders devised a plan to get rid of Muhammad once and for all. Tribal leaders convened a meeting to determine how they could murder Muhammad without exposing any individuals or tribes to revenge. It was decided that one man from each tribe would attack Muhammad at the same time, so that the guilt would be spread among them.

FACT

In 622 c.e., the entire Muslim community finally succeeded in reaching Yathrib safely. The migration itself is called the Hijrah (Arabic for "migration"), and from that point on, the city of Yathrib became known as Madinah, which literally means "the City."

On the eve of the planned attack, the Angel Gabriel reportedly appeared to Muhammad and gave him God's permission to finally leave Mecca. Aware of the plan to assassinate him, Muhammad went to Abu Bakr's home to make the final preparations for the migration. Ali stayed behind at Muhammad's own home with instructions to distribute some money that was held in trust before departing for migration the next day. When the assassins came into Muhammad's home, they were surprised to find only Ali there.

Muhammad and Abu Bakr thus escaped from Mecca unharmed. To thwart the enemies trying to kill them, they traveled south at first, and holed themselves up in a cave for three days to escape detection. They then went up a rarely traveled coastal road toward Yathrib. Ali and other stragglers joined them within days.

Muhajireen and Ansar

In Madinah, the newly arrived Muslims were each matched up with a local family, who looked after them and assisted them in settling into their new home. The emigrants from Mecca became known as the *Muhajireen* ("those who have emigrated"), and the people of Madinah became known as the *Ansar* ("the helpers"). The bonds between them were a solid brotherhood and sisterhood. The Ansar were extremely generous to their brethren in faith, many of whom had arrived from Mecca alone and penniless.

This emigration to Madinah was a turning point for the Muslim community, and for the history of the Islamic faith. No longer tortured and persecuted, the Muslims found themselves in a place of protection and liberty.

FACT

To honor the importance of Hijrah, Muslims calculate time in terms of this event. The beginning of the Islamic calendar, the Hijrah calendar, marks the year of the emigration. Year zero in the Islamic calendar thus corresponds to 622 C.E.

The Muslim State in Madinah

The new community in Madinah set about the business of living, farming, and freely practicing their faith. For the first time, the Muslims could organize society the way they believed it should be, in accordance with the guidance that Muhammad continued to receive from God. The community built a mosque for prayer, established societal rules, and set aside old tribal struggles and blood feuds.

Peace Treaties and Alliances

Shortly after arriving in Madinah, Muhammad invited representatives from neighboring tribes—Jews, Christians, and others—to discuss the idea of establishing a city-state in Madinah. With their approval, Muhammad established the first written constitution, which defined his role as leader of the community and the rights and duties of all citizens. The constitution established a justice system (there was to be no vigilante justice), and laid down the principles of foreign policy and defense. All citizens were afforded equality with the Muslims in practical affairs, and everyone enjoyed full freedom of religion.

Muhammad traveled to other cities and tribes in the area to engage them in treaties of alliance. As the alliance grew stronger, they decided to bring pressure upon the Meccans to return the confiscated property of the Muslims. The alliance began to interrupt Meccan trade caravans through the region of Madinah. At the same time, the Meccans continued to threaten and harass them, so the Muslims fortified themselves against possible attack.

Battles of Badr and Uhud

Angered by their unsuccessful attempts to stop Muhammad and the disruption of their commerce, the tribes of Mecca sent an ultimatum to Madinah demanding that Muhammad and his followers surrender or be ousted from the area. When their demands went unheeded, they organized an army to descend on Madinah. In what became known as the Battle of Badr, the Muslims miraculously came out victorious over a Meccan army three times their size. The prisoners of war that the Muslims detained were allowed to ransom themselves for as little as the price of a necklace. For some literate prisoners, their ransom was to teach ten Muslim children how to read and write.

After another year of preparation, the Meccans attempted to avenge their defeat at Badr by descending on Madinah again, this time with an army of thousands. In what became known as the Battle of Uhud, the Muslims put up a strong effort, and looked to be victorious against an army four times its size. However, some Muslim archers left their post prematurely, in anticipation of victory, and the Meccans found their advantage. They swooped in from behind and surrounded the Muslims. In the fierce battle that continued, Muhammad himself was injured and many Muslims were killed. Finally, what remained of the Muslim army managed to reach safety in the hills.

Widows and Orphans

It was during this period of defense and bloodshed that Muhammad entered into marriage contracts with several women, all but one of whom were widows. As leader of the community, Muhammad had a responsibility to set an example and care for women who had been widowed by war, and for their children. Muhammad did marry one woman who was not a widow. Her name was Aisha, and she was the daughter of Muhammad's closest companion, Abu Bakr.

According to most accounts, the marriage between Aisha and Muhammad was contracted when Aisha was a young girl of nine or ten. However, the wedding did not take place until the second year after Hijrah, when Aisha was in her teens. At that time, Muhammad was in his fifties.

Betrayals and Their Consequences

The alliance that Muhammad had forged with various tribes was very important during the period when the Madinah community was under constant attack. Eventually, however, a few tribes that had joined the alliance began to incite trouble. When they saw the strength of the Meccans, they secretly pledged their support to them, spied for them, and in one case even plotted to assassinate Muhammad. In response, Muhammad demanded that those tribes take their belongings and leave the area.

The tribes that left the Madinah alliance mobilized with the Meccans and other tribes surrounding Madinah. They planned to invade Madinah with a force much greater than during the battles of Badr and Uhud. In response, the Muslims decided to dig a ditch around the whole city, which successfully helped to protect them from the siege. This encounter became known as the Battle of the Ditch.

Conquest of Mecca

While the Meccans continued to engage the Muslims in an attempt to invade Madinah, back home their economy was suffering from the disruption in their northern trade routes (which were blocked by the Muslims from Madinah). After another series of losing battles and seeing Muhammad's strength increase rather than decrease, the Meccans finally agreed to meet Muhammad to discuss the terms of a peace agreement.

Treaty of Hudaibiyah

Muhammad traveled to Mecca, and met with representatives in the suburban area known as Hudaibiyah. They negotiated a peace treaty, including terms for a ten-year ceasefire, and agreed to remain neutral in conflicts with third parties. The armistice would allow both sides to live in happiness and to conduct their own affairs freely.

FACT

With safety secured at home, Muhammad began reaching out to neighboring states to share with them the message of Islam. He sent delegations and dictated letters to the leaders of Abyssinia, Egypt, Persia, Rome, Bahrain, Yemen, and Damascus, inviting them to faith.

Not very long after signing the treaty, a tribe that had allied with the Meccans attacked a tribe that had allied with the Muslims, in violation of the terms of the agreement. Muhammad responded by leading an army of 10,000 into Mecca. The size of the force so surprised the Meccans that the city was occupied without a single person being hurt.

Returning Home

In Mecca, Muhammad gathered all the residents of the city together. They were expecting punishment and revenge for two decades of persecution and violence. Instead, Muhammad reminded them of their misdeeds and hostility. He asked the people, "What do you expect from me?" The people were ashamed and afraid. Muhammad answered, "May God forgive you. Go in peace. There shall be no responsibility on you today—you are free!" He even released the claim to Muslim property that had been confiscated twenty years earlier by the Meccans. Muhammad then returned to Madinah, having changed the hearts of the people of Mecca.

Death of the Prophet

Muhammad returned to live in Madinah, where he led the community both materially and spiritually. Throughout this time, he continued to receive revelations from God on matters of faith and social life, and these revelations were written down and compiled into the Qur'an. Now a peaceful neighbor, the city of Mecca was open to Muslims who wanted to travel for the annual pilgrimage. Caravan routes were traveled freely in the region, and the message of Islam began to spread north into Byzantium and Iran, and south through the continent of Africa.

Last Sermon

In the tenth year after Hijrah, Muhammad made his final pilgrimage to Mecca. Over 100,000 Muslims gathered in the valley of Mount Arafat for the final stages of the annual pilgrimage. At the gathering, Muhammad rose to say a speech, which lives on as one of the greatest sermons of all time. He said:

Oh people, lend me an attentive ear, for I do not know whether after this year, I shall ever be amongst you again . . . Oh people, just as you regard this month, this day, this city as sacred, so regard the life and property of every Muslim as a sacred trust. Return the goods entrusted to you to their rightful owners. Hurt no one, so that no one may hurt you. Remember that you will indeed meet your Lord, and that He will indeed reckon all of your deeds . . . Oh people, it is true that you have certain rights with regard to women, but they also have rights over you . . . Do treat women well, and be kind to them, for they are your partners and committed helpers . . . All mankind is from Adam and Eve; an Arab has no superiority over a non-Arab, nor does a non-Arab have any superiority over an Arab. Also a white person has no superiority over a black person, nor does a black person have any superiority over a white person, except by piety and good action. Learn that every Muslim is a brother to every Muslim, and that the Muslims constitute one brotherhood . . . Remember, one day you will appear before God and answer for your deeds. So beware, do not stray from the path of righteousness after I am gone . . . Be my witness, God, that I have conveyed Your message to Your people.

Final Illness

Muhammad fell ill within months of his final pilgrimage. Too sick to get out of bed, he appointed his closest companion, Abu Bakr, to lead the community prayers. After an illness that lasted about two weeks, Muhammad died at the age of sixty-three. By that time, all of Arabia had been united under Islam, and the faith was gaining footholds in farther regions.

When the people learned of Muhammad's death, they reacted in desperation and shock. He was the prophet and leader, and they knew that with his death, revelations from God would come to an end. Many people defiantly denied that he had died. Seeing this, Abu Bakr went to the mosque and called to the people. "Oh people! If Muhammad is the sole object of your adoration, then know that he is dead. But if it is God that you worshipped, then know that He does not die!"

Abu Bakr then recited verse 3:144 of the Qur'an, which was revealed after the battle of Uhud: "Muhammad is no more than an Apostle; many were the Apostles that passed away before him. If he died or were slain, would you then turn back on your heels? If any did turn back, not the least harm would he do to God. But God will swiftly reward those who serve Him with gratitude." At this, the people were humbled and recognized the truth of Muhammad's death.

Chapter 5

Expansion of Islamic Civilization

During Muhammad's lifetime, Islam had spread to all corners of the Arabian Peninsula, bringing all the tribes together under one banner of faith. In the years following his death, Islam would unite an entire region and emerge as a great world civilization that flourished in the Middle East and gave rise to Muslim Spain and the Ottoman Empire.

The Rightly Guided Successors

After Muhammad died (in 632 C.E.), the Muslim community needed a new leader. The divine revelations did end with the death of the Final Prophet, but the community still needed a guide in more administrative areas. The Muslims needed someone to ensure that the community abided by the guidance of the Qur'an and the Prophet, to establish justice, and to create conditions whereby Islam could be fully practiced and implemented.

A leader of a Muslim community would become known as a "caliph," from the Arabic word *khalifa,* which is short for *Khalifa-tu-Rasulil-lah* (Successor to the Messenger of God).

Muhammad had not named any particular individual to succeed him, but expected the community to select a new leader from among the most pious and well-suited men among his companions. Following Muhammad's death, the debate began over who was to take over leadership of the community.

Caliph Abu Bakr

During his final illness, Muhammad had appointed his close companion Abu Bakr to lead the community in prayer, and it was understood that Muhammad approved of him as future leader. Thus, after much discussion, the community elders elected Abu Bakr as the new leader. Abu Bakr had been a rather wealthy merchant in Mecca, and was close to Muhammad in age. They grew up together, and he was always Muhammad's closest friend and companion. He was among the first people to embrace Islam, back in the days when Muhammad was preaching to only his close friends and relatives. Abu Bakr had spent much of his life at Muhammad's side.

In his first address to the Muslim community following the election, Abu Bakr reportedly told the gathered crowd: "Oh people, I have been chosen by you as your leader, although I am no better than any one of you. If I do any good, give me your support. If I do any wrong, set me right. . . . Obey me as long as I obey God and His messenger. If I disobey God and His messenger, you are free to disobey me." Abu Bakr helped to maintain the unity of the Muslim community during the potentially chaotic period following Muhammad's death.

FACT

Abu Bakr's appointment was not without detractors. Some felt that he was too soft and emotional to be a forceful or effective leader. Others felt that Muhammad's son-in-law, Ali, should be chosen successor so that leadership would remain within Muhammad's family.

After just over two years of leadership, Abu Bakr fell ill and died in 634 C.E. Before his death, he was able to consult with the senior companions of the Prophet, and Omar was chosen to succeed him as the next caliph of the Muslim state.

Caliph Omar

Omar had embraced Islam after initially denying and persecuting those who joined Muhammad in the early days. He was known to be very brave, bold, and straightforward. He was tough and disciplined, and was well respected for always telling the truth. Despite his reputation for toughness, he was concerned for the welfare of all citizens, and arbitrated in disputes with justice and fairness.

During Omar's ten years in office, the borders of the Islamic state greatly expanded. Peace treaties were signed in Damascus and Jerusalem, offering complete security for all houses of worship, and protecting the lives and property of Christian and Jewish citizens.

As the message of Islam spread, the Muslims defended themselves against aggression but did not use force to convert others to the faith. Rather, the people with whom the Muslims came into contact were inspired by their fairness and the simplicity of their faith. Many converted, and those that didn't were protected as minority communities within the Muslim state.

Omar was assassinated in 644 C.E. by a non-Muslim who had a grudge against him on a personal matter. Before his death, Omar had appointed a six-member committee to select his successor when the time came. After long deliberations, they elected Uthman to become the third caliph of Islam.

Caliph Uthman

Uthman was a close friend of Abu Bakr, and it was Abu Bakr who led him to Islam. Uthman was also a merchant, known for his generosity, integrity, and kindness. He was married to Muhammad's daughter, Ruqaiyah; when she passed away, he married another of Muhammad's daughters, Um Kulthum. He was known to be a simple man despite his wealth, and was addressed as Al-Ghani, a generous man.

During his years of leadership, Uthman made great achievements in pushing the borders against the Persian and Byzantine Empires, and establishing Muslim rule in what is now Libya and parts of Eastern Europe. Uthman also led an effort to preserve the text of the Qur'an, and it remains in its original form today.

However, it was during Uthman's rule that the first cracks in Muslim unity began to appear. Muslim representatives from Egypt accused Uthman of favoritism toward his own family, the Umayyad clan. Uthman was murdered, and his killers never fully prosecuted.

Following Uthman's death, the Prophet Muhammad's son-in-law, Ali, was chosen to be the next caliph. This opened a conflict that eventually resulted in the only major division in the Muslim community, the rift between Sunni and Shi'a (or Shi'ite) Muslims. (For more information about these two groups, see Chapter 10.)

QUESTION?

How did the conflict between the Sunni and Shi'a Muslims begin? This split began as a political difference of opinion over who should assume leadership of the Muslim community. The Shi'a believed that leadership should remain in Muhammad's family. The Sunni believed that the most qualified for the job should be selected from among the community.

According to the Shi'a Muslims, leadership of the community should have stayed within the Prophet Muhammad's own family from the very beginning and the appointment of Ali as caliph was long overdue. Others were not so supportive. One of Uthman's relatives, Mu'awiyah, was a powerful governor in Syria. He and others opposed the selection of Ali as the new leader. They were unhappy that Uthman's killers had not been brought to justice, and believed that Ali had gained support from those who were responsible for the murder.

Caliph Ali

Ali was the young first cousin of Muhammad, who grew up in his household and later married Muhammad's daughter, Fatima. Together they had two children, Hassan and Hussein. Ali was just a young boy when Muhammad began his mission, and thus he was one of the first to embrace Islam in the family. He had a deep knowledge of the Qur'an, and was often consulted by the other caliphs for advice.

Ali took over the caliphate reluctantly, and led the Muslim community from his base in Kufa, Iraq. Despite his desire to bring the community together, the conflict with Mu'awiyah continued to fester. The two sides battled in 657 C.E., and Ali began to lose strength even among his former supporters. In 661 C.E., he was killed, and his son Hassan was proclaimed the next caliph. However, Hassan deferred to Mu'awiyah, who had already been accepted as caliph in many of the Muslim territories.

The first four caliphs of Islam—Abu Bakr, Omar, Uthman, and Ali— were among Muhammad's closest companions. They were purehearted and devout, and held genuine concern for the health and welfare of the Muslim community. They are therefore known as the Rightly Guided Caliphs of Islam, and are among the best examples for Muslims regarding fair and just leadership.

The Umayyads

As the leadership of the Muslim community passed to Mu'awiyah, what became known as the Umayyad Dynasty began. The center of Umayyad rule was in Damascus, Syria, ancestral home of the Umayyad clan. By this time, the Muslim state had become a rather large empire, with governors and armies spread over much of the Middle East, western Asia, eastern Europe, and North Africa. Administration of such a large and diverse region took up much of the energy and attention of the leadership. As with any large empire, secular and practical concerns began to take precedence over more spiritual matters, although faith continued to be an important foundation.

During Mu'awiyah's rule, the division between the Sunni and Shi'a Muslims continued to grow. Ali's second son, Hussein, tried to win the caliphate from the Umayyads, but he was killed in a battle at Karbala, Iraq. He is still mourned by Shi'a Muslims in observances that mark the anniversary of his death.

The Umayyad leaders that followed Mu'awiyah introduced a number of reforms and projects, including irrigation canals, improved agriculture, and a new minted currency. As the Muslim territory continued to expand, the population became more diverse, forever coloring the mosaic that is the Muslim world. Islam continued to spread—from China and Russia to North Africa and Spain, crossing cultural and linguistic boundaries to unite people into a common community of faith.

For all their accomplishments, the Umayyad leadership had many critics. Some believed that the caliphs were more concerned with worldly gain and secular concerns, and that faith suffered at their expense. Others accused the caliphs of being lavish and self-serving. In the middle of the eighth century, a rebellion began to unfold that would bring down the Umayyad dynasty. Control of the Muslim empire fell to descendants of the Prophet's uncle, Abbas.

The Abbasids

When the Abbasids took over, they moved the capital of the Muslim empire from Damascus to Baghdad. Here they began structuring and streamlining the administration of the vast Muslim state. The Abbasids emphasized adherence to the Islamic way of life. They created written manuals that codified government procedures, a postal service, and a banking system. They also helped established trade routes and commercial ventures that connected the far corners of the vast Muslim state.

This streamlining of government and expansion of commerce brought great economic gain and prosperity to the land. Thus, more leisure time was available for scholarly and religious pursuits. Islamic civilization reached its peak during the reign of Harun al-Rashid (786–809 C.E.).

The Golden Age

The massive intellectual achievements that developed during the Abbasid period became the hallmark of what came to be called the Golden Age of Islamic civilization. Baghdad became a center for knowledge and research, literature and science. Intellectuals, writers, and students gathered in centers of learning, the world's first universities, where they made significant contributions to the studies of astronomy, medicine, mathematics, and alchemy. Muslims, Christians, and Jews from all over the world came together to share knowledge, collaborate on research, discuss and debate. They translated scientific works from Greek and introduced many original ideas and innovations.

The scholarly work that was done during this period helped propel Europe out of the Dark Ages, and preserved ancient knowledge for later generations. At this time, the Islamic world was the cradle of civilization, collecting the best minds from all corners of the earth, preserving the world's wisdom, and exploring new theories and discoveries. Chapter 23 takes a closer look at the significant achievements made during this period, and the legacy that was left behind.

Muslim Spain

At the peak of the Islamic empire, Muslims from North Africa crossed the Mediterranean to establish one of the most successful and tolerant cultural environments of all time. They called southern Spain *al-Andalus,* meaning "land of the Vandals." For eight centuries, the Muslim rulers ensured that Christians, Jews, and Muslims lived together in peaceful coexistence. Scholarship and the arts flourished.

FACT

Vandals were a Germanic people who accepted Christianity and came to the Spanish peninsula in 411 C.E. Throughout the fifth century, they plundered and ravaged North Africa, the Mediterranean, and Rome itself. The term "vandalism" was derived from the name of this warring group.

Some minority groups and the common population welcomed the Muslims who entered Andalusia because the Muslim rule brought more freedom and rights for non-Christians. The Jewish people, persecuted in Christian Europe, had the opportunity to participate in the government and academia of Muslim Spain. Indeed, there has never been a society where the three Abrahamic faiths lived together with such peace and tolerance.

Architectural Wonders

In the tenth century, the city of Cordoba was the most sophisticated city in Europe. There, wisdom and learning flourished under Muslim rule, while the rest of Europe was steeped in the ignorance of the Dark Ages. While most of the Europeans remained illiterate, Cordoba boasted seventy libraries, with over 500,000 manuscripts. There were over 600 mosques in the city, as well as hospitals and public baths. The city also provided Europe's first streetlights and paved streets.

In the eleventh century, Christian armies began forcing the Muslims out of northern Spain. The Muslim leaders retreated south, and set up a beautiful refuge in southern Spain, their last stronghold in the region. At Granada, Muslim culture continued to flourish. Muslims built one of the most glorious structures, the Alhambra—a network of courtyards, gardens, and buildings that is still hailed as one of the most beautiful examples of Islamic architecture.

Aftermath: The Inquisition

When the Christian rulers reconquered Spain, they set about ridding the land of the multicultural and tolerant attitudes of the Muslim rulers. The Catholic royalty dismissed the Muslims as heathen Africans. King

Ferdinand and Queen Isabella expelled the remaining Muslim rulers from Spain the same year that Columbus set sail for America. Eventually, the Jewish and Muslim communities were left with two options: convert to Christianity or leave Spain.

The Christian conquerors attempted to eradicate any Muslim influence from Spain, destroying thousands of libraries and converting mosques into Catholic churches. Those that did convert were called *Moriscos*—a derogatory term for baptized Christians of Muslim origin who were not considered "real" Christians by the Spanish rulers. Many of the new converts held on to their Muslim faith in secret, but if they were to be discovered practicing their faith, they would be punished or killed. Despite converting, in 1605 they too were expelled from Spain.

The Ottoman Empire

The Abbasid period was brought down in a violent confrontation with invaders from the East. Following the devastation, the Muslim state began to piece itself back together, but never fully regained the splendor and glory of its Golden Age.

Mongol Invaders

In the thirteenth century, the Muslim state began to succumb to invaders from central Asia, the Mongols. Known as fierce nomadic fighters, the Mongols invaded Baghdad and virtually destroyed the city. They continued through the region, plundering and pillaging all the way to Egypt. Mongol forces killed the last of the Abbasid caliphs in 1258. The Mongol invasions wreaked havoc on the Muslim world. The vast libraries were burned to the ground, scholars and intellectuals were murdered, and much of the cultural legacy was destroyed.

ALERT!

It is reported that the Mongols deliberately destroyed Baghdad's extensive canal system and agricultural areas. The rich cultural heritage—contained in libraries, universities, and medical schools—was destroyed. Hundreds of thousands of people were murdered, and it is said that the rivers bled red with the people's blood.

By 1300, the Mongol leaders did largely convert to Islam and ceased their attacks. In fact, they refocused their fervor on rebuilding mosques and schools. However, the damage was done. The weakened Islamic empire was left fragmented and vulnerable.

As the Muslim empire began to splinter, various local governors attempted to retain control of their own area. On the border between the Byzantine and Islamic empires, one group proved successful: the family of the Ottomans.

Rise of the Ottomans

The Ottomans had proven to be very successful in uniting the territory within their reach. By the late 1300s, they had control of what is now Turkey and Greece, and began threatening Constantinople, the heart of the Byzantine Empire. A series of early Ottoman rulers expanded their control, and after a series of battles finally conquered Constantinople in 1453. The great city, first known as Byzantium and then as Constantinople (named after Emperor Constantine), was renamed Istanbul.

The traditional symbol of Islam, the crescent moon and star, actually predates Islam by several thousand years. It was featured on the flag of Byzantium even before the birth of Christ, perhaps in honor of the Greek goddess Diana. When the Ottomans conquered Constantinople in 1453, they adopted the city's existing flag and symbol.

Suleiman the Magnificent

As a leader and statesman, Suleiman the Magnificent has the distinction of being one of the enduring figures of Ottoman history—he stayed in power for nearly fifty years, dying in 1566. During his rule, the Ottoman Empire experienced its own Golden Age.

Suleiman was known for being a balanced lawgiver who supervised some of the most beautiful Islamic construction projects. Several large monuments in Turkey were built during his reign, including the Suleiman Mosque in Istanbul. Under Suleiman's leadership, Ottoman territories nearly doubled in size. A just ruler, Suleiman ensured that all Ottoman lands respected freedom of worship, and all races and religions lived freely. His government created elaborate social welfare programs and increased commerce opportunities.

The Fall of the Ottoman Empire

During the rule of Suleiman, the Ottoman Empire was in the center of the world. Perfectly poised between Africa, Asia, and Europe, the empire served as a bridge between the East and the West. However, the peak of Ottoman civilization could not be sustained. Later rulers lacked Suleiman's ability and competence, and they failed to sustain the days of glory and achievement.

The early decline of the Ottoman Empire was brought about primarily through internal decay. Inefficiency and corruption started to become commonplace, and the rulers became more isolated and out of touch. The empire began to lose territory due to internal revolt, and later due to aggressive European expansion and colonization.

The final fall of the Ottoman Empire came about following World War I, when the Ottomans allied with Germany, which turned out to be the losing side. The Arab revolt (dramatized in the film *Lawrence of Arabia*) aided the Allied victory against the Germans and Turks. Britain and France then set about dividing up what remained of the Ottoman Empire between the allied victors. Ⓔ

Chapter 6

Six Articles of Faith

Muslims throughout the world share a common set of fundamental beliefs that are key to understanding Islam. These beliefs fall into six categories, or articles, of faith: faith in God (the key article, the one that transcends and intertwines with all others), in angels, in the prophets, in the revealed books, in the Day of Judgment, and destiny and the Divine Decree.

Faith in God

The basis of Islam is a pure, monotheistic faith in One Almighty God. Muslims believe that there is only One Supreme God, Allah, who creates and controls everything in the universe. In Islam, God is believed to be the Creator, the Sustainer, the Ruler, and the Judge. Muslims recognize that a person who believes in the Creator comes to love Him, trust in Him, hope from Him, and fear disappointing Him. The strict monotheism of Islam, called *Tawhid,* is the cornerstone of the faith.

"Allah" is the personal name of the One Almighty God, a name that is not subject to plurality ("gods") or gender ("goddess"). Therefore, even English-speaking Muslims prefer to use this personal name when referring to the Creator. Sometimes Allah is referred to as "He," and may be quoted in the royal sense, "We." These words do nothing more than expose the limits of human language. In Islam, Allah is beyond all human perception, and is neither male, female, dual, or plural. Allah is simply One. Christians and Jews in the Arabic-speaking world also use the name Allah to refer to the Almighty.

FACT

"Allah" derives from an Arabic word that means "the God." However, Muslims see it more than just a noun that could refer to any god. It is the proper name of God, which He uses in the Qur'an.

Pure Monotheism

Muslims reject all attempts to personalize the Almighty, or place intermediaries between humans and God—all idols and attempts to "reach" God through others are strictly forbidden. Islam also rejects the notion that God came to earth in the form of any man or creature.

The biggest sin in Islam, which is called *shirk,* is to associate other deities with God. In fact, Muhammad described this as the one and only sin that God will not forgive. Due to this strict prohibition against any form of idolatry, or anything that might lead to it, one will never find pictures or statues at a Muslim place of worship (the Muslim injunction against certain forms of art is discussed further in Chapter 22).

The Attributes of Allah

Throughout the Qur'an, Allah is described with ninety-nine attributes or "names." These attributes describe for human beings the nature of God—that He is the Most Merciful, the Most Gracious, the Beneficent, the All-Knowing, the Loving, the All-Wise, and so on.

In one chapter, the Qur'an describes:

Allah is He, other than Whom there is no other god, Who knows all things both open and secret, Most Gracious, Most Merciful. Allah is He, other than Whom there is no other god. The Sovereign, the Holy One, the Source of Peace, the Guardian of Faith, the Preserver of Safety, the Exalted in Might, the Irresistible, the Justly Proud. Glory to Allah! High is He above the partners they ascribe to Him. He is Allah, the Creator, the Originator, the Fashioner. To Him belong the Most Beautiful Names. Whatever is in the heavens and on earth declares His Praises and Glory. And He is the Exalted in Might, the Wise. (59:22–24)

Allah's Relationship with Humans

While Allah is fully transcendent and beyond all human attempts at understanding, Islam also teaches that Allah is near to us. Allah fully sustains each and every thing and creature on earth, and reaches out to us in mercy and compassion. "When my people ask you concerning Me, I am indeed close to them. I listen to the prayer of every supplicant when he calls on Me. Let them also, with a will, listen to My call, and believe in Me, that they may walk in the right way" (2:186). Allah knows everything about every grain of sand, every leaf, and the secret whisperings of each person's heart. One does not need any special devices or intermediaries to reach out directly to Allah.

Muslims believe that since Allah reaches out to us in compassion and mercy, it is our responsibility to respond to His call. Muslims believe that Allah is the One "Who created me, and it is Allah who guides me, and it is Allah who feeds me and gives me to drink. And when I am ill, it is

Allah who cures me. And it is Allah Who will cause me to die, and then will bring me back to life" (26:78–81).

Belief in Angels

Muslims believe that Allah created angels out of light, and that they work tirelessly to administer Allah's kingdom. Without a free will of their own, these spiritual creatures carry out Allah's orders in full obedience. "They do not disobey Allah's commands that they receive; they do precisely what they are commanded" (66:6).

The Arabic word for "angels" is *mala'ika*. This word comes from the Arabic root meaning "to help and assist," or "gathering, assembly." According to the teachings of Islam, angels give full service and devotion to God, without any hint of disobedience. It is their very nature to be Allah's faithful servants.

Named Angels

The angels surround us at all times, and they have a multitude of duties and tasks. There are angels who record our words and deeds, and angels who offer us their protection. A few angels who have special responsibilities are known to us by name. The angel Jibreel (Gabriel) has the responsibility of communicating revelation to the prophets. The angel Mikail (Michael) is in charge of the rain supply, which gives life to life. The angel Israfeel (Raphael) is in charge of blowing the trumpet that will sound to mark the Day of Judgment. The Angel of Death is responsible for taking the souls of the dying.

The Jinn

Unlike the angels, the jinn are creatures that were created from fire, and have a free will to either obey or disobey Allah. Islam teaches that Satan (called Shaytan or Iblis) is one of the jinn, and is the leader of those who disobey Allah and strive to lead human beings astray.

The jinn were the basis for the western idea of a "genie." However, Muslims do not believe that the jinn live in magic lamps or grant wishes. Rather, the jinn are a serious presence, and not to be joked about or used for entertainment purposes.

Belief in the Prophets of God

Allah communicates His commands and guidance to mankind to be revealed through human prophets. Muslims believe that it is through Allah's grace and benevolence that He sent prophets and messengers to every nation, in order to guide people to the straight path.

All prophets have been human beings who received divine revelations in order to be role models, teachers, and advisers to their people. Each prophet was born in a different time, place, and culture. However, the prophets' message has always been the same: calling people to worship the One Supreme God and to obey His commandments.

Biblical Prophets

The Qur'an makes mention of several of the Biblical prophets, including the following:

- Adam
- Alyasa (Elisha)
- Ayyub (Job)
- Dawood (David)
- Dhul-Kifl (Ezekiel)
- Esa (Jesus)
- Haroon (Aaron)
- Hud (Heber)
- Ibrahim (Abraham)
- Idrees (Enoch)
- Ilyas (Elias)
- Ishaq (Isaac)
- Ismail (Ishmael)
- Lut (Lot)
- Muhammad
- Musa (Moses)
- Nuh (Noah)
- Saleh (Methuselah)
- Shu'aib (Jethro)
- Sulayman (Solomon)
- Uzair (Ezra)
- Yahya (John the Baptist)
- Yaqub (Jacob)
- Yunus (Jonah)
- Yusuf (Joseph)
- Zakariyya (Zachariah)

The Qur'an is clear that each of the prophets communicated the message of Islam—that is, to believe in One Almighty God and to follow His guidance.

ALERT!

The word "Muslim" means "a person who submits to God." Under this definition, all of the prophets were Muslims. The Qur'an makes specific mention of the Prophet Abraham in this regard: "Abraham was not a Jew, nor yet a Christian, but he was true in faith, and bowed his will to Allah's [which is Islam], and he did not join gods with Allah" (3:67).

Muslims are advised to respect all of Allah's messengers, and not to distinguish or elevate one above another. "Say: 'We believe in Allah, and the revelation given to us, and to Abraham, Ismail, Isaac, Jacob, and the Tribes, and that given to Moses and Jesus, and that given to all prophets from their Lord. We make no difference between one and another of them, and we submit to Allah'" (2:136). The Qur'an also acknowledges that there were many more prophets, sent to all peoples through time, whose stories have not been told (4:164).

Muhammad, the Last Prophet

As Allah continued to send prophets to guide His people, each prophet was rejected, and his message either distorted or lost. Then Allah would send another prophet to renew and repeat the message of guidance. Muslims believe that after Muhammad, there was no need for Allah to send another prophet, because he left behind the protected scripture of the Qur'an to remain as a guide for mankind. According to the Qur'an, "Muhammad . . . is the messenger of God and the seal of the prophets" (33:40).

Belief in the Revealed Books of God

Muslims believe that Allah has sent human prophets in order to proclaim

His teachings throughout time and to every people. Some of these prophets had the additional responsibility of being messengers (*risalah* in Arabic), delivering the actual words of Allah to the people. Although these books were composed by different messengers, they all originate from the same divine source.

Muslims believe in the revelation of five divine books:

- Scrolls, revealed to Abraham
- Zabur (Psalms), revealed to David
- Tawrah (Torah), revealed to Moses
- Injeel (Gospels), revealed to Jesus
- Qur'an, revealed to Muhammad

Muslims believe that these original messages, at the time they were revealed, had many common teachings with Islam, with some specific guidance directed to the communities that received the revelation. However, over time the original teachings of these books became distorted or lost in human hands, and it was necessary for Allah to send another message to set the record straight and confirm His teachings. Muslims believe that the Qur'an was the final revelation God sent to mankind.

FACT

Islam's position on the Bible is that the book in circulation today does not accurately reflect the teachings of Jesus or the beliefs of his early followers. While some passages may seem to correspond with Islamic teaching, Muslims find most of the book, and certainly the modern translations and interpretations, to be corrupted.

Muslims believe that the Qur'an is the exact, authentic, and unchangeable word of Allah, as revealed to the Prophet Muhammad, and it has been protected from any change or corruption. It therefore supersedes previous revelation and is the only revealed text that Muslims turn to for guidance today.

Belief in the Day of Judgment

Muslims believe that the life of this world, and all that is in it, will come to an end on one appointed day. This day is called *Youm al-Qiyama,* or the "Day of Reckoning." At this time, every person will be raised for judgment by Allah. Allah will judge each person individually, according to his or her faith and the balance of his or her good and bad actions.

The Day of Judgment is described throughout the Qur'an as a day of peace for the righteous, and a day of despair for evildoers. "When the sky bursts apart, when the planets are dispersed, when the seas spill forth, when graves are overturned—then each soul will know what it sent forth and what it left behind" (82:1–5).

Divine Mercy and Justice

The teachings of Islam emphasize that on the Day of Judgment Allah will show mercy and justice in His judgment: "On the Day of Judgment, We shall set up scales of justice, so that not a soul will be dealt with unjustly in the least. And if there be the weight of even a mustard seed, We will bring it to account" (21:47).

QUESTION?

How is one "saved" in Islam?
"Whoever works righteousness, man or woman, and has faith, truly will Allah give a life that is good and pure, and will bestow on such their reward [in the hereafter] according to the best of their actions" (Qur'an 16:97). In Islam, faith and good works go hand in hand.

On the Day of Judgment, each person will be responsible only for his or her own faith and actions. In Islam, there is no concept of original sin or any sort of "fall from grace" of mankind. Islam rejects the notion of atonement, that someone (even God Himself) could sacrifice himself to save others. According to the Qur'an, "Who receives guidance, receives it for his own benefit; who goes astray does so to his own loss. No bearer of burdens can bear the burden of another, nor would We punish until We had sent a messenger to give warning" (17:15).

Above all, Allah is quick to forgive and show mercy to those who repent. "If anyone errs or wrongs his own soul, but afterwards seeks Allah's forgiveness, he will find Allah Oft-Forgiving, Most Merciful" (4:110). Nearly all of the chapters of the Qur'an begin with the phrase, "In the name of Allah, Most Gracious, Most Merciful."

Belief in Destiny and Divine Decree

Muslims believe that since Allah is the Sustainer of all life, nothing happens except by His Will and with His full knowledge. Divine decree, fate, or "destiny" is called *Al-Qadr* in Arabic (it comes from a word that has the meaning of "power" and "ability"). Allah thus has the power and ability to know the destiny of every creature. Everything in the world has a set, predetermined course.

This belief does not contradict with the idea of humans having free will to choose a course of action. Allah does not force us to do anything; we can choose to obey or disobey Him. However, our choice is known to Allah before we even do it, because Allah's knowledge is timeless and complete.

FACT

When discussing any event that will occur in the future, Muslims always add the phrase, *Insha'Allah,* or "God willing." This is done in accordance with Qur'anic teachings (18:23–24) that we cannot be sure of what will happen in the future.

Muslims are warned to expect difficulties and trials, in order to test and distinguish those who are patient from those who fall into despair. "And certainly, We shall test you with something of fear, hunger, loss of wealth, lives, and products—but give glad tidings to those who patiently persevere. Those who, when afflicted with calamity, say: 'To Allah we belong, and to Allah we will return.' They are those on whom descend blessings from their Lord, and mercy—those who are guided" (2:156–157).

Muslims believe, therefore, that everything that happens in life is according to Allah's will. This recognition sustains the believer through difficulties and hardships. There may be things in life that we do not understand, but Muslims trust that Allah has wisdom in all things. They believe that Allah can see the whole picture, while our vision and perception of events is limited. Ⓔ

Chapter 7

The Five Pillars of Practice

F aith in the Creator naturally leads to worship of and obedience to Him. Muslims observe five formal acts of worship, which they refer to as the five pillars of Islam. Based on the foundation of faith (discussed in Chapter 6), the pillars help build and structure a Muslim's daily life. The five pillars of Islam are the declaration of faith, prayer, fasting, almsgiving, and pilgrimage to Mecca.

A Muslim's Daily Life

From the time they wake up in the morning to the time they retire to bed, Muslims are constantly engaged in worship, mindful of Allah's laws, orders, and guidance.

The Islamic concept of worship is very broad. Anything that one does in life in accordance with Allah's guidance is an act of worship. Speaking the truth, refraining from gossip, dealing honestly in commercial affairs, treating one's parents with respect and honor, helping the poor and needy, dealing lovingly and fairly with family members—all of these actions, done for the sake of Allah, are considered worship.

The structured acts of worship occur on both a personal and community-wide level. They assure that every day, month, and year a Muslim is reminded of his or her obligations and duties, is constantly seeking the guidance of Allah, and is developing humility and consciousness of God. The five pillars of practice form the structure for a Muslim's worship and daily life.

Declaration of Faith

To emphasize that Islam is fundamentally based on a strong faith in Allah, the first pillar of practice is related to this foundation. The *shahaada,* or declaration of faith, is repeated daily throughout a Muslim's life. A Muslim declares his or her faith by saying, *La ilaha illa Allah wa Muhammad ar-rasulullah* (there is no god worthy to be worshipped except Allah, and Muhammad is the messenger of Allah).

This declaration of faith summarizes the whole of Islamic belief in the Oneness of God. Muslims also affirm faith in the prophethood, with Muhammad being the final messenger. This statement is repeated throughout the day, in formal prayers and in informal supplications. All that is necessary for a person to convert to the faith of Islam is to believe in and make this declaration.

Daily Prayer

The second pillar of Islam is *salaat* (daily prayer). Prayer is a method by which human beings can connect to Allah, and gather strength, guidance, and peace of mind. Muslims say formal prayers five times a day; they rely on these prayers to repeat and refresh their beliefs, and to help them take time out of the busy day to remember Allah and renew the effort to follow His guidance. In Islam, prayers can be performed in any clean location.

Muslim House of Worship

The Muslim house of worship is called a mosque, a term that comes from the Arabic word *masjed*. This word is based on the Arabic root S-J-D, which conveys the sense of "bowing down" or "prostration," so the mosque is the place where one bows down and prostrates in prayer.

Most mosques are open for the five daily prayers, as well as at other times for administrative or community needs. While it is not required to pray at the mosque (except for Friday noon prayer), most Muslims prefer to gain the benefit and reward of worshipping in congregation whenever possible. Details of the prayer are fully explored in Chapter 8.

ALERT!

When entering a mosque, worshippers and visitors alike are expected to remove their shoes. This is to keep the prayer area clean of soil and dirt that may be tracked in. Many Muslims follow this custom in their own homes as well.

The Fast of Ramadan

Once each year, Muslims enter a period of intense spiritual devotion known as the fast of Ramadan. Ramadan is the ninth month in the Islamic lunar calendar; it lasts for twenty-nine or thirty days, depending on the particular year's lunar cycle. Muslims are commanded to spend the daylight hours of Ramadan in fasting.

Ramadan is a period of reflection, generosity, and sacrifice observed by all Muslims at the same time, all over the world. The Islamic fast is a complete one, allowing no food, drink, smoking, or intimacy during the daytime hours of the month. From dawn until dusk, Muslims must practice self-control and focus on prayers and devotion.

During the fast, Muslims experience hunger and thirst, and learn to sympathize with those in the world who have little to eat. They come to appreciate the blessings that Allah grants them. Through increased charity during the month, Muslims develop feelings of generosity and goodwill toward others. And since all Muslims in the world are undergoing the same experience at the same time, this practice strengthens the bonds of brotherhood and sisterhood in each Muslim community and throughout the Muslim world.

FACT

Muhammad once said, "If one does not abandon falsehood in words and deeds, Allah has no need for his abandoning of food and drink." It is therefore imperative that the fasting person not only refrains from food and drink, but also from foul speech, lying, arguing, and the like.

The Islamic calendar is based on lunar cycles, so fixed times for the fasting month change from year to year. Over the course of time, the month occurs in all seasons. So all Muslims, no matter where in the world they live, have the opportunity to experience fasting during long summer days and short winter days over the course of their lifetimes.

Who Is Required to Fast?

The Qur'an commands as follows: "Ramadan is the month in which the Qur'an was sent down, as a guide to mankind, and clear signs for guidance and judgment between right and wrong. So every one of you who is present at his home during that month should spend it in fasting. But if any one is ill, or on a journey, the prescribed period should be made up by days later" (2:185). Every Muslim is required to fast, with the following exceptions.

- Travelers
- Those who are suffering from a temporary illness
- The elderly or chronically ill
- Women in menses or post-childbirth bleeding
- Pregnant or nursing women
- Children who have not yet reached adolescence

If possible, missed days are to be made up at a later time. If the reason for exception is long-term, then the missed days may be compensated for by giving in charity enough to feed one poor person for each day of fasting.

Children are not required to fast until they reach puberty. However, many children like to join in the activities of the family, and try to fast for a day or part of a day. Sometimes they will fast on the weekends, for example, or will fast from noon until sunset. This is encouraged as practice for the day that fasting will be incumbent upon them.

A Typical Day of Ramadan

On a day of fasting, Muslims rise before dawn for an early meal called *suhoor*. This light meal is intended to nourish the body through the rigorous daylong fast. With the call to prayer for the dawn prayer, the fast begins. Muslims continue through their daily lives of work, school, or other commitments, conscious of the limitations of fasting, and striving to be on their best behavior. Muslims continue to observe the daily prayers as usual, and often spend part of the day reading chapters of the Qur'an.

As sunset approaches, Muslims often gather together as family or community to break the fast and enjoy a meal together at the end of the day. Muslims break their fast just as the call to prayer for the sunset prayer is heard. Following the tradition of the Prophet Muhammad, Muslims often break their fast by eating dates and drinking some milk. After the sunset prayers, they sit down together for an evening meal called *fitoor* (technically, "breakfast").

In the evening, Muslims gather at the mosque for special prayers called *taraweeh*. These extra prayers are offered each night of Ramadan. Every evening, a section of the Qur'an will be read in a long prayer, so that by the end of the month the entire Qur'an will have been heard.

Muslims also spend time visiting with friends and relatives before retiring for the night to rest before starting the fast again the next day.

Eid al-Fitr

At the end of Ramadan, Muslims observe a three-day holiday called *Eid al-Fitr,* or the Festival of Fast-Breaking. In preparation for this holiday, Muslims give money in charity so that every family can enjoy the festivities and have a good meal. During the holiday, they try to spend time with family and friends, visit the sick and elderly, and offer games and gifts to the children. Muslims celebrate the completion of another fasting year, seek blessings and forgiveness, and look forward to the opportunity to fast again next year.

Muslims observe two holidays during the year. The first falls at the end of the fasting month of Ramadan (Eid al-Fitr, or Festival of Fast-Breaking), and the second falls at the end of the pilgrimage season (*Eid al-Adha,* or Festival of Sacrifice).

Giving Alms

Muslims recognize that all wealth and bounties in this life are theirs only by the permission of Allah, and with having them come certain duties and responsibilities. In Islam, it is the duty of the wealthy to help those who are poor and destitute. Giving in charity is emphasized again and again in the Qur'an, often hand in hand with prayer. "And be steadfast in prayer and regular in charity. And whatever good you send forth for your souls before you, you shall find it with Allah, for Allah sees well all that you do" (2:110).

While charitable giving is always encouraged in Islam, wealthier members of the community are specifically required to pay alms. This practice is known as *zakat,* which comes from an Arabic word for "purify" and "grow," for you purify your own wealth by sharing with others and allowing their wealth to grow.

Alms Recipients

As a specific religious alms, zakat is set aside for certain categories of people:

- The poor and the needy
- Those employed to collect and distribute zakat
- Converts to Islam (who may be disowned by their non-Muslim family)
- Slaves (so that they may purchase their freedom)
- Those in debt
- Those who are struggling in Allah's cause
- The wayfarer (stranded traveler)

Calculating Zakat

Zakat is required to be paid only by individuals who have wealth over a certain minimum amount (the equivalent of several ounces of gold). Income that is used to meet expenses, such as food and housing, does not figure in the calculation of zakat. Only wealth that remains after meeting one's own family expenses is considered.

FACT

Zakat is paid at the rate of 2.5 percent of remaining wealth, after the deduction of expenses. In areas without a Muslim governing body to collect the zakat, each Muslim individual is responsible for ensuring that the amount is paid.

In addition to zakat, voluntary alms (called *sadaqah*) can be given at any time, in any amount, to anyone. The Qur'an repeatedly encourages Muslims to give to the needy and care for orphans. In addition, Muhammad often said that even the smallest of good deeds can be considered charity, from smiling at your brother, to removing a harmful thing from the road. Even planting a tree, from which people or animals might one day eat, is considered charity.

Pilgrimage to Mecca

Every Muslim strives to make a once-in-a-lifetime pilgrimage to the sacred sites in Mecca, in present-day Saudi Arabia. This final pillar of Islam is required of every adult Muslim, male or female, if physically and financially possible. Many Muslims spend their entire lives saving and planning for this journey.

In recent years, over two million Muslims have gathered in Mecca for the rites of the Hajj: peasants and kings, workers and engineers, Chinese and Russians, Arabs from Canada and African-Americans from the United States. Each year, pilgrims arrive by air, road, and sea from over seventy nations.

Preparing for the Hajj

When undertaking the pilgrimage, Muslims first shed all signs of their wealth and status by donning simple white garments, called *ihram*. The required pilgrimage dress for men is two white cloths, one of which covers the body from the waist down, and one that is gathered around the shoulder. Women usually wear a simple white dress and headscarf. The ihram is a symbol of purity and equality. When wearing the ihram, the pilgrims enter a state of devotion and purity, during which quarrelling and violence (toward other people or even animals) is forbidden.

Muslims announce their arrival by calling out: "Here I am, Oh God, at Your command! Here I am at Your command! You are without associate! Here I am at Your command! To You are praise, grace, and dominion! You are without associate!" The sound of this chant (said in Arabic) rings out all over the land, as pilgrims begin arriving in Mecca for the sacred rites.

It may appear to some that the pilgrimage in Mecca is somehow associated with the importance of the city in Muhammad's life. However, most of the rites of pilgrimage date back to the Prophet Abraham, and are performed in remembrance of his life.

Rites of the Hajj

On the first day of the Hajj, the pilgrims travel from Mecca to Mina, a small village east of the city. There they spend the day and night, praying and reading the Qur'an.

On the second day of the pilgrimage, the pilgrims leave Mina just after dawn to travel to the plain of Arafat for the culminating experience of the Hajj. On what is known as the "Day of Arafat," the pilgrims spend the entire day standing near the Mount of Mercy, asking Allah for forgiveness and making supplications. After sunset on the Day of Arafat, the pilgrims leave and travel to an open plain called Muzdalifah. There they spend the night, praying, and collect small stone pebbles to be used on the next day.

On the third day, the pilgrims move before sunrise, this time back to Mina. Here they throw the stone pebbles at pillars that represent the seductions of Satan. When throwing the stones, the pilgrims remember the story of Satan's attempt to dissuade Abraham from following God's command to sacrifice his son. The stones represent Abraham's rejection of Satan and the firmness of his faith. After casting the pebbles, most pilgrims slaughter an animal (often a sheep or a goat) and give the meat to the poor—a symbolic act that shows their willingness to part with something that is precious to them, just as the Prophet Abraham was prepared to sacrifice his son at God's command.

ALERT!

Islam rejected the ancient rituals of sacrificing animals to God. According to the Qur'an, "Neither its meat nor its blood will reach Allah; it is only your piety that reaches Him" (22:37). Muslims slaughter animals at this time to remember and celebrate the piety of the Prophet Abraham, and to obtain meat to share with the poor.

The pilgrims then return to Mecca and perform seven turns around the Ka'aba, the house of worship built by Abraham and his son Ismail. In other rites, the pilgrims pray near a place called "The Station of Abraham," which is reportedly where Abraham stood while constructing the Ka'aba. The pilgrims also walk seven times between two small hills near the

Ka'aba, called Safa and Marwa, in remembrance of the plight of Abraham's wife Hajar, who searched desperately for water for herself and her son before a spring welled up in the desert for her. The pilgrims also drink from this ancient spring, which continues to flow today.

The Lesser Pilgrimage or Umrah

Hajj is required of every adult Muslim who is physically and financially able to make the journey, and must be performed during a specific period of time in the Islamic calendar. However, there is another type of pilgrimage to Mecca, known as the *umrah* (lesser pilgrimage), which may be performed any time during the year.

During umrah, Muslims observe many of the same pilgrimage rites as during Hajj. However, while this experience is commendable, it does not free one from the requirements of performing the pilgrimage during the appointed time.

QUESTION?

Why are only Muslims allowed into Mecca and Madinah?
These are cities of great importance in Islamic tradition, centers of pilgrimage and prayer, sacred places where Muslims are free from the distractions of daily life. The ban, mentioned in the Qur'an, is intended to provide a place of peace and refuge for Muslim believers.

Eid al-Adha

At the end of the pilgrimage, Muslims observe a holiday known as Eid al-Adha, or the Festival of Sacrifice. Muslims who did not attend the Hajj also slaughter meat, which they share with the poor and less fortunate. In every other way, the holiday is observed in a very similar way to the holiday at the end of Ramadan. Special prayers are said, family and friends visit each other, and gifts are given to the children. When the pilgrims return from their journey, there is much celebration to welcome them home. The pilgrims come back from Hajj spiritually refreshed, forgiven of their sins, and ready to start life anew, with a clean slate. (E)

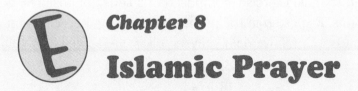

Chapter 8

Islamic Prayer

The daily prayers serve as touchstones of a Muslim's life. Five times each day, Muslims around the world break from their work and activities to turn toward God and refresh their faith. Each step in the process—the movements as well as the words—plays a role in cleansing the believer's heart and demonstrating his or her submission to God.

Five Daily Prayers

Prayer is the central act of worship for all Muslims, and is their direct contact with the Creator. Prayer is a time to thank God for His blessings and ask Him for forgiveness, guidance, and protection. A Muslim prays directly to God Alone, without any mediator. Islamic prayer is both a physical and spiritual exercise, composed of a series of postures, gestures, and recitations. Each step in the prayer expresses praise, adoration, and submission to God. All five daily prayers follow the same basic pattern.

FACT

Muhammad once compared daily prayers to a river in which people bathe five times a day. "Would you notice any dirt on such a person? That is the example of the five prayers with which God washes away evil deeds."

Why Pray?

Formal prayers are not meant to be a ritualistic or mindless activity; their role is to constantly remind Muslims of the purpose of life itself and reaffirm their faith in God. Following prayers, Muslims go back to their worldly affairs conscious of their duties and fortified against sin. Prayers said in congregation bond Muslims together in equality of their brotherhood and sisterhood. Most important, prayer is a time for direct connection to God. As Muslims say during their prayers, "God hears those who call on Him."

Timing of the Prayers

Muslims present themselves for prayer five times each day. The prayers are timed at the beginning and end of the day, as well as several times in between, to offer a refreshing break from the daily grind. The names and times of the prayers are:

1. *Fajr.* This prayer starts off the day; it is performed before sunrise.
2. *Dhuhr.* This prayer is performed just after midday.
3. *'Asr.* This prayer is performed in the late afternoon.

4. *Maghrib.* This prayer is performed just after sunset.
5. *'Isha.* This prayer ends the day; it is performed in the late evening.

There is a short window of time during which each prayer may be observed, although Muslims try not to delay the prayers so long that they miss them. In special circumstances (for example, when traveling) and under specific guidelines, it is permitted for Muslims to shorten the prayers or say two prayers at the same time.

Muslims often make use of prayer calendars and time sheets, and even computer software programs, to know the prayer timings for their locale. Muslims who live in proximity of a mosque may know that it is time to pray when they hear the call to prayer.

The Call to Prayer

When Muslims first gathered in Madinah, they established the first mosque, specifically for Muslim worship. In those early days of the Muslim community, however, the people did not have any way of knowing the exact time for gathering in the mosque for prayer. The Christians rang bells at the church, and the Jews blew on a ram's horn trumpet to call people to assembly. The Muslim community struggled to find an appropriate signal, to let the community know when to gather for prayer.

A Public Call

The problem was solved when a suggestion was made to appoint someone to call for prayer with his voice. Muhammad approved of the idea, and asked Bilal to do so. Bilal was an African convert who had been freed from slavery by the Muslims. He would climb up onto the roof of the mosque and use his beautiful and powerful voice to call out to the faithful to come for prayer. This call to prayer became known as the *adhan,* from a word that means to call or announce. Thus began the tradition that continues to this day.

The person who makes the call to prayer is called the *mu'adhin.* It is considered an honor to be selected by the community to make the call to prayer. A man is usually chosen because of his piety, as well as his powerful vocal technique. (Women do not serve as mu'adhins because it's considered inappropriate for a woman to project her voice in public.)

FACT

In earlier times, the person calling the adhan simply stood on the roof of the mosque. As mosque architecture developed, the towering minaret became a convenient place from which to make the call to prayer. In modern times, Muslims still rely on the traditional caller, although he is now assisted with loudspeakers and sometimes cassette recordings of his voice.

At the time of prayer, the mu'adhin calls out the following words:

Allahu Akbar (God is Great)
Allahu Akbar
Allahu Akbar
Allahu Akbar
Ashadu an-la illaha ill Allah (I bear witness that there is no god except Allah)
Ashadu an-la illaha ill Allah
Ashadu ana Muhammad ar-rasulullah (I bear witness that Muhammad is the messenger of Allah)
Ashadu ana Muhammad ar-rasulullah (I bear witness that Muhammad is the messenger of Allah)
Haya ala salah (Come to prayer)
Haya ala salah
Haya ala falah (Come to prosperity)
Haya ala falah
Allahu Akbar (God is Great)
Allahu Akbar
La illaha ill Allah (There is no god worthy to be worshipped except Allah)

During the predawn hours, there is an additional phrase added in the middle: *As-salaatu khayrun min'n-nawm,* which means, "Prayer is better than sleep!"

Upon hearing the adhan, Muslims make their way to the mosque for prayer, which starts after people have had time to arrive (usually about fifteen to thirty minutes after the call).

Mosques all over the Muslim world call the adhan over loudspeakers, so that everyone within traveling distance can hear. Often several mosques are located in the same vicinity, and the various sounds of the adhan echo through the land.

Performing Ablutions

Before presenting themselves for prayer, Muslims prepare by making sure that their bodies are clean of dirt and impurities. Purifying the body also helps to prepare the mind for a state of worship. The Qur'an says, "Oh you who believe! When you prepare for prayer, wash your faces, and your hands [arms] to the elbows. Rub your heads [with water], and wash your feet to the ankles. . . . Allah does not wish to place you in difficulties, but to make you clean, and to complete His favor upon you so that you may be grateful" (5:6). Ablutions are called *wudu,* from a word meaning pure, clean, and radiant.

Steps of Ablution

To perform ablution, a Muslim first takes a moment to get into the appropriate mood in preparation to wash up for prayer. Then the individual rinses with clean water the following parts of the body, starting on the right-hand side:

1. Hands
2. Mouth
3. Nose
4. Face
5. Arms, to the elbows
6. Head, including ears
7. Feet

If no clean water is available, or if one must avoid water for medical reasons, it is possible to perform a dry ablution, known as *tayamoom*. In this case, ablution is done using clean sand or dust, and only the hands and face are wiped.

Once ablutions are done, the believer remains in a state of purity until something is done to break the ablution—like using the bathroom, bleeding from a wound, vomiting, passing wind, or falling asleep. In these cases, ablutions must be redone before the next prayer.

A Full Shower

In some cases, a full bath or shower (called *ghusl*) is required before prayer. These thorough ablutions are done after intimate sexual contact and at the end of the menstrual period. After fully washing the whole body, the same process of ablution is done, with the addition of rinsing the sides of the body and the head more thoroughly.

Performing the Prayers

Once a Muslim has purified his or her mind and body, the prayer can begin. If the individual is not praying in a mosque, he or she must find a clean place to conduct the prayers. Wherever they are in the world, worshippers stand facing the Ka'aba in Mecca.

The direction that Muslims face in prayers is called the *qiblah*. The first qiblah for Muslims was the city of Jerusalem. It was over a decade into his mission that Muhammad received revelation to change the direction from Jerusalem to Mecca (Qur'an 2:142–144).

Worshiping in Congregation

If there is more than one person praying in congregation, the people stand in rows, side by side, with shoulders and feet touching each other. In a mixed-gender group, the men form separate rows from the women, to avoid distractions during the movements of prayer. Some mosques offer a separate balcony or room for women to pray, so that they may have privacy during the prayer.

In a group of worshippers, an imam is chosen to lead the prayer. The imam recites the verses and words of prayer, and the people follow his movements. During the service, he stands facing away from the worshippers, toward the direction of Mecca.

FACT

An imam is usually someone who has memorized much of the Qur'an and is considered knowledgeable and pious. There is no priesthood in Islam; the imam may change from year to year. The word "imam" means "leader" and "in front of," because he stands in front of the other worshippers during prayer.

Prayer Cycles

Each prayer is made up of cycles of movements and words, called *raka'at;* each one of the five prayers is assigned a number of cycles, anywhere from two to four raka'ats (the reasons behind the number of cycles assigned for each prayer are unknown). For each cycle of prayer, the worshipper performs certain steps while reciting the prayer.

Because Muslims pray five times a day, most of the prayers are performed alone. The following steps outline how a worshipper would perform a prayer in solitude. (Note that all prayers are said in Arabic; the following phrases are translations.)

1. Raises hands and says, "God is Great."
2. Stands with hands crossed over chest.
3. Recites the first chapter of the Qur'an, then any other small chapter or collection of verses (the choice of a particular chapter might vary according to a particular occasion or personal preference).
4. Repeats, "God is Great," then lowers into a bowing position, reciting words of praise to Allah.
5. Says, "Allah hears those who praise Him; Our Lord, You deserve our praise," and rises to a standing position.
6. Repeats, "God is Great," then lowers into a position of prostration, reciting words of praise to Allah.
7. Repeats, "God is Great," then rises to a sitting position.

8. Repeats, "God is Great," then prostrates, again reciting words of praise to Allah.
9. Either rises again for another raka'at, or remains sitting, depending on the prayer.

When the prayers are performed in a congregation, the faithful would follow the imam in their prayers—he'll make all the necessary choices, like deciding which verses from the Qur'an would be recited.

> The first chapter of the Qur'an that is repeated several times during each prayer is called Al-Fatihah (the Opening Chapter). Due to its concise summing-up of the Islamic faith, offering praise and seeking guidance, it is sometimes called the "Lord's Prayer" of Islam.

When two cycles of prayer are complete, the worshipper remains sitting for a moment. During this time, he or she recites the *tashahhud*, words of supplication and praise:

> All compliments, prayers, and pure words are due to Allah. Peace be upon you, Oh Prophet, and the mercy of God and His blessings. Peace be upon us, and on the righteous servants of God. I bear witness that none has the right to be worshipped except God Alone, and I bear witness that Muhammad is His servant and messenger.

If the prayer is longer than two cycles, the worshipper stands up again to complete the rest of the prayer, and then sits down again to recite the first tashahhud, which is then followed by the second one—in which Muslims ask God to send blessings on Muhammad:

> Oh God, send prayers on Muhammad, and on the family of Muhammad, as you sent prayers on Abraham, and on the family of Abraham. You are indeed the Praiseworthy, the Glorious. Oh God, send blessings on Muhammad, and on the family of

Muhammad, as you sent blessings on Abraham, and on the family of Abraham. You are indeed the Praiseworthy, the Glorious.

Throughout the prayer, Muslims are free to add personal supplications to seek God's forgiveness, guidance, and mercy. When finished, the worshipper does the salutation of peace (*tasleem*) by turning to the right and proclaiming, "Peace and God's mercy be with you" (in Arabic). Then he or she turns to the left and repeats the salutation.

Other Prayers

In addition to the five daily prayers, Muslims may offer extra prayers in the late night or late morning, or before or after the five formal prayers. There are also designated prayers for rain, prayers during solar and lunar eclipses, and prayers to seek guidance in decision-making.

Friday: The Day of Gathering

On Fridays, the *Dhuhr* (noon prayer) is replaced by a congregational prayer at the mosque, where worshippers also listen to a short sermon. This prayer is called *salaat-l-jumu'ah* or the gathering prayer. Attendance is required for men and optional for women.

At this prayer, Muslims gather in a central mosque in their city to pray and listen to a *khutbah* (sermon). Most often, the *khatib* (speaker) that gives the sermon is the imam; however, this duty may be performed by an invited guest or a member of the community. Usually, the speaker begins with words in praise of God, and recites and reflects on a short passage of the Qur'an. He may then address current issues or general affairs of the community and offer supplication for the welfare of all Muslims worldwide. After this, the imam leads the congregation in a short formal prayer. The whole gathering lasts for approximately one hour.

Despite the special status of salaat-l-jumu'ah, Friday is not a Sabbath or day of rest. After gathering for the community prayer, Muslims resume their work or daily routine.

Holiday Prayers

On the occasion of the two Islamic holidays, the community at large offers special holiday prayers—*salaat-l-'Eid*. On the morning of the first day of the holiday, all Muslims (men and women) gather at a large open area, dressed in their finest clothing. It is a day of celebration, happiness, and recognition of God's blessings and mercy.

The performance of the holiday prayers varies slightly from the norm. There is no adhan, and worshippers repeat the phrase *Allahu Akbar* (God is Great) several times at the beginning of each cycle of prayer. The short prayer is followed by a sermon, in which the people are reminded of the blessings of God and their duties toward Him. Again, the worshippers make special supplications to God, asking Him to look after and show mercy to the Muslims all over the world.

Muslim prayers are always said in Arabic. This allows Muslims of any nationality to join in worship in the original language of the Qur'an—no matter where they travel.

Personal Prayers and Supplications

Aside from the daily formal prayers, Muslims constantly seek forgiveness, guidance, and mercy from God through personal prayers and supplications. These personal prayers are called *du'a* (calling upon), in the sense that the supplicants are "calling upon" God.

Unlike the formal prayers, personal supplications do not have a specific time frame, format, or language. The Qur'an advises, "When My servants ask you concerning Me, [tell them] I am indeed close to them. I respond to the call [du'a] of every supplicant who calls on Me. Let them also, with a will, listen to My call, and believe in Me, that they may walk in the right way" (Qur'an 2:186).

Many Muslims follow personal prayers recommended by the Prophet Muhammad and the examples that they find in the Qur'an, such as the following.

"Our Lord! Condemn us not if we forget or fall into error. Our Lord! Do not lay on us a burden like that which You laid on those before us. Our Lord! Do not lay on us a burden greater than we have strength to bear. Blot out our sins, and grant us forgiveness. Have mercy on us. You are our Protector. Help us against those who deny faith" (2:286).

"Our Lord! Let our hearts not deviate, after You have guided us. Grant us mercy from Your grace. Verily you are the Giver of bounties without measure" (3:8).

"Our Lord! Forgive us our sins, and anything we may have done that transgressed our duty. Make our steps firm, and help us against those who deny faith" (3:147).

"Our Lord! In You we trust, and to You we turn in repentance, for unto You is the end of all journeys" (60:4).

Muslims are also free to seek help from Allah in their own language and choice of words. After all, God understands all languages and knows even the deepest secrets of our hearts.

Remembrance of God

The Qur'an reminds Muslims to be dutiful to God, and to remember Him throughout the day: "Oh you who believe! Celebrate the praises of God, and do so often, and glorify Him morning and evening" (33:41–41). All words of praise and remembrance of God are known in Islamic terminology as *dhikr*.

The Qur'an repeatedly speaks of the "remembrance of God" as a way for believers to strengthen their faith, purify their hearts, and find peace in times of turmoil. Muhammad once related that God said:

I am as my servant thinks I am. I am with him when he makes mention of Me. If he makes mention of Me to himself, I make mention of him to Myself. And if he makes mention of Me in an assembly, I make mention of him in an assembly better than it. And if he draws near to me an arm's length, I draw near to him a fathom's length. And if he comes to Me walking, I go to him at speed.

A Muslim strives to remember God throughout the day, often reciting specific phrases or words in quiet humility.

Dhikr Beads

Some Muslims carry a set of beads that are used in reciting words of remembrance. Similar to the Catholic rosary beads, *musbaha* or *tasbeeh* (Islamic prayer beads) are used to count the number of times a phrase is repeated. They consist of a string of either ninety-nine beads (for the ninety-nine names of God) or thirty-three beads (so that each bead represents three names), often made out of wood or gemstone.

ALERT!

Using the prayer beads is optional, and in fact not all Muslims accept this practice. More often, Muslims simply count the repetitions on the inside joints of their fingers.

The Qur'an reminds us that glorifying and praising God helps calm the soul: "In the remembrance of God do hearts find ease" (13:28). Muslims strive to remember God throughout the day, through formal prayers, supplications, and words of remembrance. ⒠

Chapter 9

Islamic Guidance and Law

Islam provides a framework for all aspects of life, ranging from the spiritual to the mundane, from how one should pray to what foods can be eaten and how to organize business relations. Islam lays out an entire system of life, with the rights and responsibilities of all people clearly defined.

The Lawful and Unlawful

As a fundamental principle, everything is permitted in Islam except those things that have been expressly forbidden by Allah. In Islam, forbidden things are known as *haram,* and permitted things are known as *halal.*

The word "haram" means prohibited, forbidden, or unlawful. The word "halal" means allowed, permitted, or lawful. Muslims also recognize a gray area, *makrooh,* which describes that which is not forbidden but is disliked, undesirable, or doubtful—thus, best avoided.

Muslims rely on scriptural text, reasoning, and the conclusions of scholars when deciding on the legality of a particular matter. In the end, there is no individual or governing body that has the sole duty or right to interpret Islamic law. Muslims are left to follow the clear guidance, as they best understand it.

Muhammad advised his followers to steer clear of doubtful things, and stick to what they know for sure. He said: "The lawful is clear, and the unlawful is clear, and between them are things which are doubtful and not known to most of you. So anyone who keeps away from the doubtful things, in fact he is protecting his faith and honor, and he who indulges in doubtful acts falls into fault."

ALERT!

Muslims do not have a binding religious authority, a Muslim equivalent of the Pope. Muslims read the primary Islamic sources, refer to the opinions of legal scholars, and then determine their individual course of action based on the evidence at hand, the advice of the scholars, and their own conscience.

The Qur'an warns people against making lawful things forbidden, and vice versa, based on their own opinions. "And do not say concerning the falsehood which your tongues utter, 'This is halal and that is haram,' in order to fabricate a lie against Allah. Assuredly, those who fabricate a lie against Allah will not prosper" (16:116). Muslims are always very careful when determining or instructing others about the lawfulness or unlawfulness of a course of action, for fear of leading other people astray and falling into this category of people who "lie" about God's legislation.

The Qur'an

The first and most basic source of all Islamic teaching is the Qur'an. Muslims believe the Qur'an to be the unchanging, revealed word of God. The Qur'an provides the Muslim with both guidance and inspiration: "Say: 'The holy spirit (angel Gabriel) has brought the revelation from your Lord in truth, in order to strengthen those who believe, and as a guide and glad tidings'" (16:102). The word "Qur'an" comes from the Arabic word *iqra'* (to read). You might also encounter the anglicized form "Koran," but it is not the proper, phonetic spelling of the word.

Revelation of the Qur'an

The Qur'an was revealed to Muhammad over a period of twenty-three years. In the book itself, God is quoted as proclaiming, "It is We Who have sent down the Qur'an to you in stages" (76:23).

Muhammad received the first revelation in the cave of Hira; the first phrase he heard was, "Read, in the Name of your Lord." The final verse to be revealed was: "This day I have perfected your religion for you, completed My favor upon you, and have chosen for you Islam as your religion" (5:3).

In pieces and sections, over the years, the revelations would come to Muhammad and he would recite them to his companions. Muhammad's followers would then commit the revelations to memory, reciting and reviewing the growing text. As Muhammad could neither read nor write, he also depended on scribes who wrote down the words on whatever material they could find: animal skins, pieces of tree bark, and palm branches. He would have the scribes read back to him what they wrote, to ensure that they had accurately transcribed the words.

It is also reported in Islamic sources that once a year, during the month of Ramadan, Muhammad would recite the entire Qur'an (as it had been revealed to that point) to the angel Gabriel. In what was to be the final year of Muhammad's life, the angel asked him to recite the entire text twice.

Organization of the Qur'an

As the revelations continued, Muhammad would instruct the scribes as to where to put the new verses in the body of the text, according to instructions given to him by the angel Gabriel. Thus, the verses of the Qur'an do not read from beginning to end in chronological order.

The Qur'an is composed of 114 chapters of varying lengths. The longest is 286 verses long; the shortest is merely three verses. The Qur'an is also divided into thirty equal sections, called *juz* (Arabic for "division" or "fraction"). These divisions make it easier for a person to read equal portions during each night of the month of Ramadan.

The oral tradition of the Qur'an has been passed along from generation to generation. In addition, the text itself was compiled during the lifetime of Muhammad. Scribes such as Zaid ibn Thabit kept copies in their own homes, to add to as the revelations continued.

Upon Muhammad's death, his scribes and companions compared and compiled these personal copies, reviewed them with those who had committed the Qur'an to memory, and wrote this verified text all down in one volume. This original and certified copy of the Qur'an was kept in the home of Muhammad's wife, Hafsah.

As the Islamic empire grew, two threats to the Qur'an became apparent. First of all, large numbers of believers who had memorized the Qur'an were dying in battle. And second, the growing empire began to include non-native speakers of Arabic, so there was a possibility that the text could be mispronounced or misunderstood. Early Arabic writing did not include vowel markings, so it was difficult for the non-native speaker to correctly read the words.

During his period of leadership, the Caliph Uthman took up the project of preparing a codified text of the Qur'an for dispersal throughout the growing Muslim nation. This version, based on the original copy kept with Hafsah and certified by those who had memorized the revelation, was entirely consistent with what had been revealed to Muhammad. One copy was sent to each state capital, to replace other materials that were in circulation. From these codified, original texts, multiple copies were made for distribution all over the growing Muslim world.

Themes of the Qur'an

Muslims believe that the Qur'an contains all the knowledge and wisdom that God gave us to live good lives on earth and to worship Him in the proper way: "And We have sent down to you the Book explaining all things—a guide, a mercy, and glad tidings" (16:89).

In various passages, the Qur'an tells stories and parables about previous prophets and peoples, and the lessons that can be learned from them. It provides clear instructions about what is permitted and forbidden in our daily lives. It gives encouragement, calling upon believers to put their faith and trust in Allah, and to be patient. It describes the character of righteous persons as opposed to evildoers. It warns of the punishment to come for those who reject faith and wreak havoc on earth, and sends messages of glad tidings for "believers, who do deeds of righteousness." It calls to ponder on the natural world and to wonder about the signs of Allah's creation. Above all, the Qur'an heralds Allah's mercy and perfect justice.

When first reading the Qur'an, some people are initially confused by the seemingly random order. They may have expected to read a history book, in chronological order, with chapters organized around certain themes or time periods. The Qur'an sometimes repeats particular points and recounts particular scenes in different ways throughout the different chapters. Historical accounts are interspersed with the lessons that can be learned from them. Exhortations to be kind and just are intertwined with reminders of the rewards of Paradise for those who are righteous.

Meccan and Madinan Chapters

In the early years, Muhammad and his small group of followers faced the opposition of the powerful, polytheistic Meccan tribes. The verses of revelation that came to Muhammad during this time mainly focus on matters of faith: they stress the unity of God, denounce idol worship, remind of the messages of previous prophets, and encourage the believers to persevere in patience and constancy.

After the Muslim community migrated to Madinah, the needs of the community changed. For the first time, the Muslims were able to organize a social system based in Islam. Thus, the focus of the revelation also began to shift. The chapters are longer, and go into more detail about moral and ethical codes, criminal law, economic and state policy, and guidelines for relations with other communities.

Exegesis (Tafsir)

As a person reads the Qur'an, there may be areas where a verse needs to be explained, put into historical context, or framed in reference to other verses on the same subject. Also, Muhammad may have given more insight into certain verses in his oral traditions, his personal conversations with members of the community. Muslims scholars throughout history have gathered and written commentaries on the Qur'an, called *tafsir* ("explanation" or "interpretation" in Arabic).

FACT

The most renowned and authoritative exegesis of the Qur'an was written by the scholar Ibn Kathir in the eighth century. His work fills nearly a dozen volumes of text, expanding on every verse of the entire Qur'an with history, Muhammad's teachings and words (known as *hadith*), and scholarly commentary.

The Example of the Prophet

Muslims believe that all of God's prophets brought guidance to their people, and were excellent examples to follow. As human beings, we need role models to show us how to implement certain things in our lives, and from whom to seek advice and ask questions.

When Muslims look to Muhammad as a role model, they consider the entirety of his life—the way he treated people and his family, the things he liked and disliked, the way he lived his life in general—as a legacy, which is known as the Sunnah. As the Qur'an revealed the basic principles of Islamic legislation, Muhammad played a key role in interpreting, explaining, and implementing these principles for the growing community.

A Beautiful Exemplar

The Qur'an describes Muhammad's role as follows: "Allah is the One who sent among the unlettered ones a messenger from among themselves, reciting to them Allah's verses, purifying them, and teaching them the Book and the wisdom. Truly they had been before in manifest error" (62:2). Muslims are ordered in the Qur'an to follow the words and acts of Muhammad (as presented in the Sunnah and verified by the hadith): "Whatever the Prophet ordered you to do, you should do, and whatever he forbids you, you should reject" (59:7).

Collections of Hadith

After the death of Muhammad, his companions gave direct attention to preserving his traditions. Muhammad's sayings and words were collected and written down by his companions, and then verified for authenticity with those who actually heard the Prophet with their own ears. Each written report of what Muhammad did or said is called a hadith.

An entire science of hadith then developed by scholars who investigated and verified the written transmissions on several levels. First, they examined the names of the people who reportedly heard or saw Muhammad themselves, and the reputations of those who relayed the message. The chain of narrators was examined for any breaks, or to determine if any of the narrators were considered untrustworthy or weak in memory. In addition, the text of the hadith itself was examined for contradictions against the Qur'an and other verified traditions.

Based on the results of the examination, hadith were classified into four different types: authentic, good, weak, or fabricated. Only the first two categories are used in establishing Islamic law.

Many of the criticisms of Islam come from teachings that are based on inauthentic or fabricated hadith. These sources are rejected by Muslims as Islamic law, but have been preserved as historical records.

Several early Islamic scholars dedicated their lives to investigating and verifying the hadith. Among the more notable were Imam Bukhari, from the city of Bukhara (modern-day Uzbekistan), and Imam Muslim of Persia. The hadith collections of these two scholars are widely considered to be the most authentic. They are published in print form and are widely available on the Internet.

Islamic Law

The Islamic *Shari'ah* is the entire legal system implemented in Islam. The word itself implies an endless source of water from which people satisfy their thirst; specifically, it refers to the divine law that was revealed in the Qur'an and exemplified in the life of Muhammad.

Islam is concerned with the well-being and security of every individual in society. Any behavior that threatens or violates the rights of others is prohibited in Islam, and strict punishments exist to help deter potential criminals. In this way, the lives and property of all members of society are secured and protected.

In Islam, there are penal laws for major crimes such as murder, assault, theft, and adultery. The degree of punishment depends on the magnitude of the material or emotional injury resulting from the act. At all times, only an authorized court may mete out punishment. There is no vigilantism in Islam. However, victims or their families have the final say on whether the punishment is carried out. They may, at their discretion, forgive the perpetrator and accept compensation for the crime committed.

The Islamic penal code calls for the following punishments:

- **Murder:** execution or monetary compensation to the victim's family (discretion is given to the victim's family in this choice).

- **Accidental homicide:** freedom for one of the perpetrator's slaves and monetary compensation to the victim's family; if the perpetrator has no money, he or she must fast daily for two consecutive months. (Obviously, the injunction on freeing a slave is no longer relevant.)
- **Intentional injury:** an injury equal to the one caused, or monetary compensation to the victim.
- **Land, sea, or air piracy** (this category includes terrorism and rape): execution, crucifixion, cutting off of alternate hands and feet, or exile from the land.
- **Theft:** cutting off of one hand, unless the individual stole out of true need and necessity.
- **Fornication** (premarital sex): flogging of both man and woman.
- **Adultery:** stoning to death of both man and woman.
- **False accusations about a person's chastity:** flogging and rejection of all future oaths and testimony.
- **Homosexual practices:** execution of both individuals.
- **Drinking of alcohol:** flogging.

QUESTION?

Why is homosexuality punished as a crime?

In Islam, the harshest legal punishments are reserved for crimes that affect society as a whole. Muslims believe that homosexuality is a threat to the basic family structure, and therefore, a threat to society—a crime that must be punished as other crimes that affect society.

It is important to remember that the punishments are harsh because they are meant to deter would-be criminals. Punishments such as these are meted out only for crimes that are considered transgressions against the community, because they put the entire society at risk. The punishments of the Hereafter are much more severe, but the door to forgiveness is always open through sincere repentance.

Only an Islamic court of law may order these sentences, and in reality, they are rarely carried out. Their presence in Islamic law is mainly to warn people about the consequences of wrongdoing.

Islamic Jurisprudence

Whenever Muslims are faced with an issue that is not directly addressed in either the Qur'an or the Sunnah, they may rely on laws derived by jurists, who base their opinions on the primary Islamic sources and according to methodology of reasoning and analysis. This method is called *fiqh,* or the deep understanding of something based on study and reasoning.

Sources of Fiqh

Other sources of Islamic jurisprudence include *ijmah,* the joint agreement of the companions of the Prophet for issues that came up shortly after Muhammad's death, and *qiyass,* the opinion of later scholars who research a topic and come to a conclusion based on these other main sources. These secondary sources must spring from and depend on the Qur'an and Sunnah; they may not contradict in any way either of these main sources.

Legal Opinions

A qualified scholar may issue a formal legal opinion on a topic; such a legal opinion, which must be based on sound reasoning and with evidence from primary Islamic sources, is called a *fatwa.* Examples include the prohibition to smoke and the legality of some methods of alternative reproduction.

ALERT!

A legal opinion is only that—an opinion—and is not automatically binding to all Muslims. Only persons who are qualified to interpret Islamic law may issue a valid fatwa.

Schools of Thought

Early in Islamic history, over the course of a few centuries, scholars needed to develop a system whereby they could sift through and interpret the vast amount of material in Islamic jurisprudence. The Qur'an was clear in its instructions, but did not address every possible scenario or question that may come up in a Muslim's life. The Sunnah was collected in several hundred thousand hadith reports. The challenge facing the scholars was how to go about interpreting the material for new situations that arose in the lives of believers, or in response to particular questions they had that were not addressed in the two main sources of Islamic law.

Several early scholars took up the challenge, writing about and codifying their interpretations of Islamic jurisprudence. The work based on some of these scholars has developed into several branches, or "schools of law" (called *madh'hab* in Arabic).

The Four Main Schools

The main schools of thought among Sunni Muslims were named for the scholars that founded their work, although the details were often worked out by later generations of scholars in their footsteps. They are:

- Hanafi
- Maliki
- Shafa'i
- Hanbali

Since all of the scholars based their opinions and rulings on sound Islamic primary sources, they are all regarded as valid and there is a universal acceptance of all of them. The differences among the legal rulings are generally very minor: for example, how to move one's hands during prayer, or detailed rules about fasting.

Other Schools and Deviations

Beyond the four accepted schools of legal thought in Islam, some groups have separated from the rest of the Muslim community to follow their own scholars and legal systems. These groups have generally mixed Islamic teachings with their own beliefs to come up with a new form of Islam. Some are considered to be Muslims, while others have embraced teachings that place them outside the fold of Islam. These additional divisions and deviations will be explored more fully in Chapter 10. (E)

Chapter 10

Historical Divisions and Deviations

Muslims are advised to hold together and not divide themselves in matters of faith. Nevertheless, some distinct divisions have developed within Islam, and some groups have made innovations in the faith to create new religions outside the fold. This chapter will give you a brief overview of the Sunni and Shi'a Muslims, the Sufis, Qadiani, Khalifites, the Baha'i, and the Nation of Islam.

Sunni and Shi'a Muslims

The very first division in Islam, between Sunni and Shi'a, occurred not as a matter of differing beliefs, but due to politics and the role of leadership in the community. The issue centered on the question of who was to lead the Muslim community following Muhammad's death.

When Muhammad was suffering from his final illness, he appointed his closest companion, Abu Bakr, to lead the community in prayer. After Muhammad's death, many of his companions felt that leadership of the community should go to the person most suited to the task. They consulted among themselves and selected Abu Bakr, in line with Islamic teachings about consultation and agreement among elders. Those who agreed with Abu Bakr's appointment became known as Sunni (followers of the tradition of Muhammad).

Muhammad predicted that the followers of Islam would break themselves up into seventy-three sects, and that all of them would be in the Fire (of Hell), except one. When his companions asked, "Which one?" he answered, "The one that follows my example."

Other members of the community felt that leadership of the Muslim state should stay within the bloodline of Muhammad, within his own family. This concept also became known as *Ahl-al-Bayt,* or People of the House (of Muhammad). Particularly, they felt that Muhammad's son-in-law, Ali, should have been appointed the next leader of the community, and so this group became known as Shi'ati Ali (supporters of Ali)—Shi'a or Shi'ite Muslims.

When Muhammad's bloodline died in the ninth century, Shi'a Muslims were at a loss to determine who should succeed leadership of the community. A group of Shi'a scholars gathered together to elect a new supreme imam, who was believed to possess special inspiration and served as the sole interpreter of Islamic law. In modern times, Imam Khomeini, the ayatollah of Iran from 1978 to 1989, is the most well-known Shi'a leader.

A New Form of Faith

What began as a political disagreement, a separatist movement within the political state, later turned into a new form of the faith. Due to political loyalties and deepening mutual distrust, Shi'a Muslims rejected or altered some practices of Islam.

Certainly the Shi'a religious hierarchy is very different from that of Sunni Islam. Sunni Muslims shun formal clergy status, recognizing only jurists and scholars who offer nonbinding opinions. In contrast, Shi'a Muslim leaders have popelike authority. They believe that since the leader is appointed in accordance with divine authority, he is perfect and sinless. His opinions are binding, believed to stem from prophetlike inspiration and guidance.

Shi'a Muslims also tend to focus more on the virtues of martyrdom, with particular attention to the deaths of Ali and Hussein (related in Chapter 5). On the occasion of *Ashura,* a day in the Isalmic calendar honoring Hussein's death at the hands of an opposing army, Shi'a Muslims observe mourning, gathering in the streets and publicly wailing and beating their chests.

ALERT!

Shi'a Muslims often beat themselves to great physical harm on the day of Ashura in an attempt to emulate the pain and suffering felt by Hussein. They often cut their heads and beat themselves with chains in an attempt to make the effect more dramatic.

Sunni and Shi'a Muslims also differ on some basic beliefs of the faith, including the attributes of Allah and the role of the Prophets. There are also small differences in practice between Shi'a and Sunni Muslims. The call to prayer is different (the example in Chapter 8 was the Sunni version; the Shi'a add a few phrases like a call on people to "come to the best of deeds" and another testifying that "Ali is protected by Allah"), the postures and times of prayer vary, and marriage laws have some differences.

Sunni and Shi'a Today

Today, the Shi'a Muslims make up approximately 10 percent of the Muslim world. They are mostly found in Iran, with large communities in Kuwait, Lebanon, Iraq, and Bahrain. Tensions between the two groups have varied between quiet disapproval to outright hostility. In addition to the civil wars that strengthened the divide between Sunni and Shi'a in the seventh century, the hostility is evident in modern conflicts, such as the Iran-Iraq war and tribal infighting in Afghanistan and parts of the former Soviet Union.

A Mystical Faith: Sufism

In the early centuries after Muhammad's death, some Muslims became disenchanted with the Islamic community's growing interest in worldly affairs and the rigid application of rules within the faith. These self-described purists dedicated themselves to frugal living and getting into the spirit of faith. They strived to purify the soul and develop a connection with Allah. The path of the Sufis is often called the mystic or spiritual trend within Islam.

The word "Sufi" comes from the Arabic word for wool (*suf*). Followers of this trend would often traditionally wear wool because of its simplicity and low cost. Another possible meaning comes from the word *safa* (to clean), because Sufis focus on cleansing the heart.

Over time, Sufis began organizing into various orders, each of which is called a *tariqa* (or "path"). A Sufi master, called a *shaykh,* serves as the leader and guide to his followers. Sufis develop an intense devotion to their shaykh, because they believe he can provide spiritual guidance and healing for those under his care. He is sometimes considered a "spiritual doctor" to his students.

While Sufis have maintained that they are merely continuing the simple religious lifestyle of Muhammad, many orders developed practices that were outside the fold of Islam. Some Sufi orders participate in the veneration of Sufi masters, called saints, and others follow intense devotional practices such as prolonged fasting or prayer.

The Qur'an discourages sectarianism: "As for those of you who divide their way of life and break up into sects, you have no part of them at all. Their affair is with Allah. He will tell them the truth of what they did in the end" (Qur'an 6:159).

Many Muslims reject the extremes of the Sufi path, pointing to Muhammad's teachings about moderation in matters of worship, and forbidding the veneration of others than Allah. In modern times, Sufism is often practiced in the West, but is considered sort of a "new age" philosophy. Indeed, many Western Sufis bear little resemblance to, and have little knowledge of, the practices of mainstream Islam.

The Poetry of Rumi

Among Sufis, poetry and music take on religious significance—they are seen as a way to express intense love of God (whom they often call the Beloved). One of the most famous Sufi writers, and indeed one of the most famous poets of all time, was Mevlana Jalalu'ddin Rumi. Born in Persia and raised in Turkey in the thirteenth century, Rumi wrote mystical poetry about spiritual life, practice, love, and the meaning of life. Rumi's poetry has been translated into dozens of languages; new English translations were published in the 1980s.

Whirling Dervishes

Rumi is also known for founding the Mevlevi Order of Sufism, which is now associated with the whirling dervishes. These Sufis developed a method they believed could connect them with the Divine. In an intense devotional trance, individuals twirl around in white robes with wide skirts. Their movements are intended to be relaxing and hypnotic, so that the person can become open to receiving God's energy.

The word "dervish" means doorway, and practitioners believe that the melodic trance opens up a doorway to the spiritual world, where one can commune in ecstasy with the Divine.

The Qadiani Movement

The Qadiani, or Ahmadiyyah, movement began in the late nineteenth century in the Punjab region of India, where a Muslim reformer named Mirza Ghulam Ahmed first claimed that he was the promised Messiah and later that he was a prophet of Allah who received divine revelation.

The followers of Ahmed have established what is known as the Ahmadiyyah Mission to propagate their teachings and invite others to their path. They are known for preparing and distributing multilingual translations of the Qur'an, but with variations in the text that support their own interpretations of Islamic teachings and history.

The Ahmadiyyah are also called Qadiani because their founder was from the city of Qadian in the Punjab province of India. There is a further break within the group among those who persist in the belief that Ahmed was a prophet, and those who respect him as a spiritual leader but fall short of calling him a prophet.

Muslims consider Ghulam Ahmed a false prophet, and all Muslim scholars consider Qadianis to be outside the fold of Islam.

Numerology of the Khalifites

This relatively new group believes that the Qur'an is the only source of guidance in Islam, and that the traditions of Muhammad and other prophets are irrelevant. They reject the entire Sunnah (words and acts of Muhammad), and depend solely on the Qur'an, which they believe contains a mathematical miracle to prove its authenticity as the word of God.

The Mathematical Miracle

The Khalifites claim that there is an intricate mathematical code in the Qur'an, proving that it is indeed the word of God and could not possibly have been written by any man. This mathematical "miracle" is based on the number nineteen. Letters and verses are counted, given numerological values, added and multiplied, and statistically determined to be equivalent to the number nineteen or a multiple of nineteen.

FACT

The first verse of the Qur'an has nineteen letters. The first chapter ever revealed consists of nineteen words. The Qur'an consists of 114 chapters, a number that is divisible by 19 ($19 \times 6 = 114$). However, the mathematical "miracle" of the Qur'an continues only if changes are made in the text of the Qur'an.

For some time, scholars were intrigued by and investigated this claim, not as "proof" of their faith, but as an interesting curiosity. Over time, however, the methodology used by the Khalifites came under question. It was discovered that they had revised the Qur'an, so that words and verses would fit into the formula. The statistics were determined to be false. The theory became questionable at first, and later was determined to be fraudulent.

Rashad Khalifa

At the center of this controversy was a person named Rashad Khalifa. Mr. Khalifa was an Egyptian who immigrated to the United States and took up residence in Tucson, Arizona. He published his own version of the Qur'an, with the verses manipulated to fit the mathematical theory.

Based on this numerology, Mr. Khalifa determined that there were prophetic references to himself in the Qur'an, and claimed to be a "Messenger of the Covenant." He lectured to his followers about the mathematical miracle and encouraged them to reject any source of Islamic learning other than the Qur'an. In time, Khalifa's fraudulent teachings were exposed, and his claims rejected. Rashad Khalifa was killed by an unknown assailant in 1990.

The Baha'i Faith

The Baha'i faith arose from Islam, and has now grown to be a worldwide religion. The Baha'i believe in the unity of God, and in the essential message that has been revealed through the prophets over time. They recognize Muhammad as a prophet, but also believe that Krishna, Buddha, and others were "Great Manifestations of God," culminating in the teachings of the founder of their faith, Bahaullah.

The Bab and Bahaullah

The Baha'i faith has its origins in Muslim Persia, when a young man called the Bab ("the Gate") announced the imminent arrival of a messenger of God. The Baha'i believe that the Bab himself received revelation from God, but that his main purpose was to bring attention to the messenger that would follow him. The Bab was executed as a heretic in 1850.

The Baha'i are established in 235 countries, and number five million people worldwide. To learn more about this faith, you can visit the official Baha'i Web site that operates in seven languages at ✍ www.bahai.org. The main slogan of the Baha'i is: "The earth is but one country and mankind its citizens."

In 1863, a man named Bahaullah (meaning "the Glory of God" in Arabic) announced that he was the fulfillment of the Bab's promise. His announcement resulted in his imprisonment and exile. Bahaullah began writing a series of letters and documents outlining his views of universal peace and a united world civilization. He died in 1892, with his writings and teachings in relative obscurity. He has since been embraced as a "Manifestation of God" and a spiritual guide for millions of Baha'i around the world.

The Baha'i Creeds

The Baha'i believe in the unity of the world's great religions, that they all came from the same spiritual source. The central theme of their faith is that humans form one single race and are destined to be unified in one world society. Followers of this faith are heavily involved in issues of world peace, world government, freedom, and equality.

The Baha'i may seem similar to Muslims in some aspects of faith: belief in One Almighty God and in the consistent teachings of the prophets of old. However, Islam rejects the notion that any messenger or prophet would ever follow Muhammad. The Baha'i also differ from Muslims in matters of worship, law, sacred texts, and basic creed. Indeed, the Baha'i faith is now an entirely different religion.

The Nation of Islam

In North America, one of the most well-known offshoot groups is the Nation of Islam. This movement reached its peak during the mid-twentieth century; it is associated with the black-pride and civil-rights movements of the 1960s, a period of social upheavals. While members of the Nation consider themselves Muslim, in reality their beliefs and practices have very little to do with the faith of Islam.

Main Teachings

The Nation of Islam preaches the superiority of black people. According to their doctrine, black people were the original inhabitants of the earth, the mothers and fathers of civilization, and that even God Himself appeared on earth as a black man. According to the Nation, on the Day of Judgment black people will be resurrected first, but in a "mental" resurrection rather than a physical one.

The Nation of Islam encourages discipline, the value of family, responsibility, and pride. That is the main reason it was such a draw to the disenfranchised black community; in it they found honor, respect, and hope.

History of the Nation

During the Great Depression, a mysterious figure appeared in Detroit. Calling himself Wallace Fard Muhammad, he claimed to be a mystic and a prophet from Mecca, Saudi Arabia. Many believe he was actually a con man and convicted drug dealer who had just been released from prison. One of his first followers and students was Elijah Poole, who later became known as Elijah Muhammad. When Fard disappeared in 1934, Elijah took over leadership of the growing Nation.

Elijah Muhammad began preaching that God had appeared on earth in the person of W. Fard Muhammad, who had come to call his people to faith, freedom, and independence. Elijah Muhammad came to be known as the Divine Representative, or prophet, of this god. The organization began establishing temples, and preached the sanctity of family life, the rejection of drugs and alcohol, the virtues of cleanliness and discipline, and a return to the religion of their African ancestors, Islam.

One of the most famous leaders of the Nation was Malcolm X. Malcolm credited the Nation with saving his life, turning him away from the harms of crime and drugs. Over time, he became disenchanted with Elijah Muhammad, and rejected the infallibility of this so-called prophet. Malcolm X discovered orthodox Islam during a pilgrimage to Saudi Arabia, and began to write and preach against the racist beliefs of the Nation. His public transformation and rejection of some of the Nation's basic beliefs was key in the decision of many African-Americans to turn toward traditional Islam.

ALERT!

Malcolm X's pilgrimage to Mecca was a turning point in his life; like many pilgrims before him, he returned a changed man. He reflected this new direction in a name change he undertook upon his return. He was thence known as "El-Hajj Malik Shabaaz."

After Elijah Muhammad's death, his son Imam W. Deen Mohammed also took the path of orthodox Islam. In 1992, he established the Muslim American Society, helping to steer millions of African-Americans toward mainstream Islam. In the same year, he became the first Muslim to offer an invocation at the U.S. Senate. However, Elijah Muhammad's teachings have stayed alive, most recently through the leadership of Minister Louis Farrakhan.

Building Bridges

In recent times, efforts have begun to build bridges between the Nation of Islam and members of the mainstream Muslim community. Nearly half of all Muslims in the United States are African-American, many of whom found their way to Islam through contact with the Nation.

Muslims reject the most fundamental beliefs of the Nation, and have called upon them to abandon the belief that God could appear as a man on earth, or that Elijah Muhammad was a prophet. These beliefs alone keep members of the Nation outside the fold of orthodox Islam.

In recent years, there has been increased dialogue between Louis Farrakhan and mainstream Muslim leaders in the United States. Many organizations and conferences have extended cross-invitations to participate in dialogue. In February 2000, Farrakhan formally reconciled with his longtime enemy, Imam W. Deen Mohammed, Elijah Muhammad's son. There have been recent indications that Farrakhan is trying to move the Nation away from its racist views and more fully embrace the beliefs of Islam.

Chapter 11

Islam and Other Faiths

Muslims are commanded to respect the dignity of all people, regardless of religion, race, or nationality. The Qur'an orders its followers to be just and fair with non-Muslims, even those who are considered enemies. Furthermore, special consideration is given to Jews and Christians, the People of the Book, in recognition of their faiths' divine origins and monotheistic teachings.

The Infidels

The word "infidel" is of Latin origin, and is not used by Muslims to describe those who do not share the faith. The Qur'an uses the word *kafiroon* (plural of *kafir*) to describe the people who hear the message of Islam but do not believe. The word itself means "those who reject."

ALERT!

Muslims use the word kafir—which comes from the Arabic word for covering or hiding something (as in "covering one's heart")—to refer to unbelievers. Incidentally, this word shares its root with the Arabic words for "atonement" and "penance."

The Qur'an does describe the punishment that those who reject faith will face in the Hereafter. However, Muslims are never encouraged to randomly or systematically punish, wage war against, or kill people simply because they do not believe in the message of Islam. Such behavior would be the antithesis of the Qur'anic injunction: "Let there be no compulsion in religion" (2:256).

The Qur'an gives clear instructions to Muslims on how they should interact with those who do not believe, in a chapter of the Qur'an aptly titled *Al-Kafiroon* (Those Who Reject Faith): "Say: 'Oh you who reject faith! I do not worship what you worship, and you will not worship what I worship. And I will never worship that which you worship, nor will you ever worship that which I worship. You have your faith, and I have mine'" (109:1–6).

Mushrikoon

The Qur'an describes those people who worship idols and other false gods rather than the One Almighty God as *mushrikoon,* which literally means, "those who perform shirk," or associate others with Allah. In English, you might translate mushrikoon as "pagans."

At the time Muhammad was preaching in Mecca, the leaders and most of the people fell into this category. They fashioned idols of wood and clay, and brought them food and drink in the hopes of intercession. Muhammad chastised them for worshipping objects that could do nothing to protect or help themselves, much less others. Angry at his words, the Meccans set out to torture, persecute, and attempt to destroy the Muslim community.

There are a few verses of the Qur'an that encourage the Muslims to fight firmly against the mushrikoon, but they must be understood in the terms of the historical events surrounding the revelation of these verses. The Muslims were commanded to defend themselves against "those who fight you" (2:190). These verses refer specifically to those Meccan tribes and their allies, and others who tried to systematically destroy the Muslim community or suppress their rights to freedom of worship. In no case may a Muslim initiate aggression against a people who are not hostile; in fact, the Qur'an encourages Muslims to "deal kindly and justly with them, for Allah loves those who are just" (60:8).

The People of the Book

According to the Qur'an, the People of the Book are those who believe in previous prophets and messengers and they deserve particular respect and consideration. Christians, Jews, and other monotheists fall into this category.

The Qur'an acknowledges that among these groups, there are people who truly practice faith in God and strive to be righteous:

> Of the People of the Book are a portion who stands for the right. They rehearse the signs of Allah all night long, and they prostrate themselves in adoration. They believe in Allah and the Last Day; they enjoin what is right and forbid what is wrong; and they hasten in the emulation of all good works. They are in the ranks of the righteous. Of the good they do, nothing will be rejected of them, for Allah knows well those that do right. (3:113–115)

Accusations of Anti-Semitism

There has been some criticism that the Qur'an encourages Muslims to be anti-Semitic. Technically, that's impossible—the Prophet Muhammad himself was an Arab of the Semitic race. There are a few verses in the Qur'an that are very critical of hypocrisy among "the Children of Israel."

The Qur'an makes the charge that some among them were guilty of changing their divine laws, practicing racial discrimination, and rejecting Jesus as a prophet. All of the criticisms were based on practical and theological reasons, which were very much in evidence at the time of the revelation. The Qur'an calls on those Jewish people to evaluate themselves, and to come back into obedience to God's laws.

FACT

"Those who believe, and those who follow the Jewish scriptures, and the Christians, and the Sabians—any who believe in Allah and the Last Day, and work righteousness—shall have their reward with their Lord. On them shall be no fear, nor shall they grieve" (2:62).

The Christian Faith

The Qur'an speaks highly of Jesus, the disciples, and those Christians who believe in God and work righteousness. However, there is also criticism of what Muslims believe to be misinterpretation of Jesus' divinity and role on earth:

Oh People of the Book! Commit no excesses in your religion, nor say of Allah anything but the truth. Christ Jesus, the son of Mary, was no more than a messenger of Allah, and His Word, which He bestowed on Mary, and a Spirit proceeding from Him. So believe in Allah and his messengers. Say not "Three" (of a Trinity). Desist—it will be better for you, for Allah is but One God. Glory be to Him! Far exalted is He above having a son. To Him belong all things in the heavens and on earth. (4:171)

The Qur'an explains that the miraculous virgin birth accords no special status to Jesus. Just like Adam, God simply created him. "The similitude of Jesus before Allah is as that of Adam. He created him from dust, then said to him: 'Be.' And he was" (3:59).

Muslims also take issue with the Biblical account of Jesus' death and resurrection. The Qur'an makes it clear that Jesus was not killed, but was raised up to God. Muslims believe in the Second Coming, that Jesus will reappear on earth to fight the Anti-Christ and lead his true followers during a time of felicity before the Day of Resurrection. More detail about the Islamic view of Jesus can be found in Chapter 12.

The Same Message

Muslims believe that all prophets of God taught essentially the same message to their people. "The same religion has He established for you as that which He enjoined on Noah, which we have sent by inspiration to thee, and that which We enjoined on Abraham, Moses, and Jesus. Namely, that you should remain steadfast in religion, and make no divisions therein" (42:13). Muslims believe that the message of Muhammad was fundamentally the same message taught by Moses to his people, and by Jesus to his followers: to believe in One Almighty God, worship Him alone, seek help from Him alone, and follow His guidance in every matter of life.

Differences from Judaism and Christianity

Muslims recognize that Judaism, Christianity, and Islam all teach that there is but One God. All faiths teach that we should follow God's guidance, do good deeds, and avoid evil. However, the faiths differ about some fundamental issues, including God's attributes, His prophets and books of revelation, and the concept of salvation.

The Story of Creation

Muslims believe that Allah created all that is in the heavens and on earth in perfect balance, order, and harmony. The Qur'anic description of creation is similar to the biblical one, with one fundamental difference. Whereas the Bible indicates that God created the world in six days and then "rested on the seventh day" (Genesis 2:2), the Qur'an states that "We created the heavens and the earth and all that is between them in six days, nor did any sense of weariness touch Us" (50:38). This is a direct challenge to the idea that God, the Almighty, would have been in need of rest after fulfilling the creation.

Each of the six days of creation are "like a thousand years of your reckoning" (22:47) or even "as fifty-thousand years" (70:4). The word "day" connotes a long period of time that does not contradict the current scientific thought about the evolution of the earth.

Oneness of God

The most fundamental teaching of Islam is that there is but One Almighty God, who has no partner, no associate, and no incarnation. The Qur'an makes a challenge against Trinitarian Christian beliefs. The very first law of Moses was that the "Lord our God, the Lord is One," and Muslims view the concept of the Trinity as a violation of that most basic precept.

While Christians would try to explain that the Truine God is in fact One, or that the three "persons" of God do not constitute three separate deities, Islam rejects these explanations. Muslims believe that Jesus himself claimed no divinity, and he worshipped Almighty God alone. In the chapter *Al-Ikhlas* (Purity of Faith), the Qur'an sums it up as follows. "Say: 'He is Allah, the One. Allah, the Eternal, Absolute. He begets not, nor is He begotten. And there is none like unto Him'" (112:1–4).

Salvation Based on Faith and Works

The most fundamental theological difference between Christians and Muslims surrounds the question of salvation. Muslims proclaim that God is Merciful, but also Just, and that every soul will be rewarded or punished based on tests during our lifetime. If one has faith, believes in Allah, and does works of righteousness, it is in Allah's Mercy to save that person from punishment. On the other hand, if a person is wicked, rejects faith, and harms everyone in his or her path, then it would not be just for God to give that person the same reward. Faith alone is not enough; one must follow up with good actions that are the embodiment of that faith. Likewise, good works mean nothing unless based on the foundation of a sincere faith in God.

Original Sin

One cannot understand the varying views of salvation without an understanding of the concept of original sin and separation from God in the two faiths. Muslims believe that when Adam and Eve sinned in the Garden, God forgave them their sins in His Mercy. There is no burden placed on all mankind that needs redemption; therefore, there is no need for a Savior. All people are born sinless.

Interfaith Discussions

Muslims are encouraged to engage in respectful dialogue with People of the Book and those of other religions. "And do not dispute with the People of the Book, except in ways that are best" (29:46). Muslims generally try to avoid heated arguments or endless debate about matters of faith.

Muslims are also encouraged to invite others to the faith, but do not have organized missionary programs. The Arabic word for inviting others to Islam is *da'wah,* which means "calling others to faith." Muslims are instructed to use good manners when talking with others about their faith. "Invite to the Way of thy Lord with wisdom and beautiful preaching, and discuss with them in ways that are best and most gracious. For thy Lord knows best who have strayed from His path, and who receive guidance" (16:125).

Most Muslims are happy to answer questions about their faith, as long as the questioner has a genuine desire to learn and not ridicule. Certainly, mutual dialogue and respectful discussion is the best way to learn about another people, so that we can build bridges and create a more civilized and peaceful community. Ignorance breeds prejudice, which only leads to more hatred and conflict.

There are over 1,200 mosques in North America, many of which hold regular open houses or introductory classes about Islam. To find a local mosque or Islamic Center, check your local telephone book or the organizations listed in Appendix B.

Non-Muslims in Muslim Countries

Within a Muslim state, all people are to enjoy freedom, honor, and protection from aggression. History has shown that these ideals can be fulfilled and enhanced in an Islamic state. Unfortunately, many of today's so-called "Muslim countries" violate even these basic human rights, which should be guaranteed under any Islamic system.

Freedom of Worship

Non-Muslims have the right to perform their religious rites without interference or prejudice. Their places of worship are to be protected and respected. As a minority religious community, they are permitted to regulate their personal matters (such as marriage, divorce, dietary laws, and so on) according to the teaching of their own faith. In turn, they must honor the same societal and civic responsibilities as those that are expected of the Muslim population (for example, being fair in business practices).

During the lifetime of Muhammad, leaders of the Muslim state signed treaties with neighboring Jewish and Christian tribes. These treaties and others that came after them ensured freedom of worship, and forbade the destruction of houses of worship. Notably, one treaty that was signed between the Muslim community and the Jewish people who lived in Madinah proclaimed: "Whoever stays with the Muslims from all Jewish tribes shall have help and aid, and shall not be the victims of injustice nor vengeance. They are all safe; they have their religion and Muslims have theirs."

During the time of the second caliph, Omar, a treaty was drawn up between Muslims and Christians in Jerusalem. The opening paragraph read: "This is the security that is given to the people of Elia (Jerusalem). It grants them security to all, sick or sound, security for their lives, their wealth, their churches, their crosses, and for all that relates to their religion. Their churches shall not be changed to dwelling places, nor destroyed, and nothing shall be taken from them, neither from their churches nor their surroundings. Nothing shall be taken from their wealth, and no constraint shall be placed upon anyone in matters of their religion, nor shall anyone be harmed." Jerusalem remained under Muslim rule for several hundred years during which time the rites of all faiths were respected.

FACT

In the twelfth century, the key to the Church of the Holy Sepulcher in Jerusalem was entrusted to two Muslim families by the names of Joudeh and Nusseibeh. To this day, these Muslim families are entrusted with doorkeeper duties and guardianship of the church key.

The Jizyah Tax

In an Islamic state, all Muslims have the duty to protect the community from outside aggression, including the duty to bear arms if necessary. In addition, wealthy Muslims are required in the faith to pay alms (zakat). Minority religious communities enjoy the protection of the Islamic state, but are exempt from these requirements. To balance these rights and duties, the Islamic state imposes a small tax (called *jizyah*) on non-Muslims within its borders, to fund the army and ensure their continued protection.

The word "jizyah" itself means to "compensate" or "repay." The non-Muslims who enjoy the freedoms of living in the Islamic state need to compensate for their exemption from military duty and the payment of alms. Those who are old, sick, or unable to pay are exempt from the jizyah. The amount has always been minimal, based on a person's ability to pay. Once a person pays this amount, it becomes the obligation of the Muslim state to protect them from any aggressor, either from within the community or outside of it.

Muslims in Non-Muslim Countries

Muslims are instructed to respect the cultures and traditions of other people, do good, prevent harm, and help in any situation where their assistance is needed, no matter where they live. The hospitality of the Muslim people is well recognized, and this kindness and generosity extends beyond borders of land or family.

Muslims are reminded in the Qur'an that the world is spacious, and people are free to travel to and live in a safe place. "He who forsakes his home for the sake of Allah, finds in the earth many a refuge, wide and spacious" (4:100). Thus, if Muslims face persecution due to their faith, they are encouraged to immigrate to a place of protection, wherever it might be. After all, it was a Christian king who gave refuge to the small, persecuted Muslim community during the early years of Muhammad's mission.

It is certainly preferable for Muslims to live in an Islamic environment with other Muslims. There, a Muslim can be assured of freedom of faith, justice, and friendship with others who share the same faith and worldview. However, it is also commendable for Muslims to live throughout the world as teachers and examples for others, or even to receive an education or earn a lawful living to support their families.

FACT

Since 1994, the Council on American-Islamic Relations has advocated for Muslims in issues of workplace or educational discrimination. In 2001, the organization helped to resolve over 300 complaints, all through negotiation, letters of protest, and other peaceful means.

When living among non-Muslims, Muslims are obliged to abide by the laws governing the country in which they live as long as they do not violate Islamic principles. When a local law does violate Islamic principles (for example, the ban on wearing a head scarf in some jurisdictions), Muslims try to negotiate for their rights and perform acts of civil disobedience in protest. Under no circumstances is violence or anarchy permitted.

Chapter 12

The Muslim Perception of Jesus

Muslims respect Jesus as an honorable prophet and messenger of God. According to Islamic teachings, Jesus is not rejected, but neither is he considered to be a part of God Himself. Islam considers Jesus to be one of the great prophets of God, in the company of Abraham, Moses, and Muhammad.

A Miraculous Birth

The story of Jesus' birth in the Qur'an begins with the story of Mary, his mother, in the chapter named after her (called "Miriam" in Arabic). In the Qur'anic account, Mary's mother dedicated her daughter to the service of God. Zachariah took charge of Mary's care, and found that God indeed met her every need. The Qur'an tells of one occasion when Zachariah found Mary in her room with fresh fruit that was out of season. He asked where it came from, and Mary replied: "From God, for God provides sustenance to whom He pleases, without measure" (3:37). Mary's faith was strong, and she constantly thanked God for his blessings and favors.

ALERT!

In the Qur'an, Jesus is known by the name "Esa" (alternatively spelled "Isa"). The Aramaic language of Jesus contained no sound or letter "J," so this spelling more accurately reflects the way that the name was likely pronounced.

The Announcement

One day while she was praying in seclusion, an angel appeared before Mary in the form of a man. Frightened, she tried to flee. "Verily! I seek refuge with the Most Beneficent from you, if you do fear God!" (Qur'an 19:18). The Qur'an relates what happened next: "He (the angel) said, 'I am only a messenger from your Lord, to announce to you the gift of a righteous son.' She said, 'How can I have a son, seeing that no man has touched me, and I am not unchaste?' He said, 'So it will be. Your Lord said, 'That is easy for Me, and We wish to appoint him as a sign unto men, and a mercy from Us. It is a matter so decreed'" (19:19–21).

In another section of the Qur'an, the angels indicate to Mary the honor in which her son would be held: "Behold! The angels said, 'Oh Mary! God gives you glad tidings of a Word from Him. His name will be Christ Jesus, the son of Mary, held in honor in this world and the Hereafter, and of the company of those nearest to God. He shall speak to the people in childhood and maturity. And he shall be of the company of the righteous'" (3:45–46). When she protested that she could not have a child, as no man had touched her, the angels replied, "Even so, God creates what He wills. When He has decreed a matter, He says to it, 'Be!' and it is" (3:47).

The Birth

After hearing the angel's words, Mary was left anxious and concerned. She was a pious and honorable woman. People would talk and make accusations against her if she showed up with a newborn child and no husband. So Mary chose to leave and seclude herself away from the people. She wandered about the barren valleys, finally resting against a dry palm tree in the middle of nowhere. It was here that she gave birth to her son.

At this point, Mary was overwhelmed with anguish and cried out that she wished she were dead. The Qur'an relates that a voice then called out to calm her. "Grieve not! For your Lord has provided a stream beneath you. Shake the trunk of the palm tree towards yourself; it will let fall fresh, ripe dates upon you. So eat and drink, and cool your eye" (19:24–26). She thus refreshed herself, and prepared to face her community.

The Baby Speaks

Mary decided to return to her people, but worried about what she would tell them. The angels instructed her to take a vow of silence, and not to answer anyone who addressed her. When Mary arrived, the people naturally questioned her about this apparent sin. "Oh, sister of Aaron! Your father was not a man of evil, nor was your mother a woman unchaste!" they scolded her (19:28). The Qur'an then relates that Mary then put her finger to her lips and pointed to the child. The people asked how they could talk to a newborn baby. It was then that Jesus spoke, fulfilling the miracle that had been mentioned when the angels first appeared to Mary. He said:

I am indeed a servant of God. He has given me revelation, and made me a prophet. And He has made me blessed wherever I may be, and has enjoined on me prayer and almsgiving as long as I live. He has made me kind to my mother, and not overbearing or unblessed. So peace is on me the day I was born, the day that I die, and the day that I shall be raised up to life. (19:30–33)

While some people disregarded this miracle as a strange trick, most realized that the baby was unique and destined for a special mission. They left Mary alone thereafter, and did not harass her.

Other Miracles

The Qur'an confirms that Jesus performed miracles by the power of God. The Qur'an relates that Jesus said:

I have come to you with a sign from your Lord, in that I make for you out of clay, as it were, the figure of a bird. Then I breathe into it, and it becomes a bird, by God's leave. And I heal those born blind, and the lepers, and I bring the dead into life, by God's leave. And I declare to you what you eat, and what you store in your houses. Surely therein is a sign for you, if you did believe. (3:49)

Here the Qur'an makes clear that Jesus' miracles were all done "by God's leave," or permission. Of his own power, Jesus could do nothing. He performed miracles by the grace and power of God alone, as testament to the Almighty Creator behind all things.

Monotheistic Teachings

Islam teaches that from the beginning of time, prophets have been sent to teach their people to believe in the One True God, and obey His commandments. The message that Jesus brought to his people was no different. Jesus emphasized that his mission did not cancel the laws received by Moses, but fulfilled them. "And in the footsteps [of the previous prophets], We sent Jesus the son of Mary, confirming the Torah that had come before him. We sent him the Gospel; therein was guidance and light, and confirmation of the Torah that had come before him—a guidance and an admonition to those who fear God" (Qur'an 5:46).

According to Islam, Jesus was thus a link in a long chain of prophets and messengers sent by God to their people. Jesus was sent to the Children of Israel, who had deviated from the teachings of Moses and other messengers. He was supported by miracles, to prove that he was a messenger of God. However, the majority of people rejected his ministry.

Messenger of God

Islam rejects any notion that Jesus was anything more than a human messenger of God. Muslims do not believe that Jesus was "God on earth," or a part of the Trinity. The Qur'an is very clear:

> Christ the son of Mary was no more than a messenger. Many were the messengers that passed away before him. His mother was a woman of truth. They both had to eat their daily food. See how God makes his signs clear to them, yet see in what ways they are deluded away from the truth! Say, "Will we worship, besides God, something that has no power either to harm or benefit you? But God Alone, He it is that hears and knows all things" (5:75–76).

"Son of God"

Islam rejects the idea that Jesus was somehow part of God, or a "begotten son of God." The title "son of God" had been given to others before him, and merely indicated that a person was a "servant of God." This person was close and dear to God because of his faithful service, but there is no connotation that such a servant is actually part of God Himself. Muslims believe that this term became misused and misinterpreted by monotheists through the influence of the Greek and Roman pagan theology.

FACT

It is blasphemous to say that a human being is an "incarnation" of God or the product of a union between God and any other life form. The Qur'an makes it very clear: "For it is not consonant with the Majesty of the Most Gracious that He should beget a son. Not one of the beings in the heavens and the earth must come to the Most Gracious but as a servant" (19:92–93).

The Qur'an recognizes that Jesus had no human father, but this miracle is not reason to call Jesus the son of God, or God Himself. The Qur'an points out that Adam had neither a father nor a mother (3:59). In Islam, God Alone is the Almighty, and is able to create as He wills.

The "Messiah"

The Qur'an does call Jesus the "Messiah," from the Semitic word, *maseeh*. This term comes from a root word (*masaha*) that means "to rub" or "to anoint." Historically, priests and kings were anointed when being consecrated to their offices. The Greek word for "anointed" is Christos, from which the name "Christ" developed. In Islamic terms, every prophet of God is anointed or appointed for religious service.

Muslim Rejection of the Trinity

Islam flatly rejects the concept of the Trinity, equating it with polytheism. The Oneness of God is the fundamental basis of all monotheistic teaching, and Islam is very strict about this interpretation. The Qur'an calls upon people to reflect on and purify their faith: "Oh People of the Book! Commit no excesses in your religion, nor say of God anything but the truth. Christ Jesus, the son of Mary, was no more than a messenger of God . . . so believe in God and His messengers. Say not, 'Three.' Desist— it will be better for you. For God is One God, glory be to Him!" (4:171).

Another verse is more direct and clear: "They disbelieve who say, 'God is one of three in a Trinity.' There is no god except One God. If they desist not from their word of blasphemy, truly a grievous chastisement will befall the disbelievers among them [in the Hereafter]" (5:73).

Muslims point out that there were many people in the early Christian communities who did not believe in the Trinity. Even today, there are some Christian congregations that reject or de-emphasize this teaching.

In Islam, the Holy Spirit is understood to be the Angel Gabriel. Gabriel was used as the conduit for messages from God to all of his prophets and messengers. Thus, the Holy Spirit is considered distinct and separate from God, not part of God.

Return to God

Muslims and Christians disagree about the circumstances surrounding the end of Jesus' life on earth. According to Islamic teaching, the crucifixion of Jesus never took place. The Qur'an states very clearly that the plot to kill Jesus failed because God saved Jesus from his enemies by raising him up to heaven.

The Qur'an condemns the actions of some disbelievers among the Children of Israel, who rejected Jesus' mission, made false charges of fornication against Mary, and boasted about killing Jesus:

> They rejected faith. They uttered against Mary a grave, false charge. They said (in boast), "We killed Christ Jesus, the son of Mary, the messenger of God." But they killed him not, nor crucified him. Only a likeness of that was shown to them. And those who debate about this are full of doubts, with no certain knowledge, but only conjecture to follow. Surely, they did not kill him. No, God raised him up unto Himself, and God is Exalted in Power, Wise. (4:156–158)

Who do Muslims believe was crucified instead of Jesus?
The Qur'an does not elaborate, but only points out that it was someone who looked like him, who "appeared" to be him. Indeed, there is as much mystery about the "death" of Jesus as there is about his birth.

The Second Coming

Islam teaches that Jesus will return to earth before the Day of Judgment. While the second coming is not specifically mentioned in the Qur'an, it does say that Jesus is a "sign" for the coming of the Hour (43:61). This is interpreted to mean that Jesus will come back at the end of times.

More detailed information about Jesus' return to earth is given in the Sunnah. On one occasion, Muhammad came upon a group of people who were discussing the Day of Judgment. He told them that it would not come until the people see ten signs. Among them, he mentioned, "the descent of Jesus, the son of Mary." Muhammad also told his followers that Jesus would descend among the people as a just judge close to the end of time. He will follow the laws of Islam, and all Jewish and Christian people will believe in him before his death: "And there is none of the People of the Book but must believe in him before his death. And on the Day of Judgment he will be a witness against them" (4:159).

The Injeel

Islam teaches that Jesus brought revelation to his people in the form of the Injeel (Gospels). Muslims believe that the original teachings of Jesus called upon people to believe in One God and follow His commandments, but these revelations became distorted—the later interpretations of Jesus' mission, by Paul and others, essentially changed his pure and simple message.

The Gospel According to Jesus

According to the Muslim faith, the revelations that Jesus gave to his followers can no longer be found; the Bible of today does not accurately reflect his mission and teachings. That is, Muslims believe in the "Gospel according to Jesus," not according to Matthew, Mark, Luke, John, or anyone else. While the New Testament contains many verses and stories that Muslims may find to be true, the book itself is not considered by Muslims to be God's revelation. Any contradictions between the Bible and Islamic teachings are viewed as man-made elements introduced after Jesus' departure.

FACT

Most of the disagreements between Muslims and Christians center on the person and role of Jesus. Muslims believe that Jesus was an important link in the long line of prophets who brought God's message of monotheism to the world, and they find that Christian teachings overexhalt Jesus above what God intended his role to be.

Despite the theological differences between Christianity and Islam, Muslims try to focus on the commonalities between themselves and the People of the Book, particularly the Christians. The Qur'an reminds, "Nearest among them in love to the believers will you find those who say, 'We are Christians.' Because among these are men devoted to learning, and men who have renounced the world, and they are not arrogant." Muslims and Christians would all agree that this is how Jesus wanted his followers to be.

Chapter 13

The Muslim View of Creation

Muslims believe that Allah is the Creator and Sustainer of the universe; nothing exists except by His power and mercy. However, the process of creation was a slow process of development, taking place over many periods or eons. Muslims recognize the order and balance in the natural world and see it as a sign of Allah's wisdom and power.

Creation in the Qur'an

The act of creation is frequently spoken of in the Qur'an in order to draw the reader into thinking about the order in all things and about the All-Knowing Creator who is behind it.

The Qur'an calls upon people to study the natural world and its history in order to find signs of God's wisdom. By pondering the perfect, intricate, natural laws, an individual may come to realize that an infinitely Wise and All-Powerful Creator must be ordering the universe. According to the Qur'an, God proclaimed, "We will show them Our Signs, in the horizons and in their own selves, until it becomes manifest that it is the truth" (41:53).

The Islamic term for creation is *khaliqa,* and Allah is known as Al-Khaliq (the Creator). These words come from an Arabic root word that refers to the act of creation or molding into form. Other Arabic words derived from this root are "nature," "morality," and "ethics."

No Book of Genesis

In the Bible, one can simply open to page one and find an entire chapter that explains, step by step, the theological teachings about God's process of creation, from beginning to end. Not so with the Qur'an. The Qur'an contains the same level of detail, but the story must be pieced together from many verses, dispersed throughout dozens of different chapters.

Why? Because the purpose is not to give the reader a factual historical account, but rather to engage the reader in contemplating the lessons to be learned from the story of Creation. Thus, the descriptions of the process of creation are interspersed with verses extolling the wisdom of God, lamenting mankind's ingratitude, and calling upon people to open their eyes and look around them. How can this wonderful universe be under the power of anyone other than an Almighty, All-Knowing God?

Descriptions of Creation

The Qur'an talks about the creation of the heavens and the earth, the mountains, the diversity of life, and the special gifts and role that human beings have.

> He it is Who created the heavens and the earth in six days, then established Himself on the Throne. He knows what enters within the earth and what comes forth out of it, what comes down from heaven and what mounts up to it. And He is with you wherever you may be. And Allah sees well all that you do. To Him belongs the dominion of the heavens and the earth, and all affairs go back to Allah. He merges night into day, and He merges day into night, and He has full knowledge of the secrets of all hearts. (57:4–6)

> Verily in the heavens and the earth are signs for those who believe. And in the creation of yourselves, and the fact that animals are scattered (through the earth), are signs for those of assured faith. And in the alternation of night and day, and the fact that Allah sends down sustenance from the sky, and revives therewith the earth after its death, and in the change of the winds, are signs for those that are wise. (45:3–5)

> Allah is He Who raised the heavens without any pillars that you can see; then He established Himself on the Throne. He has subjected the sun and the moon; each one runs its course for a term appointed. He regulates all affairs, explaining the signs in detail, that you may believe with certainty in the meeting with your Lord. And it is He Who spread out the earth, and set thereon mountains standing firm, and flowing rivers, and fruit of every kind He made in pairs. He draws the night as a veil over the day. Behold! Verily in these things there are signs for those who consider! And in the earth are tracts, diverse though neighboring, and gardens of vines and fields sown with corn, and palm trees—growing out of single roots or otherwise—watered with

the same water, yet some of them We make more excellent than others to eat. Behold! Verily in these things are signs for those who understand! (13:2–4)

Has there not been over man a long period of time when he was nothing, not even mentioned? Verily, We created man from a drop of mingled liquid, in order to try him. So We gave him the gifts of hearing and sight. We showed him the Way, whether he be grateful or ungrateful. (76:1–3)

The Big Bang

When describing the creation of the "heavens and the earth," the Qur'an does not discount the theory of a Big Bang explosion at the start of it all. In fact, the Qur'an says that "the heavens and the earth were joined together as one unit, before We clove them asunder" (21:30). Following this big explosion, Allah "turned to the sky, and it had been (as) smoke: He said to it and to the earth: 'Come together, willingly or unwillingly.' They said: 'We come (together), in willing obedience'" (41:11). Thus the elements of what was to become the planets began to cool, come together, and form into shape, following the natural laws that Allah established in the universe.

FACT

Muslim author Harun Yahya, a native of Turkey, has written more than 200 books about creation, science, and evolution based on Qur'anic teachings and the work of previous Islamic scholars. His work has been translated into over a dozen languages.

The Qur'an states that God created the sun, the moon, and the planets, each with their own individual courses, or orbits. "It is He Who created the night and the day, and the sun and the moon; all [the celestial bodies] swim along, each in its rounded course" (21:33). In another verse, it describes that the sun and the moon will run their course for a term appointed by God (13:2).

Continuous Expansion of the Universe

The Qur'an also does not rule out the idea that the universe is continuing to expand. "The heavens, We have built them with power. And verily, We are expanding it" (Qur'an 51:47). There has been some historical debate among Muslim scholars about the precise meaning of this verse, since knowledge of the universe's expansion was only recently discovered. Theories about the expansion of the universe were confirmed only when Edwin P. Hubble made his observations in the 1930s, noting that the galaxies are indeed moving away from each other.

In Just Six Days?

The Qur'an states that "Allah created the heavens and the earth, and all that is between them, in six days" (7:54), and this information is repeated in other verses as well. On the surface, it seems remarkably similar to the time frame given in the Jewish and Christian Book of Genesis. Does such a teaching contradict the scientific evidence that the universe developed over billions of years?

It Depends on Your "Day"

The verses that mention "six days" use the Arabic word *youm* (day). This word appears several other times in the Qur'an. One verse describes the Day of Resurrection as "a Day the measure whereof is [as] fifty thousand years" (70:4). Another verse clearly states that "a Day in the sight of your Lord is like a thousand years of your reckoning" (22:47). The word "youm" is thus understood to be a long period of time, an era or eon.

Therefore, Muslims interpret the description of a "six-day" creation to mean that God created the universe in six distinct periods, or eons. The length of these periods is not precisely identified, nor are the specific developments that took place during each period. The Qur'an also describes how Allah created the universe and the physical earth in two "days," and then populated it with life in the subsequent four "days" (41:9–12).

Did God Rest?

One distinct difference between the Creation story in Islam, as opposed to that given in the Book of Genesis, is what happened at the end of the sixth "day," when the creation was finished. According to the Bible, God looked over His creation, and "saw that it was good." God was finished, and on the seventh day He rested.

In the Qur'an, a distinct point is made that the Almighty Creator is beyond any need for rest. "We created the heavens and the earth and all between them in six days, nor did any sense of weariness touch Us" (50:38). In the Islamic story, God established Himself on the Throne, to oversee all of creation.

ALERT!

Friday is the day when Muslims gather for congregational worship during the noon prayer time. However, it is not a day of rest. The community gathers to pray and then returns to normal daily routines and work. Muslims do not observe a Sabbath.

God is not "done" with His work because the process of creation is ongoing—every minute of the day, every day of every year. Each new child who is born, every seed that sprouts into a sapling, every new species that appears on earth, is a part of the ongoing process of God's creation. "He it is Who created the heavens and the earth in six days, then established Himself on the Throne. He knows what enters within the heart of the earth, and what comes forth out of it, what comes down from heaven, and what mounts up to it. And He is with you wherever you may be. And God sees well all that you do" (Qur'an 57:4).

Creation versus Evolution

As we have seen thus far, the Qur'anic account of creation is in line with modern scientific thought about the development of the universe and life on earth. Muslims acknowledge that life developed over a long period of time, but see Allah's hand behind it all. The diversity of life that has cropped up over time is a sign pointing to God, not away from Him.

What is the matter with you, that ye are not conscious of Allah's majesty, seeing that it is He that has created you in diverse stages? See you not how Allah has created the seven heavens one above another, and made the moon a light in their midst, and made the sun as a [Glorious] Lamp? And Allah has produced you from the earth, growing [gradually]. (71:13–17)

There is much debate, in both religious and nonreligious circles, about the validity of modern theories of evolution. Many Muslims flatly reject any notion of evolution, simply because of its association with those who deny God's existence. In general, they also reject that evolution is a random act, devoid of an All-Knowing Creator. However, many Muslims do recognize the possibility that Allah planned some forms of evolution.

Life Sprung from Water

The Qur'an describes that all particles that make up the universe were joined together in one celestial cloud, before they were "cloven asunder" or exploded. In the same verse, the Qur'an says that God "made from water every living thing" (21:30).

Another verse describes how "God has created every animal from water. Of them are some that creep on their bellies, some that walk on two legs, and some that walk on four. God creates what He wills, for truly God has power over all things" (24:45). These verses support the scientific theory that life began in the Earth's oceans.

Adam or Apes?

Where do human beings fit into the development of life on earth? Scientific theories currently hold that *Homo sapiens* evolved from earlier forms of hominoid primates approximately three to six million years ago. However, the lines of descent between species are widely debated and not proven.

The Qur'an makes brief mention of a group of people who were punished by God for their disobedience and transgression. "When in their insolence they transgressed [all] prohibitions, We said to them: 'Be ye apes, despised and rejected'" (7:166). Many Muslim scholars interpret this to mean that these human beings were literally turned into apes by God.

While Islam recognizes the general idea of the development of life over a period of time, human beings are considered different. Islam teaches that human beings are a unique life form that was created by God in a special way, with unique gifts and abilities that had not yet been seen on earth. In short, Muslims do not believe that human beings randomly evolved from apes.

Islam teaches that human beings are a special creation of God, given a special nature and an important role. The life of human beings began with the creation of two people, a male and a female named Adam and Hawwa (Eve).

Adam and Eve

When the earth had been prepared—blessed with sustenance, rain, and abundant plant and animal life—everything was ready for the entrance of a new creature, a special being that God would endow with gifts: a soul and conscience, knowledge, and the free choice to follow God's guidance.

Allah created the angels from light, the jinn from fire, and human beings from the "salt of the earth" (clay, in the Qur'an). While the angels were created to serve God and have no free will, human beings were given both the freedom of choice and the knowledge, so that they might choose to serve God.

The Qur'an describes how God created Adam: "We created man from sounding clay, from mud molded into shape. And the jinn race, We had created before, from the fire of a scorching wind" (15:26–27). In another verse, the Qur'an describes that the first human beings were created from clay, and that their descendants would be created from "fluid": "He began the creation of man from clay, and made his progeny from a quintessence of fluid" (32:7–8). Thus from the very beginning, human beings had an intimate attachment to the earth.

Knowledge and Free Will

Allah created the human to be a "vicegerent" or "authority" on the earth. In order to fulfill this role, the first human being (Adam) needed knowledge, so the first thing that God did upon creating Adam was to teach him the "names" of all things—to give him knowledge of the world. Human beings were endowed with a reasoning and intelligent mind, unique among the creatures of the earth.

God also created human beings with the conscious knowledge of right from wrong and the free choice to follow one path or the other. At the time of Adam's creation, the Qur'an describes that the angels were worried about the mischief that these new beings could cause:

> Behold! Your Lord said to the angels, "I will create a vicegerent on earth." They said: "Will You place therein one who will make mischief and shed blood, while we celebrate Your praises and glorify Your Holy name?" He said, "I know what you know not." And He taught Adam the names of all things [gave him knowledge]. Then He placed them before the angels, and said: "Tell me the names of these if you are right." They said, "Glory to You! Of knowledge We have none, save what You have taught us. In truth it is You Who are perfect in knowledge and wisdom." (2:30–32)

Then God asked Adam to tell the names, to demonstrate the gifts that God had given him, placing him above all the rest of creation.

Satan's Temptation

In the Qur'anic account, God then ordered all of the angels and the jinn to bow down to Adam, to recognize humanity's superiority over them, and in obedience to God's command. One of the jinn, Iblis (Satan), refused.

The Qur'an describes what took place next. Allah asked Iblis why he did not obey. Iblis replied with arrogance, saying: "I am better than him! You created me from fire, and You created him from clay" (7:12). Allah then rejected Iblis, casting him out and cursing him.

Iblis then asked for respite, until the Day of Resurrection, so that he could try to bring some of the humans along with him. "Then I will assault them from before them and behind them, from their right and their left. Nor will You find, in most of them, gratitude for Your mercies" (7:17). Allah granted this respite, adding: "If any of them follow you, I will fill Hell with all of you" (7:18).

Creation of the First Woman

While the creation of Eve is not described in detail, the Qur'an does make it clear that a "mate" was created for Adam, from the same nature and soul. "It is He Who created you from a single person, and made his mate of like nature, in order that he might dwell with her [in love]" (7:189). She is not mentioned by name in the Qur'an, but in Islamic tradition she is known as Hawwa (Eve).

The "Fall" of Mankind

After Satan was rejected, God allowed Adam and Eve to live in the Garden of Paradise. "Oh, Adam! Live, you and your wife, in the Garden. And enjoy [its good things] as ye wish: but approach not this tree, lest you become of the unjust" (7:19). In fulfillment of his promise, Satan began immediately to try to interfere and cause the human beings to become disobedient. The Qur'an says that Satan began whispering suggestions to them, that the fruit of the forbidden tree was actually the best kind. Adam and Eve then chose to eat from the tree, which they realized immediately was a mistake.

Forgiveness

At this point, the story begins to differ greatly from the Biblical account. After Adam and Eve realized their mistake, they immediately sought forgiveness from God. "They said: 'Our Lord! We have wronged our souls. If You forgive us not, and bestow not upon us Your Mercy, we shall certainly be lost'" (7:23). The Qur'an describes that Allah taught Adam some words to use, to seek repentance. "Then learned Adam from his Lord certain words, and Allah accepted his repentance, for He is Oft-Forgiving, Most Merciful" (2:37).

In Islam, there is no concept of "original sin." The first human beings made a mistake, asked for forgiveness, and God showed them mercy. This is a pattern that would endure throughout time. Islam teaches that God created us and therefore knows our weaknesses and vulnerabilities. He does not hold us accountable for what we cannot uphold, nor does He accept atonement on behalf of someone else. But in His Grace and Mercy, those who believe and repent may be forgiven for their misdeeds.

ALERT!

In Islam, each person is responsible for himself; there is no inherited sinfulness in mankind. "Who receives guidance, receives it for his own benefit; who goes astray does so to his own loss. No bearer of burdens can bear the burden of another" (Qur'an 17:15).

Life on Earth

After accepting their repentance, God ordered Adam and Eve to go down to earth to do their work, worship God, and await their return to Him. Allah promised them that guidance will be sent, and that any who believe in God and follow His guidance will see joy and happiness in the Hereafter. "We said, 'Get you down all from here. And if, as is sure, there comes to you guidance from Me, whoever follows My guidance, on them shall be no fear, nor shall they grieve. But those who reject faith and belie Our signs, they shall be companions of the Fire; they shall abide therein'" (2:38–39).

Throughout these accounts of Adam and Eve's creation and fall are several underlying lessons:

- God created human beings with a special nature and responsibility toward the earth.
- Satan was rejected because of his arrogance and disobedience of God.
- All human beings should strive to follow God, and reject attempts to dissuade them from the Straight Path.
- God's Mercy and Grace are abundant and limitless, so we should seek His guidance and protection.

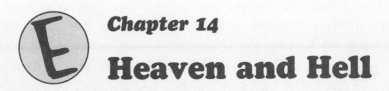

Chapter 14

Heaven and Hell

Muslims believe that the life of this world is only a temporary refuge, and that one day everyone will face God to account for their choices in life. God is a fair but merciful Judge. Those who are good will be rewarded with admission into the "gardens, beneath which rivers flow." Those who are evil will be doomed to punishment in Hellfire.

Life after Death

Death is a natural event that none of us can escape. Throughout time, religions have always pursued the following question: What happens to us after death?

In Islam, the belief is that a person's soul leaves the body and awaits a final Day of Judgment before God. At the time of that Judgment, God will show mercy and justice, and decide who will be rewarded and who will be punished. He will reward those who have "believed and worked deeds of righteousness" with eternal paradise, called Jannah (the Garden). Of those who have rejected faith and done evil, Allah will either forgive them in His mercy, or punish them in eternal Hellfire, called *Jahannam* (a word related to other Arabic words that mean "displeasure," "ignorance," and "frown").

This Life and the Hereafter

Muslims live their lives—work, marry, and raise children—with a thought to the Hereafter. They strive to use every opportunity to deepen their faith in God, follow His guidance, and do good deeds. It is very easy to get caught up in the hustle and bustle of life without a thought to what comes next. In Islamic terms, the life we are living now is called the *dunya*—something earthly, temporal, and low.

FACT

The Islamic term *taqwa* is used to describe how human beings should relate to God. While it is often translated as "fear God," a more accurate meaning would be to approach God with piety and reverence. Muslims are not afraid of God, but revere Him and strive to do His will.

The Hereafter is what Muslims believe is most important; in Islamic terminology, it is called the *akhirah*, "the end" or "the last." The akhirah is what's to come at the end of our lives here, and the final aim of all believers is to be in a good place for the rest of eternity. To this end, Muslims try not to get distracted from their true purpose: to worship God

and to strive in righteousness. The Qur'an reminds: "Oh you who believe!
Revere God, and let every soul look to what he has sent forth for tomorrow
[the Hereafter]. Yes, revere God, for God is Well-Acquainted with all that you
do. And do not be like those who forgot God, and He made them forget
themselves. Such are the rebellious transgressors" (59:18–19).

Salvation in God

Muslims believe that God is Merciful and Compassionate, and does
not require of us more than what we can do. In Islam, salvation requires
piety and good action, but is only possible through the Mercy of God. In
the Qur'an, God promises the reward of Paradise for those who show
piety and reverence to Him, who conduct themselves in accordance with
their faith, who obey His will and law, who make sacrifices for His sake,
and who repent of their misconduct. The important thing is to make a
sincere effort to live as God has requested, for God knows our hearts
and our intentions.

ALERT!

Despite our best efforts, we will always fall short. We are human
and make mistakes. Muslims believe that God Who created us
knows this and shows us mercy. We do not "earn" our way into
Heaven; only by the Mercy and Grace of God does He reward our
efforts.

The Soul's Temporary Dwelling Place

So what actually happens to our souls when we die? Islam teaches that
at the moment of death, the Angel of Death comes to remove the soul
from the body. The souls of good people are lifted out gently, while the
souls of wicked people are yanked out with terrifying force.

After the soul is lifted from the body, the angels carry it up to the
gates of Heaven. There the person will become aware of whether he or
she is destined for Heaven or Hell. Then God orders the soul to be
returned to earth.

In the Company of Angels

When the soul is returned to the earth, it rests in the grave until the Day of Resurrection. Muhammad taught that the soul rests in the company of angels, who question the person about his or her beliefs. They ask three questions: "Who is your Lord? What was your way of life? Who was your prophet?"

If the soul answers properly, then the angels give it pleasant company, and the grave begins to seem spacious and comfortable. If it shows rejection of God in its answers, then the space of the grave begins to seem tight and suffocating. The angels will torment such souls until the Day of Judgment. This is known as the punishment of the grave.

The Day of Resurrection

Muslims believe that the entire world will come to an end on one appointed day, when everything will be annihilated. The Qur'an describes the Day of Resurrection (*Youm al-Qiyama*) as follows: "When the sky bursts apart, when planets are dispersed, when the seas spill forth, when graves are overturned, then each soul will know what it sent forward and what it left behind" (82:1–5).

Signs of the Hour

When will this Day come? When people asked Muhammad, he would always answer that this knowledge was with God alone. Yet, according to several traditions, he did indicate some signs that would appear before the day arrived. Several "minor" signs will appear as the end times approach. Among them:

- Shepherds will begin competing in the construction of tall buildings.
- Drinking and fornication will increase; killing will increase.
- Earthquakes will increase in number.
- Knowledge of Islam will be taken away, while ignorance will increase.
- Time will be shortened so that a year will be like a month, a month like a day, a day like an hour.

There are dozens more of the minor signs, and many of them have already begun to appear. But that doesn't necessarily mean that the Day of Judgment could come at any moment. There will be more "major" signs that signify that the Hour is imminent. These include:

- Dajjal (the anti-Christ) will appear, claiming to be God and trying to deceive people away from true faith. Only unbelievers will follow him.
- Jesus Christ will return to earth.
- Two tribes of people (Gog and Magog) will ravage the earth.
- The sun will rise from the west.

FACT

The Muslim counterparts to the Bible's Gog and Magog are known as Yajuj and Mujuj. The Qur'an does not go into detail about who these people are or from where they will come. They are described as a savage, unruly tribe of people, who will break free from bondage and ravage the earth before the end of the world.

At the moment of the final Hour, a trumpet will call the people to assembly. This trumpet will be blown by the Angel Israfeel, and will notify people that the time of Judgment has arrived. All living creatures, all people past and present, will be gathered together before God. There will be a mass panic, as everyone starts worrying about the coming Judgment. "Then when the Trumpet is blown, there will be no more relationships between them that day, nor will one ask after another" (23:101).

The Day of Judgment

The Qur'an describes the Day of Judgment as a day of happiness for the believers and a day of panic and fear for those who rejected God. God will sort out the people into groups, review their records, and either bless them with His Mercy, or punish them. God is a perfect Judge, and will be balanced and fair, taking into account every aspect of a person's life. "On that Day will men proceed in groups sorted out, to be shown the deeds that they had done. Then shall anyone who has done an atom's weight of good, see it! And anyone who has done an atom's weight of evil shall see it" (99:6–8).

Islam contends that it is not consistent with God's perfect Justice that all people be treated the same, whether they were good or bad, whether they believed or disbelieved. Rather, God's Justice requires that there should be reward for faith and good works, and punishment for disbelief and evil works. Yet, God's Mercy overshadows all.

The Book of Deeds

Every person on earth will have a book that contains a record of everything he or she said or did during his or her lifetime. The Qur'an explains the reaction people will have when reading their own book: "And the Book will be placed before you. And you will see the sinful in great terror, because of what is recorded therein. They will say, 'Oh, woe to us! What book is this? It leaves out nothing, great or small, but takes account of it.' They will find all that they did, placed before them. And not one will your Lord treat with injustice" (18:49).

The Scales of Justice

The Qur'an describes how God will use perfect scales of justice to weigh a person's good and evil deeds. "We shall set up scales of justice for the Day of Judgment, so that not a soul will be dealt with unjustly in the least. And if there be no more than the weight of a mustard seed, We will bring it into account" (21:47).

Based on the results, a person will find reward in Paradise, or punishment in Hell. "Then those whose balance of good deeds is heavy, they will be successful. But those whose balance is light will be those who have lost their souls. In Hell will they abide" (23:102–103). Throughout this process, God will show compassion and mercy to those who strived to believe and do the right thing.

The Bridge over Hell

Islam teaches that following the Judgment, people will cross a bridge called *As-Siraat* (the Path). This bridge is described as being sharper than a sword and thinner than a strand of hair. Those crossing the bridge will look down and see the horrors of Hell. Then, the blessed will go on, and the gates of Paradise will be open, and angels will greet them in peace and welcome them. Those who are destined for punishment in Hell will fall off the bridge into the pit below.

In Heaven

The Qur'an describes a beautiful and wonderful place that awaits those who believe in God and do righteous good deeds. It is a place of peace, with rivers and fruits, sweet smells, goblets of gold, and the shade of God Himself. The Qur'an warns that there is more to Paradise that is beyond our knowledge or comprehension. "No person knows what delights of the eye are kept hidden in reserve for them, as a reward for their good deeds" (32:17). Muhammad also reported that God said, "I have prepared for My righteous slaves that which no eye has seen, no ear has heard and has never crossed the mind of any human being."

The Qur'an is clear that both men and women will dwell in the Garden. "God has promised to believers, men and women, Gardens underneath which rivers flow, to dwell therein, and beautiful mansions in Gardens everlasting. But the greatest bliss is the good pleasure of God; that is the supreme felicity" (9:72).

Peace in Paradise

The people of the Garden will be happy and peaceful. "The righteous will be amid gardens and fountains. Their greeting will be, 'Enter here, in peace and security.' And We shall remove from their hearts any lurking sense of injury. They will be like brothers, joyfully facing each other on thrones [of dignity]. There, no sense of fatigue shall touch them, nor shall they ever be asked to leave" (15:45–48).

The Qur'an also describes that they will experience pure joy and no sense of wickedness. "No frivolity will they hear therein, nor any mischief. Only the saying, 'Peace! Peace!'" (56:25–26). "Verily the companions of the Garden shall that day have joy in all that they do. They and their associates will be in pleasant shade, reclining on couches of dignity. Every fruit will be there for them; they shall have whatever they call for. 'Peace!'—a word of salutation from a Lord Most Merciful" (36:55–58).

God's Company

The greatest reward for those in the Garden will be the company and pleasure of God. Beyond the comfortable surroundings, people will feel peaceful joy in the presence of their Lord. Muhammad said, "Then the screen will be removed and they will look towards Him. By God, He will not give them a thing more beloved to them and more comforting to their eyes, than the gaze of Himself." Heaven in Islam is not merely a physical reward; spiritual redemption is the highest goal.

The Levels of Paradise

The Qur'an indicates that some people will be higher (more respected and closer to God) than others. There will be different levels, and people will be assigned to these levels based on the strength of their faith and the purity of their hearts. "And those foremost (in faith) will be foremost (in the Hereafter). These will be those nearest to God, in Gardens of Bliss" (56:10–12).

FACT

The idea that there are seventy-two virgins awaiting each righteous man in Paradise is a misinterpretation of Islamic teaching. The Qur'an mentions "companions" for all believers, men and women. The Arabic word for "companions" (plural of *houri*) does not have a sexual connotation. Indeed, the Qur'an uses the same word to refer to the disciples of Jesus.

Muhammad once told his followers that the highest level of Paradise is reserved for those who sacrifice their lives for the sake of God, martyred for a righteous cause. A person who helps widows and the poor will be at the same level. "They will have the pleasure of occupying the highest dwellings in Paradise. Your Lord will smile at them, and whenever your Lord smiles upon any of His servants, that person will not be brought to account," he said.

In the Fire of Hell

Just as those who believe and do good are rewarded for their efforts, those who reject God and rebel against His laws will face punishment in the Hereafter. Called Jahannam in Arabic, Hell is described as a fierce fire that will consume and punish those within it. But beyond the pain and torment of the fire, the ultimate punishment is the shame and disgrace before God. "Our Lord! Any whom You admit to the Fire, truly You cover them with shame. And never will wrongdoers find any helpers" (Qur'an 3:192).

Just as Paradise contains levels within it, the Fire of Hell contains levels with varying degrees of heat and intensity. People will be placed therein depending on the extent of their disbelief and sins. The Qur'an indicates that "the hypocrites will be in the lowest depths of the Fire" (4:145).

Descriptions of the Fire

The Fire of Hell is described throughout the Qur'an as a warning to people about the consequences of the choices they make in life. It is said to be a place of intense heat and suffering, with boiling water, hot wind, and black smoke. People are punished with burns, dragged along in chains, and constantly tormented. They are given putrid liquid to drink, and thorny, bitter plants to eat. There is no relief for those who are consumed by the punishment: "So taste the results of your evil; no increase shall We give you, except in torment" (78:30). Indeed, people themselves will supply the fuel for the Fire; the Qur'an repeatedly says that Hellfire is "fueled by men and stones."

Who Will Be Punished?

The only people who will be punished in Hell eternally, with no chance of escape, are those who disbelieve in God and associate others with Him in their worship. The Qur'an says, "But those who reject God, for them will be the Fire of Hell. No term shall be appointed for them, so they should die, nor shall its punishment be lightened for them. Thus do We reward every ungrateful one!" (35:36).

"Those who reject faith, and die rejecting, on them is God's curse, and the curse of the angels, and of all mankind. They will abide therein [Hell]. Their penalty will not be lightened, nor will respite be their lot" (2:161–162).

Hypocrites are equated with disbelievers, and face the same punishment. "The hypocrites, men and women, are alike. They enjoin evil, and forbid what is just, and tighten their purse strings. They have forgotten God, so He has forgotten them. Verily the hypocrites are rebellious and perverse. God has promised the hypocrites, men and women, and the rejecters of faith, the Fire of Hell. Therein shall they dwell; sufficient is it for them. For them is the curse of God, and an enduring punishment" (9:68–69).

Those who believe in God may spend a short time in Hell, in punishment for sins they committed during their lives. Sins such as arrogance, pride, murder, envy, lying, oppression, promiscuity, slander, miserliness, or cowardice may be punished, if not repented before death. Similarly, one may be punished for transgressing God's limits or for being neglectful of one's duties to God.

Despite the vivid and horrific images of the punishment of Hell, the overwhelming message in the Qur'an is one of God's Mercy and Compassion. Nearly every chapter of the Qur'an begins with the phrase, "In the Name of God, the Compassionate, the Merciful." That message is repeated throughout the Qur'an, to offer hope to those who turn to Him in repentance and humility.

Chapter 15

Islamic Manners and Morals

I slam provides clear guidance to its followers on how they should conduct themselves in their daily lives. In his or her interactions with others, a Muslim is to have the best of manners. The root of the word "Islam" is "peace," and Muslims are to be peaceful in word and deed, treat people with kindness and mercy, and be tolerant and just.

Equality and Tolerance

Islam is known for its teachings about the equality of all people, regardless of race, ethnicity, or linguistic background. Muslims regard the diversity of life as a sign of the beauty of Allah's creation: "And among His Signs is the creation of the heavens and the earth, and the variations in your languages and your colors. Verily in that are signs for those who know" (Qur'an 30:22). Many of the first Muslims were from the lowest classes of society—slaves, women, and orphans—who were attracted by Muhammad's message of human worth and equality.

The Golden Rule, "do unto others as you do unto yourself," is a universal value in all major faiths, and Islam is no exception. Muhammad once said, "Not one of you is a believer until he desires for his brother that which he desires for himself."

Arrogance of Satan

Indeed, Satan's major sin was arrogance—his belief that he was better than Allah's other creation, the human being (the story of Satan's insubordination is described in Chapter 13). Arrogance and pride led to Satan's fall, and likewise will be the cause of suffering and destruction in the world if left unchecked. When we devalue others because of the way that Allah created them, we question Allah's judgment and wisdom.

The Lessons of the Hajj

Hajj is the ultimate expression of the equality of all people in the eyes of God. It is the one time and place on earth when kings stand barefoot, side by side with peasants and artisans. Looking at the people, in their seamless white clothes, one would not be able to tell the difference. Worldly riches, status, family background—all are erased in the eyes of God—and they should be so in our own eyes as well.

Renowned black activist Malcolm X had a life-changing experience in 1964, when he traveled to Mecca, Saudi Arabia, for the annual pilgrimage. He was especially struck by the true sense of brotherhood and the absolute love between all those assembled, which challenged his previous beliefs that equality among the races was impossible to achieve. He wrote about his experience in a letter, which was later published in *The Autobiography of Malcolm X* (African American Images, reprinted 1989).

Tolerance of Diversity

Diversity in Allah's creation is not only in colors and languages, but also in ideas and ways of life. The Qur'an makes clear that Allah intentionally did not create us all as carbon copies of each other. We have the opportunity to learn from each other and gain a new perspective, particularly when learning about people who are different from ourselves. As the Qur'an proclaims God's words, "Oh mankind! We created you from a single soul, male and female, and made you into nations and tribes, so that you may come to know one another. Truly, the most honored of you in God's sight is the greatest of you in piety. God is All-Knowing, All-Aware" (49:13).

There are places in time and history when Muslims were known to be the most tolerant nation on earth. Unfortunately, there are also many examples of Muslims who have allowed arrogance, pride, and greed to get the better of them.

Kindness and Generosity

Muhammad always commanded his followers to treat everyone with kindness, and to give to others in charity. There are countless stories of Muhammad exhorting the benefits of charity, for both individuals and society at large.

Muslims are reminded in the Qur'an not to be boastful about their charitable donations: "O you who believe! Do not cancel your charity, by giving reminders of your generosity, or by injury, like those who spend their wealth to be seen by men, but believe neither in God nor in the Last Day" (2:264).

In many traditions, Muhammad reminded his followers that the bounties we have in this world do not belong to us, but are a trust from Allah. It is our duty to share with those less fortunate. In addition to the institution of zakat (almsgiving), Islam implemented systems whereby slaves would be set free, and neighbors would care for neighbors. Even those who are limited in means can give in charity. Muhammad instructed them: "Help someone in his work, or make something for someone who cannot make it himself. If you cannot, then at least restrain yourself from doing harm to anyone, for that also is a charity." On another occasion, he said, "Each person's every joint must perform an act of charity every day the sun comes up. To act justly between two people is a charity. To help a man with his mount, helping him onto it, or hoisting up his belongings onto it, is a charity. A good word is a charity. Every step you take towards prayer is a charity. And removing a harmful thing from the road is a charity."

The Virtue of Mercy

Muhammad often told stories of people, to serve as examples to others. In one case, he told a story of a man who passed by a road and found a thorny branch in the middle of the path. He removed the branch so that it would not be an inconvenience to people. When Muhammad told the story, he added, "Allah appreciated his action and forgave his sins."

The Qur'an is filled with messages of the mercy of Allah, and exhorts its followers to be merciful and just. Muhammad once told a man, "Whoever is not merciful to others will not be treated mercifully [by Allah on the Day of Judgment]." He particularly disliked those who did not show mercy to children and the elderly.

Treatment of Animals

A Muslim's kindness should not only extend to other people but also to animals, which are deserving of kind treatment and mercy. In another story, Muhammad told of a dog that was circling around a well, suffering from extreme thirst. A woman saw the animal in this condition, so she lowered her leather sock into the well, drew some water, and gave it to the dog to drink. "Allah appreciated her action and forgave her sins, simply on account of this kindness," he said. His companions who were listening to the story asked Muhammad, "Are we rewarded for our kindness towards animals as well?" He answered, "There are rewards for kindness to every living thing."

FACT

While in the company of Muhammad, a man once took an egg from a bird's nest. This caused the mother bird to get upset and begin circling around Muhammad's head. He asked, "Who stole this bird's egg?" The man admitted that he took the egg. Muhammad then told him, "Put it back, and have mercy."

In another account, Muhammad warned those people who treat animals with cruelty. He told his companions, "A woman was doomed to Hellfire because she put a cat in a closet until the cat died from starvation. She did not give the cat anything to eat or drink, nor did she let the cat free to hunt for its food."

Honesty and Trustworthiness

It is often said that a "man is only as good as his word." This held true in pre-Islamic Arabic culture, when trust and loyalty were matters of life and death. In Islam, honesty gained additional importance as a matter of faith. Believers are described as being truthful and upright; they must keep their promises and fulfill their trusts. "Oh you who believe! Fear Allah and be with those who are truthful" (Qur'an 9:119). Those who reject faith are often described as liars and hypocrites, and Muslims are warned against following in their footsteps. Islam considers giving false testimony one of the worst sins committed by men.

Backbiting

Muslims are instructed not to talk about people behind their backs, speaking ill of others not in their presence. "Oh you who believe! Avoid suspicion as much as possible, for suspicion in some cases is a sin. And do not spy on each other, nor speak ill of each other behind their backs. Would any of you like to eat the flesh of his dead brother? No, you would abhor it" (49:12).

When his companions asked, Muhammad said that backbiting is "to say something about your brother which he dislikes." They asked about the case in which what they are saying about the person is true. He responded, "If what you say is true about him, you have backbitten against him, and if it is not true then you have committed slander against him." Either case is a serious sin. Muslims are advised again and again to be careful of their tongue. "Whosoever believes in Allah and the Last Day should say what is good, or keep silent," Muhammad advised.

Oaths and Promises

Muslims are obliged to fulfill their promises, and meet the terms of contracts or agreements. When we make agreements, the other party trusts us to fulfill our end of the bargain. Muslims are forbidden from reneging on promises. The Qur'an says, "And those who respect their trusts and covenants; and those who stand firm in their testimonies; and those who strictly guard their worship—such will be the honored ones in the Gardens of Bliss" (Qur'an 70:32–35). Muhammad also taught, "Speak the truth when you talk, keep your promise when you make it, fulfill your trust when you are trusted, and restrain your hands from injustice."

When called upon to arbitrate in disputes, Muslims are required to be fair and equitable to both parties. The Qur'an advises: "And when you judge between people, that you judge with justice" (4:58).

Hypocrisy

Muslims are further advised to "practice what they preach." Muslims should not be advising people to do things that they themselves do not do. This is another sign of hypocrisy. "Oh you who believe! Why do you say, that which you do not? Grievously hateful is it, in the sight of Allah, that you say that which you do not" (Qur'an 61:2–3).

Muhammad described the characteristics of a hypocrite: "Whenever he is entrusted, he betrays his trust. Whenever he speaks, he tells a lie. Whenever he makes a covenant, he breaks it. Whenever he quarrels, he behaves in an evil and insulting manner."

Justice and Forgiveness

Before Islam, vengeance killings and inter-tribal feuds were common and accepted. Islam broke this cycle by instructing Muslims to seek equal justice only, and encouraged forgiveness as the admirable high road.

> Oh you who believe! Stand out firmly for justice, as witnesses to Allah, as against yourselves, or your parents, or your kin; and whether it be against rich or poor. For Allah can best protect both. Follow not the lusts of your own hearts, lest you swerve, and if you distort justice or decline to do justice, verily Allah is well acquainted with all that you do. (Qur'an 4:135)

Eye for an Eye

The rules of Islamic justice stopped the common practice of massive vengeance killings, where a murder would be revenged through deaths of dozens of the perpetrator's family and tribe members. Islam taught that justice must be proportional to the harm done.

Even with the rules of justice in place, the Qur'an reminds Muslims of the value and benefits of forgiveness as opposed to punishment: "Let them forgive and overlook. Do you not wish that Allah should forgive you? For Allah is Oft-Forgiving, Most Merciful" (24:22).

The Three-Day Rule

It is an established Muslim tradition based on Muhammad's example that no Muslim should argue or keep away from another for an extended period of time. If Muslims have a disagreement with each other, they may observe a brief cooling-off period. However, as Muhammad instructed, "It is not permissible for a Muslim to be estranged from his brother for more than three days, both of them turning away from the other when they meet. The better of them is the one who is the first to greet the other."

Modesty and Humility

Muslims are reminded that Allah is their Creator, and that they should humbly submit to and worship Him Alone. In English, the word "humility" is based on a Latin word for "ground." Being humble means acting modestly and with respect, avoiding arrogance and boasting. One is lowered to the ground, rather than put up on a pedestal.

In prayer, Muslims humbly prostrate to the ground, in symbolic recognition that without Allah's constant guidance and support, we would be lost. The Qur'an advises: "Call on your Lord with humility and in private, for Allah loves not those who transgress beyond bounds" (7:55).

Modesty and Decency

Modesty is an attitude, a demeanor; in Arabic, the term used for modesty is *haya,* which also means to be bashful or shy—the opposite of arrogant. Both men and women are commanded in Islam to be modest, to observe humility in our interactions with each other, and to be quiet and humble in demeanor.

The Qur'an tells the story of the Prophet Luqman and the advice that he gave his son:

Oh my son! Establish regular prayer, enjoin what is just, and forbid what is wrong, and bear with patient constancy whatever befalls you, for this is firmness in the conduct of affairs. And swell not your cheek for pride at men, nor walk in insolence through the earth, for Allah loves not any arrogant boaster. And be moderate in your pace, and lower your voice, for the harshest of sounds, without doubt, is the braying of the donkey. (31:17–19)

The dress of a Muslim is a means to observe modesty, decency, and respect. But beyond clothing and dress, Muslims try to be decent in their behavior as well. Foul language is discouraged, as is excessive joking and noisy banter. Muslims strive toward humility in their worship of God and in their conduct with others on earth.

Fair Business Practices

In Islam, business and trade are highly encouraged, as long as they are conducted by lawful means and through lawful channels. It is expected that any earnings be made through decent and honest labor. A Muslim is to be self-supporting, and avoid becoming a liability on any person or the society at large.

Business practices must be conducted with frankness and honesty. Islam encourages that contracts and agreements should be written down, and witnessed by two trustworthy persons, so that neither party later tries to take advantage of the other or make false claims.

FACT

Muslims are encouraged to pay for services as soon as they are performed, and not to withhold or delay payment. Muhammad instructed that when Muslims hire laborers to do some work, they should "compensate them before the sweat dries."

Muslims are forbidden from cheating, hiding defects in merchandise, exploitation, monopoly, and fraud. There is a chapter of the Qur'an named Al-Mutaffifin, or "Dealing in Fraud." It begins, "Woe to those that deal in fraud. Those who, when they have to receive some measure from men, exact full measure, but when they have to give by measure or weight to men, give less than due" (83:1–3).

In another section, the Qur'an commands the Muslims: "Give just measure, and cause no loss to others by fraud. And weigh with scales true and upright. And do not withhold things that are justly due to men, nor do evil in the land, working mischief" (26:181–3). It was common practice in ancient times to "tip the scales" or to hide defective merchandise underneath a pile of quality goods. These practices were strictly forbidden in Islam.

Forbidden Industries

Muslims are prohibited from working with illegal industries, or trading in substances that are forbidden in Islam. For example, working in factories that make alcohol, meat-packing plants that package pork, or working in nightclubs are all forbidden. Muhammad once said, "When Allah prohibits a thing, He prohibits giving and receiving the price of it as well."

Lending with Interest

Islam absolutely prohibits the lending of money for a price or with interest. This prohibition is based on a concern for the moral and economic welfare of society. Interest creates an atmosphere where the wealthy exploit those who are weaker, creating greed and hatred in people's hearts.

QUESTION?

How can Muslims buy real estate if interest-based mortgages are forbidden?
Many Muslim families are forced to rent their homes, while some finance through Islamic organizations. Muslims may use other financial tools that do not depend on interest, such as installment sales or equity participation.

Muslims are forbidden from collecting interest, paying interest, or having anything to do with it. "Those who devour usury [interest] will not stand, except as the one whom the devil by his touch has driven to madness. That is because they say, 'Trade is like usury.' But Allah has permitted trade, and forbidden usury" (2:274).

Muhammad emphasized the prohibition when he told his followers, "Allah has cursed the one who takes interest, the one who pays it, the one who writes it, and the one who witnesses the contract." This guideline, like all of the others in Islam, are in place to help people engage in trusting and fair relationships with each other, and to avoid the possibilities of exploitation and abuse.

Chapter 16

Dietary Laws, Health Care, and Funeral Services

I slam calls upon people to take care of their health, avoid harmful substances, and to seek appropriate medical treatment when necessary. Muslims follow these guidelines laid out in the Qur'an because they believe that God, the Creator, knows what is best for human well-being.

Dietary Laws

Muslims believe that God made each creature with an intended purpose and way of life. Cows eat grass; lions eat meat. In the Qur'an, Muslims find guidelines about what sort of food is fit for human consumption. In general, Islam permits people to eat what is healthy and lawful on the earth, and prohibits all things that are harmful or unlawful. While there may be health reasons for avoiding certain foods, Muslims follow these regulations in accordance with Islamic law without question, trusting in the guidance of Allah.

Food that meets general Islamic dietary guidelines is called *halal* (permissible). Meat that is slaughtered in accordance with Islamic custom is called *zabihah*. Food that is prohibited to Muslims is called *haram* (forbidden).

Forbidden Foods

The Qur'an specifies certain foods that Muslims are prohibited from eating, including the following:

- Swine (pork), including all pork by-products
- Animals slaughtered in dedication to false gods
- Blood or dead carcasses
- Animals that have been strangled, beaten to death, gored, eaten by wild animals, or have died as the result of a fall
- Predatory animals (meat eaters such as lions, dogs, eagles, owls, and others)

Any food that is not specifically forbidden is considered lawful for Muslims. While the dietary restrictions may seem similar to Jewish law, there are some differences. In Islam, all marine animals are lawful, including game found in the waters of seas, rivers, and lakes. Muslims do not observe regulations of Kashrut (Jewish dietary laws) about mixing dairy and meat, and most will eat shellfish.

ALERT!

In recognition of their similarities in faith, the Qur'an permits Muslims to eat food provided by the "People of the Book" (Jews and Christians), as long as the other Islamic dietary conditions are also met.

Muslims strive to follow these guidelines, but also recognize that God is merciful and does not wish harm on human beings. Therefore, if a person finds himself in a situation where he is starving and nothing is available except unlawful food, he is allowed to eat the food in order to save his life.

Islamic Slaughter

When slaughtering animals for food, Muslims recognize that they are taking life, which God has made sacred. They thus invoke God's name, as a reminder that they are killing with His permission, only to meet the need for food. Any adult Muslim, male or female, may slaughter an animal for food—there is no need to have a special status or title.

According to Islam, the animal should be treated with kindness and consideration, and when the time comes to slaughter, one should follow these steps:

1. Shelter the animal kindly, and do not expose it to the slaughtering tool, other slaughtered animals, or blood.
2. Put the animal at ease and comfort it.
3. Place the animal on its right side, facing the Ka'aba.
4. Utter the words, *Bismillah, Allahu Akbar* (In the name of God, God is Most Great.)
5. Using a very sharp knife, cut the throat of the animal firmly and swiftly, to minimize and end the animal's pain quickly.
6. Leave the animal alone until it is completely dead.

Only meat that is slaughtered while invoking God's name is considered lawful to Muslims. Some Muslims believe that invoking God's name at the time of eating renders the food lawful, even if it was not mentioned at the time of slaughter.

Hunting for Food

Hunting is permitted in Islam only when necessary for food. Taking the life of an animal for sport, without intending to eat from it or otherwise benefit from it, is prohibited. It was related that Muhammad once said, "If someone kills a sparrow for sport, the sparrow will cry out on the Day of Judgment, 'Oh Lord! This person killed me in vain and wasted my body; he did not kill me for any useful purpose.' Then Allah will hold the hunter accountable." Waste is frowned upon in Islam, so hunters are encouraged to use all parts of the animal for food, clothing, or other useful purposes.

Drugs and Alcohol

There is a zero-tolerance policy toward alcohol and drugs. Nowadays, many medical doctors propose that there are benefits in moderate consumption of some substances (wine, marijuana). However, Islam takes the strong prohibitive stance that any substance that intoxicates or harms the body in a large amount is unlawful even in a small amount. Islam prohibits all intoxicants, regardless of the quantity or kind. In general, any substance that harms the body is considered unlawful in Islam.

Alcohol Is Prohibited

Alcohol is clearly forbidden in several verses of the Qur'an, including the following:

Oh you who believe! Intoxicants and gambling . . . are an abomination, of Satan's handiwork. Eschew such abomination, that you may prosper. Satan's plan is but to excite enmity and hatred between you, with intoxicants and gambling, and hinder you from the remembrance of Allah, and from prayer. Will you not then abstain? (5:90–91)

It is reported that Muhammad once said: "Allah curses all people who deal with intoxicants: the one who produces it, the one for whom it is produced, the one who drinks it, the one who serves it, the one who carries it, the one for whom it is carried, the one who sells it, the one who earns from the sale of it, the one who buys it, and the one for whom it is bought." The prohibition could not be any clearer.

Since intoxicants are prohibited in amounts both large and small, Muslims avoid alcohol even in baking, cooking, or in medicinal substances. The Qur'an acknowledges that there may be some benefit in alcohol (2:219), but emphasizes that the harm is more serious than any transitional benefit.

Smoking and Illicit Drugs

Many Muslims believe that tobacco and nicotine are poisons to the body, and are therefore to be avoided. The strong link between smoking and serious health problems, such as cancer and heart disease, are the main reasons cited for its prohibition. Other reasons are also mentioned:

- Money spent on smoking is squandered and wasted, when it could be used for worthy causes.
- The unpleasant smell of tobacco smoke annoys other people.
- The Qur'an commands people not to kill themselves (4:29), and not to make their hands contribute to their own destruction (2:195).
- Secondhand smoke is also dangerous, and Muhammad called upon believers not to harm themselves or others.

However, tobacco smoking is a relatively modern practice, and the early Muslim community did not have any contact with tobacco. There is no conclusive ruling about it in the primary sources of Islamic law, the Qur'an or the Sunnah. Therefore, some Muslims contend that it is a personal choice. Indeed, in some parts of the Muslim world, cigarette-smoking rates are very high.

FACT

Early Muslim jurists who ruled that cigarette smoking is allowed in Islam did so prior to the discovery of the many health hazards of smoking. A group of Muslim scholars recently polled by the World Health Organization was almost unanimous in declaring that smoking was impermissible or abominable.

As for illicit drugs, the clear prohibitions about alcohol extend to any intoxicating substance. Unlawful drugs in Islam therefore include marijuana, cocaine, opium, heroin, and the like. Any substances that can cause harm to the body, or impair a person's judgment, are considered poisons to be avoided.

Personal Cleanliness

Muslims strive to high standards of personal hygiene. In Islam, cleanliness and purification are not only requirements for worship, but are part of a Muslim's daily life. Muhammad once said that "cleanliness is a sign of faith." Cleanliness and purity are known in Arabic as *tahaarah*. As a religious concept, hygiene is not just a matter of washing your hands and taking daily showers. A Muslim strives to be pure morally, spiritually, and physically. The Qur'an commends those people who keep themselves pure and clean (2:22).

In daily life, Muslims are encouraged to trim their nails, remove body hair, observe good dental hygiene, keep their clothes clean, and apply perfume. Also, their homes and places of prayer must be clean and free from impurities. Before prayer, Muslims should purify their body through ablutions.

The Practice of Circumcision

Male circumcision, a well-established tradition in Islam, is another aspect of tahaarah. Circumcision is not mentioned in the Qur'an, but it is established Muslim tradition that Muslim boys are circumcised at birth to promote good health and cleanliness. In Islam, any qualified doctor may perform a circumcision.

ALERT!

Female circumcision is neither mandated nor condoned by Islam. It is a pre-Islamic cultural tradition practiced in some parts of sub-Saharan Africa by both Muslims and non-Muslims alike.

There is ongoing debate on the value of male circumcision. The American Academy of Pediatrics finds that "circumcision is not essential to a child's well-being at birth, even though it does have some potential medical benefits." Some clinical studies have found a decreased rate of urinary tract infections and cancer in circumcised boys. Muslims are likely to continue the practice regardless of the debate, as a religious tradition that was practiced and approved by the Prophet Muhammad.

Reproductive Issues

The introduction of modern medical technology has presented new questions about medical ethics and responsibility. When evaluating these new medical techniques, Muslims refer to the Qur'an and Sunnah for guidance. When it comes to reproductive issues, two main standards need to be met: no destruction of life that God has made sacred, and no disruption of parental and blood family bonds.

Contraception and Abortion

Most Muslim couples desire a family, because children are considered a blessing from God and raising children is one of the main goals of the family. Some couples may wish to time pregnancies for health or other reasons. In general, contraception is permitted in Islam, as long as the method only temporarily prevents fertilization and does not disrupt the growth of an already fertilized embryo.

In the early days of Islam, coitus interruptus was widely practiced, with the knowledge and approval of the Prophet Muhammad. Modern methods such as barriers, the pill, and even modern IUDs are generally considered to be permissible, because they disrupt the process by which the egg first meets the sperm. Sterilization is forbidden on the grounds that it permanently scars a person, leaving no future option to change one's mind.

There are differences of opinion in Islam on whether or not it is wrong to disrupt a pregnancy after fertilization. In general, abortion is considered a sin, the murder of an innocent unborn life. However, the magnitude of the sin varies according to the age of the pregnancy. Muhammad once said:

Each one of you collected in the womb of his mother for forty days, and then turns into a clot for an equal period [of forty days], and then turns into a piece of flesh for a similar period [of forty days]. Then Allah sends an angel and orders him to write four things [regarding the destiny of the child's life]. Then the soul is breathed into him. (Bukhari)

QUESTION?

Are Muslims allowed to use birth control?
Islam encourages a strong family life, and reminds Muslims that God is the One who creates and provides for new life. Nevertheless, contraception is generally permitted in Islam, as long as the method causes only temporary infertility, and both the husband and wife agree on its use.

According to this narration, the soul is breathed into the fetus at 120 days after gestation. Muslim jurists acknowledge this turning point when making rulings about abortion.

During the first four months (120 days) of gestation, the growing fetus is a potential life whose growth should not be interrupted. These months allow plenty of time for medical tests and evaluations of the mother and child. If there is solid evidence that the mother is in danger, or that the fetus has a major abnormality that will cause him or her to suffer and live in agony, then most scholars agree that abortion is permissible. Abortion becomes a major sin (murder) if it is done after 120 days of gestation, unless the life of the mother is in certain danger.

Under no circumstances is a Muslim to perform an abortion because a pregnancy is inconvenient or the parents fear that they will not be able to support a child financially. Muslims are reminded in the Qur'an that it is God who gives life and death, and that the creation of a child is in His hands. Muslims always keep in mind the possibility that no matter what they do, if God decrees a child for them, they will have one. Muslims are advised to seek help from God if they fear that they cannot care for a child. "Kill not your children for fear of want. We will provide sustenance for them as well as for you. Verily, the killing of them is a great sin" (Qur'an 17:31).

Infertility and Reproductive Technology

Muslims acknowledge that all life comes from God and that the inability to have a child is a test in this life. Islam encourages believers to look for a healthy balance between striving for pregnancy and accepting what God has ordained for them. As the Qur'an admonishes, "To Allah belongs the dominion of the heavens and the earth. He creates what He wills. He bestows children, male or female, according to His Will, or He bestows both males and females, and He leaves barren whom He will" (42:49–50).

When facing any medical issue, Muslims believe in seeking medical treatment in the hopes of a good outcome. However, that treatment needs to fall within the ethics and dictates of Islamic law. When treating infertility, the main Islamic rule is that one must honor the blood parental relationship within the bonds of marriage. Any reproductive technology (in vitro fertilization, hormonal treatments, and so on) that is sought by a Muslim couple with no third-party intervention is permissible. However, some modern reproductive techniques cloud the parental relationship and are forbidden in Islam. This includes surrogate parenting and the use of donor sperm or eggs.

Euthanasia and Organ Donation

Just as Muslims acknowledge that all life comes from God, they also believe that death comes at a time appointed by God alone. Muslims believe that human life is sacred, a trust given to us by God, and that one should be patient in the face of death, and respectful of the deceased. God Alone is the One who gives and takes life at a term appointed by Him. The duration of life is not for us to determine or control. It is not permitted for a Muslim to give up and take his own life by any means. The deliberate ending of a life is suicide or murder, both of which are grave sins in Islam and are strictly prohibited.

Organ Donation

Many Muslims abhor the idea of disturbing the human body in death, and believe organ donation to be forbidden. The traditional burial practices of Islam require Muslims to be respectful of the deceased and keep the body intact. However, some Muslims believe that in this case, the good of helping another person through organ donation outweighs the bad.

FACT

Several Islamic councils and jurists have recently ruled that there is nothing wrong with organ donation in Islam, as long as the procedure poses no danger to a living donor, and is performed respectfully on a deceased donor. The scholars agreed that saving a life carries more weight than preserving a body.

Death and Funeral Rituals

Islam sees death not as an end to life but rather as the beginning of the world to come. Muslims recognize that all creatures will die and believe that God determines our time and place of death. "Every soul shall have a taste of death; in the end to Us shall you be brought back. . . . Nor does any one know in what land he is to die. Verily, with Allah is full knowledge, and He is acquainted with all things" (Qur'an 29:57, 31:34).

Death Rites

Muslims see death as a natural event, and they prefer to face death in the company of friends and loved ones, not among strangers in a sterile medical ward. When a Muslim nears death, his friends and loved ones gather around to help him turn his thoughts to God, encourage him to repent his sins, remind him about the good things he did during his life, and give him hope about the mercy of God. They may also prompt him, very gently, to utter words of faith as his last words.

After death has been confirmed, those present close the eyes of the deceased, cover the body with a clean sheet, and supplicate for God to forgive him for anything he did wrong during his life. They then hasten to prepare the body for washing, shrouding, and burial.

Islamic Burial

Muslims strive to bury the dead as soon as possible after death, and many Islamic burials occur within twenty-four hours. Family members or other members of the Muslim community care for the deceased. They wash the body several times with water, following the same general procedure as in the ablutions for prayer. In the final wash, perfume or camphor is added to the water. Finally, the body is dried with a towel and shrouded in plain white cloths.

At the time of burial, Muslims gather to pray the funeral prayer, called *salaat-l-janazah*. This is a congregational prayer that asks God for forgiveness and mercy for the deceased. The congregation gathers in front of the body, standing in rows. The funeral prayer is said silently, but for a few words. After the prayer, the body is transferred directly to the cemetery for burial.

If permitted by local law, Muslims are buried without a casket. The body is placed in the grave on its right side, facing Mecca. Muslim cemeteries are characterized by simplicity, humility, and economy. One will not find ornate monuments or elaborate floral displays. Usually the grave is marked with a simple stone marker, level to the ground.

The official mourning period in Islam is three days. For widows, this period is extended to four months and ten days, as described in the Qur'an (2:234). The Prophet Muhammad advised his followers to be humble and patient in mourning. Grief at the death of a loved one is natural, but Muslims are not to despair or lose faith.

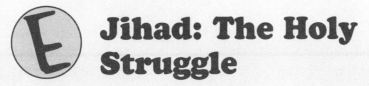 Jihad: The Holy Struggle

Perhaps one of the most controversial and misunderstood aspects of Islam is the concept of jihad. References to a "jihad against the West" coupled with phrases like "Islamic militancy" run freely through the media and in politics, and some Muslim groups would concur, but this concept of jihad is a distorted, misunderstood version of the term's original Islamic meaning.

What It Means

So what is jihad anyway? The actual word comes from the Arabic root J-H-D, which carries the meaning "struggle" or "strive." Other words derived from this root include "effort," "fatigue," and "labor." The essential meaning is this: Jihad is a struggle to practice one's faith in the face of obstacles.

ALERT!

The translation of "jihad" as "holy war" is incorrect. In Arabic, you would translate "holy war" as *harbun muqaddasatu,* a phrase that is not found in the Qur'an or in any other form of Islamic literature.

Jihad in the Qur'an

The word "jihad" appears in the Qur'an several times, where it is used to describe the efforts of the believers to resist pressure from others to give up their faith, and to defend themselves against oppressors. In one instance, the Muslims are encouraged to strive against falsehood with the "weapon" of the Qur'an: "Therefore listen not to the unbelievers, but strive against them with it [the Qur'an] with the utmost strenuousness" (25:52).

In some passages, the Qur'an uses other forms of the root J-H-D to describe the efforts of non-Muslims who strive against the believers. For example: "We have enjoined on people kindness to parents. But if they strive [*jahadaka*] to make you ascribe partners with Me . . . then obey them not" (29:8).

Jihad can be a struggle within one's self—to keep one's heart, tongue, and mind free from evil. One can struggle to do good and to avoid evil in society. One can struggle with money and possessions, to support good causes. As a final resort, one may struggle in the battlefield against opposing forces.

Jihad in Practice

During the lifetime of the Prophet Muhammad, the Muslim community was in a struggle for its very survival. Faced with the persecution and cruelty of the people of Mecca and their endless pursuit to destroy them, the Muslims sought alternative means of defense. They immigrated to Abyssinia and then to Madinah, enforced economic blockades, and formed peace treaties and alliances.

There were times when the Muslims were forced to engage in battle. In these cases, verses of the Qur'an were revealed, advising them to fight strong and hard: "When an oppressive wrong is inflicted on them, are not cowed but help and defend themselves" (42:39). Without exception, the early Muslims fought in battles only to defend themselves against unprovoked attack or the betrayal of allies.

The Qur'an repeatedly stresses the value of forgiveness, even toward one's enemies. While Islam generally holds to the ancient teaching of "an eye for an eye," there is an emphasis on the blessings of forgiveness. The teachings are summed up in these verses:

Indeed, if any do help and defend himself, after a wrong done to him, against such there is no cause of blame. The blame is only against those who oppress men with wrongdoing, and insolently transgress beyond bounds through the land, defying right and justice. For such there will be a chastisement grievous [in the Hereafter]. But indeed if any show patience and forgive, that would truly be an affair of great resolution. (42:41–43)

This was indeed the practice of the early Muslim community, and it continues to serve as an example for later generations of Muslims to follow.

FACT

Muslims recognize that the struggle within one's self—making the moral effort to overcome difficulties and temptations of arrogance, jealousy, or selfishness—is often more rigorous than physical battle. According to the Prophet Muhammad, "The greatest jihad is to speak the truth in the face of a tyrannical ruler."

Jihad Is Not a Struggle to Force Conversion

To many in the West, jihad is associated with such images as a horde of Muslim armies offering the conquered nations "Islam or the sword."

Although in Islam jihad refers to the spiritual struggle of a believer rather than the physical, violent struggles of war, jihad today is most often understood as the latter.

According to Islamic doctrine, however, if faith does not emerge from deep personal conviction, it is neither truthful nor acceptable to God. Quite simply, a person cannot be forced into Islam—or any other religion, for that matter. Faith is a matter of the heart, between one's self and God. "Let there be no compulsion in religion," the Qur'an commands (2:256).

The Qur'an re-emphasizes this point in several other verses. For example: "Say, 'The truth is from Your Lord.' Let him who will, believe, and let him who will, reject it" (18:29). Finally, the Muslims are advised in the Qur'an to respond to non-Muslims with these words, "You have your religion, and I have mine" (109:6).

The Qur'an also advises Muslims to speak with people with wisdom and sweet words, to discuss issues of religion in a respectful and polite way, and to be patient with those who ridicule them. Historically, there is not a single community of people that was forced to embrace Islam or face death.

> Invite all to the Way of your Lord with wisdom and beautiful preaching, and argue with them in ways that are best and most gracious. For your Lord knows best who have strayed from His path, and who receive guidance. And if you punish, let your punishment be proportional to the wrong that has been done to you. But if you show patience, that is indeed the best course for those who are patient. And do be patient, for patience is from Allah. Nor grieve over them, and do not distress yourself because of their plots. For Allah is with those who restrain themselves, and those who do good. (16:125–128)

For Defense of Whom?

The Qur'an often describes defensive jihad as a system of checks and balances, a way that Allah set up to "check one set of people by means of another" (2:251 and other verses). When one person or group transgresses their limits and violates the rights of others, Muslims have not only the right, but the duty to "check" them and bring them back into line. Injustice would be triumphant in this world if good people were not prepared to risk much, even their lives, to prevent it. Muslims are called upon to respond to aggression and persecution, and take it as their duty to stop anyone who is transgressing justice. Muslims are called upon to help anyone who is facing these hardships, regardless of their religious or political affiliation.

The Qur'an commands the defense of all houses of worship, even those of other faiths: "Did not Allah check one set of people by means of another, there would surely have been pulled down monasteries, churches, synagogues, and mosques, in which the name of Allah is commemorated in abundant measure" (22:40).

The Qur'an specifically encourages Muslims to come to the defense of those who have been expelled from their homes, are oppressed and tortured, and those who are weak. "Why should you not fight in the cause of Allah and of those who, being weak, are ill-treated and oppressed? Men, women, and children whose cry is, 'Our Lord! Rescue us from this town, whose people are oppressors! Raise for us from You one who will protect, and raise for us from You one who will help!'" (4:75).

In another verse, the Qur'an specifically gives permission: "To those against whom war is made, permission is given to fight back, because they are wronged. And truly, Allah is most powerful for their aid. They are those who have been expelled from their homes in defiance of right, for no cause except that they say, 'Our Lord is Allah'" (22:39–40).

With all of this in mind, the aim of Islam is to remove persecution and oppression, so that freedom may be restored and justice may flourish. At all times, physical battle is the last resort, and is to be used only under the most extraordinary circumstances, when all other attempts at just and peaceful solutions to the dispute fail. If non-Muslims are living peacefully, or even indifferently, with the Muslims, there are no grounds or justification to declare war on them. Muslims are commanded to avoid initiating hostilities, embarking on any act of aggression, or violating the rights of others.

Rules of Engagement

Even during the times when Muslims are engaged in battles of a military nature, they must follow certain codes of ethics and rules of engagement laid down in the Qur'an and exemplified by the life of the Prophet Muhammad. It is human nature to become agitated and seek revenge when one is wronged, so Islam lays out very strict rules to ensure the legitimate and proper conduct of Muslim soldiers.

The "Geneva Conventions" of Islam

Muslims adhered to strict rules of combat long before such agreements were common. These rules are outlined in the following list:

- Give diplomacy a chance before battle starts; respect all treaties.
- Do not harm those who are not physically involved in fighting— women, children, the elderly, and religious persons.
- Do not destroy property, including real estate, infrastructure, trees, farms, animals, and orchards.
- Protect all places of worship.
- Treat well all prisoners of war.
- Allow the bodies of soldiers slain in battle to be buried in dignity.
- Stop fighting when the enemy ceases hostilities and negotiate for peace.

FACT

After reaching a peace treaty with the pagan leadership, Muhammad was able to lead the Muslim community back to Mecca in a peaceful manner. At that time, Muhammad granted amnesty to all the residents of Mecca, even those who had gravely persecuted the Muslims in the past.

Islam recognizes that kind treatment toward one's enemies is a way to bring a lasting peace. The Qur'an says the following:

It may be that Allah will establish friendship between you and those whom you now hold as enemies. For Allah has power over all things, and Allah is Oft-Forgiving, Most Merciful. Allah forbids you not—with regard to those who do not fight you for your faith, nor drive you out of your homes—from dealing kindly and justly with them. For Allah loves those who are just. (60:7–8)

Suicide and Martyrdom

In Islam, it is a grave sin to kill someone unjustly. "Nor take life, which Allah has made sacred, except for just cause" (17:33). The phrase "just cause" refers to criminal justice, particularly the death penalty for certain crimes, such as murder. These punishments may be assigned only by a court of law.

The Qur'an reiterates the ancient law that killing one person is like killing the whole community, while saving a life is like saving the whole community (5:32). Any life taken must be in accordance with the law, and carried out by the proper authorities. There is no vigilantism in Islam.

Suicide Is a Sin

It is particularly sinful to deliberately kill one's self. Usually such people act out of desperation, with no sense of the value of their own lives. Allah advises Muslims to be patient, hopeful, and confident of the mercy of Allah, and not to despair or lose hope. The Qur'an's message is clear: "Do not kill yourselves, for surely Allah is Most Merciful to you" (4:29).

According to Islamic tradition, people who commit suicide will spend the time in Hell torturing themselves with their chosen method or weapon. A person who jumps off a cliff, for example, will spend eternity jumping off cliffs and feeling the agony of death over and over again.

Martyrdom

Islam teaches that sacrifice, bravery, and sincere effort will be rewarded by Allah in the Hereafter. The Arabic word for martyr is *shaheed,* which means "witness." A martyr witnesses the truth, and gives up his or her life for it, dying under brave or heroic circumstances; martyrs may be killed while legitimately defending the Muslim community or fighting against tyranny. According to one tradition, Muhammad also describes the following groups of people as martyrs:

- One who dies of a plague.
- One who drowns.
- One who dies from a stomach ailment.
- One who dies from internal disease.
- One who is crushed to death when a building collapses.
- A woman who dies in childbirth.

Muhammad once said that there are people who kill in the name of Islam, but still go to Hellfire. When asked why, he answered, "Because they were not truly fighting for the sake of God." To be considered a martyr, one must be acting within the bounds of Islamic law and have pure intentions.

Fundamentalism and Extremism

The words "fundamentalist" and "extremist" are often used interchangeably in today's world. Muslims prefer to draw a distinction between those who follow the basic principles (fundamentals) of their faith and those who join the extreme, fanatic fringe.

The Middle Path

In the Qur'an, Muslims are instructed to be moderate in all affairs of life, especially on issues concerning religion. Muslims should eat well, but not to the point of satiation. They should spend money on their families, but also donate a share of their wealth to the poor. They should pray during the night, but also sleep.

Muhammad advised his followers to practice kindness and bring people together. In one tradition, he told the people to "make things easy and convenient, and do not make them hard or difficult. Give cheers and glad tidings, and do not create tension or hatred, nor repel others."

Muhammad once told his followers, "Observe moderation in deeds." He specifically warned against extremism when he told his companions: "Be aware of extremism in your religion; people before you were destroyed because of that."

Returning to the Fundamentals

The term "fundamentalism" as we often use it today came into usage in relation to a Protestant Christian movement of the early twentieth century, and it does not apply to Muslims in the same sense. For Muslims, "fundamentalism" means going back to the basics or strictly following one's religious text. In this sense, Muslims are fundamentalist by nature, because they do strive to adhere to the basic principles of their faith.

Many people would argue that if Muslims better adhered to the fundamental principles of their faith, the world would be better off. If a person pays taxes and drives according to the speed limit, in accordance with the law, we call him a good citizen. Likewise, if a Muslim follows the fundamental precepts of Islam—helping the needy and poor, assisting his neighbors, taking care of his family—then he would be considered a contributing member of society. However, being a fundamentalist does not mean being an extremist. There are many Muslims who follow the fundamental teachings of Islam, but are unfairly stereotyped as radical extremists.

No Room for Terrorism

The Qur'an clearly condemns actions that transgress beyond what is considered lawful and just. "Fight in the cause of Allah those who fight you, but do not transgress limits, for Allah loves not the transgressors" (2:190). Certainly acts of terrorism, including the murder of innocent civilians, would be considered transgressions beyond the limits of justice.

Muslims are commanded to be on the side of justice, even if it means turning against those closest to us. "Oh you who believe! Stand out firmly for justice, as witnesses to Allah, even as against yourselves, or your parents, or your kin, and whether it be against rich or poor—for Allah can best protect both. Do not follow the lusts of your own hearts, lest you swerve. And if you distort justice, or decline to do justice, truly Allah is well-acquainted with all that you do" (4:135).

How Is Terrorism Justified?

It's clear that terrorism can never be justified by Islamic teaching. Many people invoke religion as justification for their actions when in fact those actions violate the very principles the faith stands for, and unfortunately Muslims are no exception. Those who transgress the limits of justice may try to justify their actions and achieve their goals in the name of Islam. It is not difficult to take verses and teachings out of context and distort their meaning. Many people have been led astray, in all religions and throughout the ages, by misinterpretations and distortions in matters of faith.

The Qur'an warns Muslims not to let anger and hatred overcome them and cause them to do wrong against others. "Oh you who believe! Stand out firmly for Allah, as witnesses to fair-dealing, and let not the hatred of others towards you make you swerve to wrong and depart from justice. Be just—that is next to piety—and fear Allah. For Allah is well-acquainted with all that you do" (5:8).

Punishment for Terrorism

Throughout Islamic history, acts of transgression were dealt with harshly, to deter anyone else from believing that such actions have merit or are useful ways to further their cause.

Islamic courts have upheld capital punishment for those convicted of piracy, airplane hijacking, kidnapping, and genocide. Muslim leaders and individuals all over the world express condemnation and outrage when acts of terrorism are perpetrated upon innocent people, whether the terrorists are so-called Muslims or not. (E)

Chapter 18

Shrouded in Mystery: Women and Islam

Another issue that's been a point of much debate and misunderstanding is the position of women in Islam. Many people see Muslim women as meek and subservient, objects worthy of pity. However, the weak position of women in some Muslim societies does not represent the teachings of the faith of Islam. Islam honors women and advocates their full and equitable rights.

Historical Background

Throughout history, from ancient times until today, women have been struggling to free themselves from abuse and mistreatment. In most ancient cultures, and even some modern ones, women have been considered property to be bought, sold, or inherited like animals. They were looked down upon morally, socially, and spiritually, and were considered inferior to men in every way. They were blamed for all human misfortune. In order to atone for their despicable nature, women were expected to serve and please men.

Women of Pre-Islamic Arabia

The position of women in the Arabian Peninsula was no exception. At the birth of a girl child, families would go into mourning and hide themselves from the community in shame. Many girls were buried alive in infancy. Those who grew up were treated as slaves or servants until they reached the age of marriage. Then they were sold as wives or slaves to their husbands, who could sell, trade, use, or abuse them as they wished.

Women Today

In most of the world, gains in women's rights have been realized just in the past 100 years. In France, women were finally granted the right to own property in 1938. American women gained the right to vote in 1920, after a long and arduous struggle. Despite these advances, women today are still objectified in the media and popular culture. From cosmetics to fashion, diet plans to cosmetic surgery, women are pressured to look a certain way, to fit a certain image of the ideal woman. These pressures are internalized by young women, to the point that millions of young women suffer from eating disorders and low self-esteem.

In the United States, women don't fare much better. Statistics show that one in three American women are physically or sexually abused at home, and one in five will be raped in her lifetime. All over the world, women are still engaged in a constant struggle for their God-given status and rights.

Equal in the Eyes of God

In Islam, men and women have equal rights and obligations, and are equally rewarded by Allah. The Qur'an states:

> The believers, men and women, are protectors of one another.
> They enjoin what is just, and forbid what is evil, and observe
> regular prayers, pay alms, and obey Allah and His Messenger.
> On them will Allah pour His mercy, for Allah is Exalted in power,
> Wise. Allah has promised to the believers, men and women,
> gardens under which rivers flow [in Paradise]." (9:71–72)

Note that the verse says that men and women are protectors of "one another"—the relationship is mutual.

The Qur'an describes the creation of man and woman as comparable to the creation of night and day. Neither is better than the other, because they serve different yet equally important roles.

> By the night, as it conceals the day; by the day as it appears in
> glory; by the creation of male and female—truly, the ends for which
> you strive are diverse. So the one who gives in charity, and is
> conscious of Allah, and in all sincerity testifies to the best—We will
> indeed make smooth for such a one the path to ease. (92:1–7)

On one occasion, Muhammad told his followers, "Women are the *shaqa'iq* of men." The word "shaqa'iq" means the exact half of something, which completes the first half to make a whole.

From the Beginning

The equality of men and women in Islam goes back to the very beginning, to the description of Adam and Eve in the Qur'an. Muslims believe that Adam and Eve were both created from the same origin, equal but not identical, as complements to each other. "It is Allah Who created you from a single soul, and then created, of like nature, his mate" (Qur'an 7:189).

Eve is the temptress of the Garden of Eden who aided Satan in enticing Adam to disobey God. In the Qur'anic account, Allah dealt with both Adam and Eve with perfect equality. Both were equally guilty of disobeying Allah, both recognized and repented their mistake, and Allah forgave them both. Thus, Eve's disobedience to Allah's command was not related to her femininity, nor was she solely to blame. Menstruation and childbearing are not considered as punishment from Allah on every woman. Rather, these are part of women's nature, the way that Allah created women so that they can play a critical role in family life.

FACT

Discharge of blood (from a man or a woman) exempts a Muslim from prayer and fasting. This is a health precaution, and also because the presence of blood itself is considered a violation of ablutions. A bleeding person is not considered "unclean." Only the blood itself is.

Equal Rewards

In the Qur'an, Allah mentions with honor all of mankind, especially women. Verses of the Qur'an establish that women are on an equal footing with men in terms of reward for their good deeds. Qur'anic descriptions of heaven make no differentiation between men's rewards and women's rewards. In many verses of the Qur'an, "the believers" are addressed as a whole, with no differentiation between men and women. In other verses, men and women are specifically addressed, to emphasize the point that both are blessed by Allah and equal in His eyes. One key verse describes the believers:

> For Muslim men and women, for believing men and women, for devout men and women, for true men and women, for men and women who are patient and constant, for men and women who humble themselves, for men and women who give in charity, for men and women who fast, for men and women who guard their chastity, and for men and women who engage much in Allah's remembrance—for them Allah has prepared forgiveness and great reward. (33:35)

Women's Rights

In Islam, a woman is seen as an individual in her own right, an independent person, and not as a shadow or adjunct to her husband or any other man. Muslim women are fully entitled to education, work, business ownership, and inheritance. At the time of Muhammad, just these rights alone were considered revolutionary. Even in marriage, the Muslim woman retains full rights to own and dispose of her own property and earnings, without any interference from her husband or anyone else. Women are perfectly free to work and earn a living, but are not obligated to support themselves from those earnings.

A Muslim woman retains her own family name upon marriage, rather than taking the name of her husband. This symbolic act emphasizes that she remains her own person, with her own valid identity.

The Islamic system sets up an overlapping circle of relatives to guarantee the financial security of women. The obligation is on these relatives, not the woman herself, to cover expenses such as housing and food. Thus any money that a woman earns is hers to keep or spend as she sees fit.

There are many women in history who serve as successful role models to Muslim women. Khadijah, the first wife of Muhammad, was a successful businesswoman. During the lifetime of the Prophet Muhammad, women endured persecution, exile, and martyrdom side by side with their male counterparts. In the battlefield, women carried water to the wounded, tended the injured, and even participated in actual fighting. Among the scholars of Islamic learning were Aisha and Asmaa bint Zayd, who shared their knowledge with men and women alike.

Women are active in politics and education throughout the Muslim world. The Iranian parliament has more female members than the U.S. Senate. Muslim countries like Pakistan, Bangladesh, Indonesia, and Turkey have had female prime ministers or presidents. In many Muslim countries, women make up the majority of college and graduate school students.

Women's Duties

As with anything in life, a person's rights are balanced by the responsibilities that correspond to those rights. Islam gave rights and duties to both men and women, so that they can live in mutual harmony and respect.

Duty to Allah

Any Muslim's first responsibility is to follow the guidance of Allah, to worship Allah alone, and to avoid violating any of Allah's injunctions. A Muslim woman is dutiful to Allah, and seeks knowledge so that she can better follow His guidance.

This duty supersedes all others. If her husband or parents require her to go against the teachings of her faith, her first responsibility is to her faith. In these circumstances, she is required to disobey those that would have her act against Islamic teachings.

Duty to Family

Islam recognizes that women were created with a special gift, the gift of carrying and nurturing new life. In the Islamic framework, the family is the foundation of society, and women are the firmest rocks in that foundation. Muslim women consider it an honor to play such an important role in family life. While many Muslim women work outside the home, and are perfectly entitled to do so, they are also cautious that their family responsibilities are not neglected.

Cultural Traditions

While all of these rights and responsibilities are specified in Islam, they are not always adhered to in some places and during some periods of time. In the diverse Muslim world, local cultural influences are sometimes confused with Islamic practice.

When discussing Islam (or any other faith), it's important to differentiate between the teachings of the faith and the practices of some people who claim to practice it. If a practice is truly based in Islamic teaching, one will be able to research it in authentic sources of Islamic knowledge. By the same token, one must understand that our own backgrounds and experiences may cause us to have different interpretations of the same practice. While we may see something as outdated or conservative, the people who actually believe in and practice it see things in an entirely different light. We must all constantly seek knowledge to aid in our understanding.

Culture and traditions often interfere with a faith, or even overshadow the faith's true teachings. The adherence to Islam varies with the strength of the beliefs and knowledge of the people. In some instances, local practices have no justification in the faith, or violate the faith's teachings altogether.

The Dress Codes

Islam requires that all people pay attention to their appearance, dress decently, maintain dignity, and enjoy what Allah has provided for clothing and adornment. In Islam, the human body is a sacred trust that should be maintained, protected, and nourished.

From the Islamic point of view, clothing serves the purposes of protecting, covering, and beautifying our appearance. The Qur'an encourages us to dress in beautiful clothing: "Oh children of Adam! Wear your beautiful apparel" (7:31). However, the Qur'an also warns against neglect in appearance and public nudity. "Oh children of Adam! Do not let Satan seduce you, in the same manner as he got your parents out of the Garden, stripping them of their raiment" (7:27).

Muslim men and women observe a standard of modesty that may be considered conservative, but they feel that these guidelines, established by Allah, are for the benefit of both individuals and the society in general.

General Modesty

Islam teaches men and women to coexist in cooperation, without exceeding the limits defined for them in Islam. When Muslim men and women are in the presence of each other, they must observe guidelines that help them to retain an air of respect, politeness, and honor. Islam forbids any situation that may lead to improper, unlawful, or even suspicious circumstances.

In the Qur'an, both men and women are commanded to be modest and "lower their eyes." This means that they should be humble, and not gaze at each other in an immodest way. This does not mean that Muslims have to walk around looking at the ground, but rather that they should restrain their glances, and not look each other over in a longing way. Lowering the gaze is also a sign of respect in many cultures, especially toward the elders. In many societies, making eye contact is an act of hostility and challenge.

All cultures have a notion that certain parts of the human body are considered private. In some cultures, these guidelines may change over time. Victorian women would never be seen in bathing suits, and even in our grandmothers' time it was considered inappropriate to wear skirts above the knees. In Islam, the standards of decency have been fixed and standardized, and are not subject to human whims or the fashion industry.

Dress Code for Women

Islam prohibits all forms of public nudity and exploitation of the female body. In addition to lowering their gazes, Muslim women are advised in the Qur'an not to make a display of their beauty in public. They are further advised to "draw their head coverings over their chests" (24:33), and to "cast their outer garments over them when outdoors" (33:59).

In ancient times, it was customary for women to wear a head covering, but they often pulled the ends back behind the neck to expose dresses with plunging necklines. The first verse makes reference to this, asking women to use those same head coverings, but to pull the ends forward so that the chest is covered. This head covering is often called a *hijab* or *khimar.*

QUESTION?

What does "hijab" mean?
"Hijab" is a general term that literally means "screen" or "cover." Variations of the word can also mean to obscure from view, hide, or vanish. It is a general term that describes Muslim women's clothing, but commonly refers specifically to a headscarf or veil.

In the second verse, women are advised to wear garments over their house clothes when they leave the house. This outer garment is often called a *jilbab, abaya,* or *chador,* depending on the area of the world where it is found.

These are the minimum requirements laid out in the Qur'an. The Qur'an makes no reference to color or style, so one will find many local variations that meet these basic standards. In the Arabian Peninsula, it is customary for women to wear black. In western Africa, women wear colorful dresses and turbans. In Southeast Asia, women often wear *shalwar kameez,* tunics and pants of bright colors and designs. Again, Islam allows for local variations as an expression of the diversity of the Muslim community, as long as minimum standards are observed.

One may also find women who believe that it is even more modest for them to be completely covered, including the face. Face veiling is not predominant in the Muslim world, but may be customary in certain places or practiced by choice by some individuals. Most Muslims believe that this practice goes beyond the minimum standards, but is respected as the choice or cultural norm of some people.

FACT

In the predominantly Muslim country of Turkey, women are forbidden from wearing a headscarf in government buildings and universities. In 1999, a democratically elected Parliament member was removed from office because she refused to remove her headscarf at the swearing-in ceremony.

In the privacy of the home, or in the presence only of family members and close female friends, Muslim women are free to remove their head coverings and outer garments, and adorn themselves with makeup and jewelry.

In the vast majority of Muslim nations, women are free to choose whether they would like to "cover" or not, and the style of dress they wear. It is a personal choice based on piety and modesty, and is not considered a sign of women's inferiority by those who practice it.

Dress Code for Men

Islam also prohibits all forms of nudity and exploitation of the male figure. Men are also advised to cover their bodies modestly, particularly from the navel to the knee. Indeed, in the traditional dress of many Muslim countries, men wear long flowing robes and perhaps a head covering as well. Like women, Muslim men may not wear clothing that is tight, transparent, or extravagant.

Why Modesty in Dress?

Islam prescribes modesty in dress and action to preserve dignity and respect between men and women in society. Muslims believe that a person's beauty is not for public display and that one should look best for family and close friends, not strangers on the street.

For women, distinctive dress offers protection from unwanted advances and makes it clear to others that she is a modest and religious woman. The differences between male and female minimum dress requirements have simply to do with the biological differences between men and women. Even in American culture, it is considered appropriate for a man to be in public without a shirt on, but women never go out topless.

Both Muslim men and women are forbidden from dressing like or imitating the opposite sex. For this reason, Muslim men are forbidden from wearing gold, silk, or "feminine" jewelry such as earrings.

With dignity in manners and dress, both men and women are free to go about their daily lives as contributing members of society, without issues of sexuality interfering or becoming a distraction. Many Muslim women are of the opinion that modest dress allows them to be recognized for their intelligence and contributions to society, not judged by their beauty or lack thereof. In the end, most feel that we should all be appreciated for our minds and hearts, not judged by what we look like on the outside. (E)

Chapter 19

Islamic Married Life

According to the teachings of Islam, family is the main structure of society, and a strong family must rest on two equal, mature, capable, and cooperative partners. Marriage provides a stable base for a good Muslim family, an environment for raising children, extended relations between families, and a substructure for society as a whole.

Choosing a Spouse

Islam considers marriage to be the most important act in the life of both men and women, and it is not to be entered into lightly. The choice of a spouse is one of the most important decisions in life, and Muslims enter into this life choice with guidance and support.

Permitted Relationships

The Qur'an makes clear that certain categories of people cannot be married to one another. This is a moral protection, as well as a biological one—to prevent incest relationships. Specifically, the following groups of people cannot marry each other in Islam:

- Stepmothers and stepsons; stepfathers and stepdaughters
- Mothers and children; fathers and children
- Sisters and brothers
- Aunts and nephews; uncles and nieces
- Grandmothers/grandfathers and grandchildren
- Mothers-in-law and sons-in-law; fathers-in-law and daughters-in-law

It may seem unnecessary to even say this. However, some of these relationships were common in pre-Islamic Arabia and in other cultures throughout time.

Beyond these restrictions, Muslims are encouraged to marry someone who is suitable and equivalent. Factors of religion, social status, and culture may come into play, but the most important is that both partners have a similar religious outlook.

Parental Involvement

Choosing a spouse is a major life decision that should not be taken lightly or left to chance or hormones. In Islam, it is taken as seriously as any other decision in life—with prayer, careful investigation, and family involvement. Muslim parents play an important role in the screening process of potential spouses, because they know their children extremely well—their personalities, their likes and dislikes, and their possible pitfalls. They may look at a potential suitor objectively with these aspects in mind. While parents are not permitted to randomly reject suitors without Islamic justification, they play an important role in narrowing down potential prospects.

Dating and Arranged Marriage

In the process of choosing a spouse, Islam institutes several guidelines aimed at protecting the honor and chastity of the young couple. Dating, as it is often practiced in today's western world, does not exist among Muslims. Young men and women do not engage in one-on-one intimate relationships to "get to know each other" in a very deep way without a commitment of marriage. Young people approach courtship with the ultimate goal of marriage in mind. Islam requires chastity before marriage for both men and women, and strict fidelity to one's spouse upon marriage.

The Prophet Muhammad once said, "Whenever a man is alone with a woman, Satan is the third among them." When young people are getting to know each other, being alone together is a temptation. To ward off this temptation, courting couples always meet in a group environment.

When a young person decides that he or she is ready and would like to be married, the following steps often take place:

- The family makes inquiries about other young people they know that might be suitable. Usually the father or mother approaches the other family to suggest a meeting.
- The couple agrees to meet in a chaperoned group environment. Often they visit in the company of other relatives or close friends to talk and get to know each other.
- The family investigates the candidate further. They may talk with friends, other family members, leaders in the Muslim community, coworkers, or anyone else who may know about the candidate's personality and character.
- The couple prays a special prayer for guidance, seeking Allah's help in making a decision.

- The couple agrees to pursue marriage or part ways. Islam has given this freedom of choice to both young men and women. They cannot be forced into a marriage that they do not want.

This type of focused courtship helps to ensure the strength of any future marriage by drawing upon the wisdom and guidance of family elders. Family involvement in the choice of a marriage partner helps assure that this choice is based not on romantic notions, but rather on a careful, objective evaluation of the compatibility of the couple. Such an approach helps minimize the chance for later marital conflicts and divorce.

Forced Marriage

Muhammad once said, "A previously married woman without a husband (a divorcée or widow) must not be married until she is consulted, and a virgin (never before married) must not be married until her permission is sought." One of the main conditions needed for a marriage to be valid is the free consent of both parties. Both women and men must be consulted before marriage can take place. Families are involved in the early selection process that is really "arranged introduction" and not "arranged marriage." Under no circumstances can a parent force one's child to submit to his or her choice.

The practice of forced marriage was common during the pre-Islamic era, and Muhammad had many opportunities to confront and condemn it. In one instance, a young woman came to Muhammad and complained that her father had married her off to his nephew. Muhammad first told her to "accept what your father has arranged," but she complained that she did not accept the arrangement. Muhammad then said, "Then this marriage is invalid. Go and marry whomever you wish." The girl then responded that she did in fact agree to the marriage, but that she raised the issue because she "wanted women to know that fathers have no right in their daughters' matters" (that is, they have no right to force a marriage on them).

While parents are actively involved in the process of screening suitors and suggesting prospects, it is ultimately the decision of the couple whether they will agree to be married or not.

The Marriage Contract

In Islam, marriage is not merely a sacrament, but also a legally binding contract between two partners. A written contract establishes the couple's acceptance of one another as spouses and outlines their responsibilities to one another in all aspects of their interaction. A marriage contract is like a very detailed prenuptial agreement that is there to help minimize misunderstandings and false hopes in the relationship.

In order to be a valid contract, the marriage must be attested to by two Muslim witnesses, have the consent of both parties, and include the offer of a marriage gift.

Marriage Gift

In order for the marriage to be valid, the groom must present the new bride with a gift, called a *mahr*. This gift is for her enjoyment alone, and acts to protect her from violations in the marriage contract. There are no specifications for the minimum or maximum worth of the mahr; it may be in the form of cash, property, or intangible assets. The mahr may be given at the time of the marriage, or if both parties agree, all or part of it may be deferred to a later time. Unlike a traditional dowry, the mahr is for the bride alone. Her father or other family members share no part of it.

Marriage Conditions

Both the man and the woman may make certain stipulations in the marriage contract that outline conditions to be fulfilled for the marriage to remain valid. These conditions are put into writing at the time of marriage and agreed to by both parties.

It's not necessary to lay out all aspects of Islamic marriage law, as those rights and responsibilities are understood and enforceable without being specified. But if either spouse would like to include additional conditions that would not violate Islamic law, that are to their own personal taste and needs, this is acceptable. Such conditions may include where the couple will live, clarification of the woman's right to education and employment, or any other issues of concern to either party. The open discussion of these issues prior to marriage helps the couple to identify problem areas and come to an understanding on these issues before entering into the marriage.

The Islamic Marriage Ceremony

When both parties agree to marry, the families decide on a date for the marriage ceremony. The actual ceremony is usually a private affair, with just the immediate family and witnesses in attendance. The bride is represented by a guardian, called a *Wali*—usually her father, brother, or uncle.

QUESTION?

What is the role of a Wali?
The word "Wali" means "protector" or "supporter," a person who represents the bride in the marriage negotiations. The bride's Wali must be a Muslim. If a woman's family members are not Muslim, then a Muslim man of her choosing may represent her.

The Wali is charged with ensuring that the bride's rights are not violated and to look after her interests in the contract negotiations. Islam does not have a religious priesthood, so any trustworthy Muslim can officiate over the ceremony, provided that all other requirements are met.

At the actual ceremony, there may be a brief sermon about the importance of marriage and the rights and duties involved. Verses from the Qur'an may be read that pertain to this subject. Then the bride and her representative are asked if she agrees to marry the groom. She is asked what her requested mahr is, and what conditions she would like to include in the contract. The groom is offered the opportunity to agree to these, and to request his own conditions. Once all parties agree, the marriage ceremony is concluded and witnessed, and the couple is officially married. Then the marriage is announced and celebrated in the greater community.

FACT

In many countries, the civil marriage ceremony is not sufficient to meet Islamic requirements for marriage. In these cases, Muslim couples often have both a religious ceremony and a civil ceremony, to protect the couple's legal rights in that country. In some jurisdictions, Muslim leaders have clergy rights to perform marriages so one ceremony fulfills both state and legal requirements.

The Wedding Celebration

In Islam, weddings are joyous occasions, celebrated by the entire community. Since the actual ceremony is usually done privately, the public celebration is similar to a wedding reception. This celebration, called a *walimah,* is often observed as a wedding dinner, with food, singing, and congratulations all around.

The actual nature of the wedding celebration varies from country to country, and according to the cultural norms of the couple. The Prophet Muhammad advised his followers not to be too extravagant in the wedding celebrations. Indeed, it was the common practice of the time to simply invite guests for a dinner of rice and lamb, or even just dates and milk, if that's all that was available.

Muslim Weddings Around the World

In many Muslim countries, wedding celebrations may take place over a series of days, accompanied by back-to-back celebrations and feasts. One common tradition is for the women to gather in the home of the bride a few days before the wedding, to apply henna and prepare her for the upcoming marriage.

Men and women celebrate marriage parties separately, in accordance with the Islamic principles of modesty. Among themselves, women may dress up and sing, dance, and laugh. Guests wear their best clothing, and the women don their gold. The bride often has a series of wedding dresses: one for the henna party, and one or two for the walimah. Traditionally, wedding dresses vary in color, including red, green, or other bright colors. Some dresses include elaborate embroidery or sequin decorations.

In modern times, many Muslim women wear a white wedding gown for at least part of the celebrations.

As long as people stay within Islamic limits, variations in celebrations are expected and honored as cultural expressions. The various wedding traditions reflect the diversity of the Muslim world.

Rights and Duties of Husband and Wife

Marriage is a relationship of comfort, trust, confidence, mercy, loyalty, affection, and love. It can also involve frustration and mutual compromise. In order to provide structure and balance to the marital relationship, Islam specifies certain rights and obligations for both husband and wife.

The Ideal Relationship

The Qur'an describes the marital relationship as one of warmth and security. "Among His signs is this—that Allah created for you spouses from among yourselves, that you may dwell with them in tranquility, and Allah has put love and mercy between your hearts" (30:21).

The Qur'an describes husbands and wives: "They are garments for you, and you are garments for them" (2:187). A garment, used as a metaphor in this verse, gives a person warmth, protection, comfort, and decency. Ideally, this is what a husband and wife offer each other.

Couples are bound to face difficulties and get frustrated with one another from time to time. The Qur'an advises that even in these situations, we should "Live with them on a footing of kindness and equity" and remember that "even if you dislike them, perhaps you dislike something in which Allah has placed much good" (4:19). Couples should always try to see the best in each other.

On many occasions, Muhammad advised his companions to treat their wives with respect, honor, and tenderness. He said, "The most perfect man in his faith is the one whose behavior is most excellent, and the best of you are those who are best to their wives." In another circumstance, he advised: "Only an honorable man treats his wife honorably, and only a wicked man humiliates his wife."

Roles and Responsibilities

Marriage in Islam is described as a partnership, with each spouse contributing to the common welfare and health of the family unit. Cooperation between husband and wife is required, and each couple has some flexibility in their own family arrangements.

In marriage, a woman retains the same rights she had as a single woman, including the full rights to own and dispose of her own property as she sees fit, and to earn and retain her own income. Once the couple has children, however, she needs to balance her rights with her responsibilities toward her children. The wife has the right to a comfortable place to live, provided by the husband, with all financial needs taken care of. In return, she has a responsibility to be loyal to her husband, and to maintain a relaxing home atmosphere.

The husband, in turn, is entirely responsible for the financial needs of the family. In return for this responsibility, he has the right to be the final arbiter in family disputes. His authority, however, is neither absolute nor unchecked. As long as his final decisions are in accordance with Islam, then his wife should willingly cooperate, out of love, respect, and honor for him. A husband should be kind and understanding with his wife, and treat her in a tender and loving manner.

Many people today have come to realize that it is not easy to "have it all" in terms of career, parenthood, social life, and so on. In Islam, the basic duties are divided so that no one person feels responsible for it all. Within this framework, each couple is free to discuss and choose any type of arrangement that meets their personal needs or unique situation. Overall, Muslims believe that the system is balanced and fair, with each person afforded both rights and corresponding responsibilities.

The Practice of Polygamy

Polygamy has been practiced in various cultures and societies for thousands of years. Many ancient rulers had hundreds of wives and concubines, whom they freely took or discarded according to their whims. No ancient society placed restrictions on the practice, either in the number of wives or the manner in which they should be treated.

The word "polygamy" can refer to either a man or a woman having more than one spouse. In Islam, women may not have more than one partner. What is permitted in Islam is officially termed "polygyny," a practice of men having multiple wives.

Islam brought severe restrictions on the practice of marrying more than one wife, neither outlawing nor promoting it. This legal provision must be understood in the context of Islam's position on several important issues. First, Islam is a faith for all cultures and time periods, and thus must take into consideration all possible circumstances. The laws must accommodate all possible individual and social conditions.

Also, Islam strongly prohibits extramarital relationships, and encourages all men and women to marry.

The Qur'an indicates that under specific, restricted circumstances, a Muslim man may marry two, three, or a maximum of four wives. This permission is restricted with conditions of financial, physical, and emotional fairness. Any woman involved in such a marriage must give her approval; it is a free choice of all parties.

While polygyny has been abused in some instances, the practice can have a valuable function in certain circumstances. The obvious example of this is in wartime, when there are large numbers of widows and orphans left without means of support, protection, and companionship. It was in this context that the Qur'anic verses allowing more than one wife were revealed.

At the Battle of Uhud, thousands of Muslim men were killed; their widows and orphaned children were left alone. At this time, the following verses were revealed:

> To orphans restore their property . . . nor substitute your worthless things for their good ones, and devour not their substance by mixing it up with your own. For this is indeed a great sin. If you fear that you will not be able to deal justly with orphans, marry women of your choice—two, three, or four. But if you fear that you will not be able to deal justly with them, then marry only one . . . (4:2–3)

When looking at these verses, a number of facts are evident:

- The practice is not mandatory, but merely permitted in certain circumstances.
- This practice is not associated with passion or lust. It is rather based on compassion toward widows and orphans, a matter that is confirmed by the atmosphere in which these verses were revealed.
- Even in such a situation, the permission is far more restricted than what was common practice at the time—an unlimited number of wives with no conditions.
- Dealing justly with one's wives is a condition and obligation.

This applies to equal housing, food, and kind treatment without discrimination.

- If a man doubts that he can be fair and even between more than one wife, he is encouraged to marry only one.

This permission is consistent with the realistic Islamic view of the varying social needs, problems, and cultural variations throughout time and in all places. Islam did not invent or require polygyny; it merely regulated the long-common practice to ensure equal rights and status for all parties concerned. In today's world, polygyny is not a common practice among all Muslims.

ALERT!

The Qur'an warns that, "you will never be able to be fair and just between women, even if it is your ardent desire" (4:129). Based on this verse, many Muslims believe that monogamy is encouraged, and men are warned about the possible consequences of their choice.

Getting a Divorce

Islam provides many safeguards to ensure a happy and stable marriage. Nevertheless, conflicts can arise, and Muslims are given guidance on what to do when a marriage seems doomed. Even in divorce, the Qur'an encourages kind treatment of one's spouse: "Hold together on equitable terms, or separate with kindness" (2:229).

Steps to Divorce

When a couple is having difficulties, the Qur'an lays out a series of steps to follow in an attempt toward reconciliation. First, the couple should try to work things out themselves. If that doesn't work, then arbitrators from both the husband and wife's families can get together to try to solve the problem peacefully and justly. "If you fear a breach between them [the spouses], then appoint two arbiters, one from his family and the other from hers. If they seek to set things aright, Allah will cause their reconciliation.

For Allah has full knowledge and is acquainted with all things" (4:35).

If all attempts at reconciliation fail, divorce is permitted (although it is discouraged). Muhammad once described divorce as "the most hated in the sight of Allah, among all the things that are permissible." Upon divorce, there is a three-month waiting period (called the *iddah*) during which the couple still has an opportunity to reconcile. This gives the couple ample time to calm themselves, evaluate the relationship, and determine if the wife is expecting a child.

When divorce is final, the couple is advised to part ways in kindness; there is to be no game playing or yo-yoing. "And when you have divorced women . . . either retain them honorably or release them honorably. But do not retain them in order to injure them, for this is transgression, and whoever does this has wronged his own soul" (Qur'an 2:231).

Can Women Initiate Divorce?

If a woman no longer wishes to be married to her husband, she can initiate divorce by returning the mahr (the gift that her husband gave to her at the time of marriage) to her husband. In addition, a woman may include provisions in the marriage contract that pertain to her right to divorce, and under what certain circumstances. As a final option, a woman may also appeal to a judge to grant a divorce, if there is evidence that her husband is unjust, is mistreating her, or has violated the terms of their marriage agreement.

Spousal Abuse

One verse of the Qur'an is often misinterpreted as to allow for physical abuse of a wayward spouse. The verse in question addresses the instance when a woman is guilty of serious illegal conduct: "As to those women on whose part you fear disloyalty and ill-conduct, admonish them first, then do not share their beds, and at last tap them lightly; but if they return to obedience, seek not against them means of annoyance, for Allah is Most High, Great" (4:34).

In many English translations of the Qur'an, the phrase "tap them lightly" is written as "beat them." This is a misinterpretation of the words *darban gharyra mubarrih* in Arabic. Muslims who lived at the time of the verse's revelation and early jurists understood this phrase to mean a light tapping, with something no bigger than a toothbrush, that leaves not even a mark on the body.

ALERT!

As an example for Muslims to follow, the Prophet Muhammad never resorted to that measure, and rather advised his followers, "Do not strike the female servants of Allah."

This verse provides a rare exception to the rule of kindness and tenderness, applying only to those cases where the wife is guilty of an extreme infraction or lewdness, and the husband is innocent and well behaved. If the husband is the cause of the problem, he has no right to do any of these steps.

As a last resort, after peaceful means have failed, the husband may resort to this symbolic expression of his disapproval. Under no circumstances is any Muslim at any time permitted to strike someone in the face or cause any bodily harm. This final step is intended as an extreme expression of disapproval, with hopes that the wife will come around, cease the disruptive behavior, and prevent the marriage from ending up in divorce.

Child Custody

In the event of divorce, children often bear the most painful consequences. Islamic law takes their needs into account and makes sure that they are cared for.

The financial support of any children, during marriage or after divorce, rests solely with the father. This is the children's right upon their father, and courts have the power to enforce this responsibility upon the father, if necessary.

Islamic law maintains that physical custody of the children must go to a Muslim that is in good physical and mental health and is in the best position to meet the children's needs. Islamic law takes into account the differing needs of children depending on their stage of development. Young children, under the age of seven, are generally cared for by the mother. At this stage in life, mothers have the best ability to nurture and tend to the child. If the mother remarries, however, then the father may make a claim of custody.

For children over the age of seven who have not yet reached adolescence, boys are given a choice while girls stay with their mother. This is because the mother plays a critical role in teaching her daughters about their bodies and growing into womanhood, and it is in a girl's best interest to be with her mother during this time.

After a child has reached puberty, both boys and girls are given the choice of which parent to live with. At this age, the children have reached a level of maturity and independence where their opinions and comfort can be expressed and respected.

There are some differences among Islamic scholars about child custody, so you might find small differences in local law and the application of it. However, the overwhelming concern is that the children are cared for by the parent most fit for custody, and that their emotional and physical needs are fully met.

Interfaith Marriage

When choosing a marriage partner, compatible religious outlook is one of the main factors to consider. As a general rule, it is preferable for Muslims to marry other Muslims. The Qur'an emphasizes this: "Do not marry unbelieving women until they believe; a slave woman who believes is better than an unbelieving woman, even if you are attracted to her" (2:221). At the time of this verse's revelation, marrying a slave was considered a great humiliation. However, Islam establishes that a person's faith is more important than social status or any other factor.

Under no circumstances is a Muslim, man or woman, allowed to marry a polytheist. However, under certain circumstances Muslim men are permitted to marry Jewish or Christian women: "Lawful for you in marriage are not only chaste women who are believers, but chaste women from among the people of the book revealed before your time, when you give them their due dowers" (5:5). Regardless of the faith of one's spouse, Muslims are still held to the standard of kindness, tenderness, and mutual respect in the marriage relationship.

Muslim women may marry only Muslim men. "They are not lawful wives for the unbelievers, nor are the unbelievers lawful husbands for them" (60:11). Muslims perceive this rule as a protection for the woman in marriage. If a Muslim woman were to marry outside the faith, her husband would neither understand nor follow Islamic teachings about fair treatment of women, her rights and responsibilities. Such a marriage would put her at risk to abuse or the pressure to give up her faith. (E)

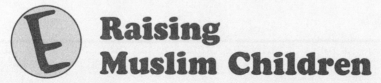

Chapter 20

Raising Muslim Children

One of the main purposes of the family in Islam is to provide an appropriate environment for raising young children. Muslims consider their children to be precious treasures, gifts from Allah, a source of tremendous joy but also a trial and responsibility.

The Birth of a Child

The birth of a child is an event of great joy and gratitude. This happy occasion is shared with relatives, friends, and the community at large. The newborn child is welcomed into the community, and everyone prays for the child's future health, happiness, and well-being.

Birth Rites

At the moment of birth, the father, mother, or other close relative will whisper the Islamic call to prayer in the newborn's ear. Thus, the Muslim child's life begins with words of Allah's praise and a call to faith in Him.

A welcoming celebration is often observed in the first weeks of the child's life, on the seventh, fourteenth, or twenty-first day after birth. This celebration is called the *aqiqah,* from the word *aqqa,* "to slaughter an animal." For this celebration, the parents slaughter a lamb (or perhaps a cow or goat, if lamb is not available) and invite the entire community for a meal. This traditional observance is an opportunity for the parents to show their gratitude, express their happiness, and celebrate their joy with the whole community.

It is also traditional for the newborn child's head to be shaved in the early days or weeks. The hair is then weighed, and the value of its weight in gold is given in charity. This is also an expression of thankfulness, and the desire to share joy with others at this happy occasion.

For newborn boys, circumcision is usually performed in these early days and weeks as well. There is no Islamic ceremony or ritual associated with this process, and any adult (Muslim or not) may perform the surgery. In Islam, circumcision is more related to hygiene than to any religious significance.

ALERT!

Circumcision of girls is not an Islamic practice. This procedure, which often causes irreparable harm to young girls, is based in local cultural beliefs that predate Islam. Indeed, the practice is observed in many parts of Africa by people of Christian, Jewish, Muslim, and animist faiths.

Breastfeeding

In Islam, breastfeeding is considered the best and most proper way to nourish a baby. The Qur'an encourages Muslim women to breastfeed their infants for up to two years. "Mothers shall breastfeed their children for two whole years, for those that desire to complete the term" (2:233).

Islam gives so much value to the breastfeeding relationship that any woman who nurses another's child in infancy is considered that child's foster mother. If that woman nurses other children, as well, those children are all considered "milk" brothers and sisters. Their bond is so close that they enjoy the same relationship as blood siblings under Islamic law.

Naming a Muslim Child

Muslims are encouraged to give their children a meaningful and appropriate name, reflecting good qualities and virtues. The child's name does not necessarily have to be Arabic in origin, as long as it holds a nice meaning and does not subject the child to ridicule.

Muslim parents are often given a *kunya,* that is, an honorable nickname that is based on the name of their firstborn child. The father of a child named Hamzah would be known as Abu Hamzah (the father of Hamzah). His mother would be known as Um Hamzah (the mother of Hamzah).

In Muslim families, parents often choose a single first name for the newborn child. A child may then have several middle names that list the family's history: the name of the father, grandfather, great-grandfather, and so on. The family surname (or historically, the tribal name) comes at the end. The words *bint* (daughter of) or *ibn* (son of) may also be included somewhere in the name, to denote relationship. Thus, a boy named Abdullah ibn Qais Al-Ashari is Abdullah, the son of Qais (his father's name), of the tribe or family called Al-Ashari.

This system of naming a child after the father is also part of the English naming system. Historically, a person named Timothy, who was the son of John, became known as "Timothy, John's son," and later simply "Timothy Johnson." Similarly, over time the historical bint or ibn has been generally removed from Arabic names, so the family ancestral names read simply like a long series of middle names.

Prohibited Names

Muslims are forbidden from calling their children names that denote worship of something or someone other than Allah. In ancient Arabia, it was common for people to be named "Sun-worshipper" and the like; Muhammad changed their names to more appropriate ones once they embraced Islam. Any names that show reverence to false gods are forbidden. In addition, Muslims should name their children with names of honor. It is forbidden to call one's child a name that means "ugly" or "dirty." Muhammad once changed a person's name from Harb (war) to Silm (peace), and from 'Asiyah (tough or hard) to Jamilah (beautiful).

It is also forbidden for Muslims to give their children names that are befitting of Allah alone. Muslims must refrain from names such as Al-Khaliq (The Creator) or Malik al-Mulook (King of Kings), as these should be used to describe only Allah.

Recommended Names

The most honorable names in Islam are those that denote worship of Allah. Other common names remind us of the character of previous prophets, and valuable Islamic virtues. Muhammad used to recommend that Muslims name their sons Abdullah (worshipper of Allah) or Abdel-Rahman (worshipper of the Most Merciful). Indeed, the prefix "Abd" can be attached to any of the names or attributes of Allah to mean, for example, "Worshipper of the Mighty" (Abdel-Aziz) or "Worshipper of the Truth" (Abdel-Haqq).

Muslims often name their children after the companions of the Prophet Muhammad, members of the earliest Muslim community, as well as after previous prophets. Muhammad is the most common example, but

Muslims also name their children Musa (Moses), Isa (Jesus), Ibrahim (Abraham), and Yahya (John the Baptist), among others.

It is also common to name girls after well-known women in history, including Maryam (Mary, mother of Jesus) and Khadijah (the first wife of Muhammad). Many girls are named for values and virtues that are respected in Islam.

QUESTION?

Does a Muslim convert have to change his or her name?
Only if the name has a meaning offensive to Isam. Many new Muslims keep their given names, some change them, and others take on Islamic "nicknames" by which they are known among their Muslim family and friends. Converts to Islam should always retain their family surname.

Common Muslim Names

While traditional names are always popular, Muslims also are inventive and can use more modern names, as long as they have a positive Islamic meaning. While most are based in the Arabic language, there is also some borrowing from other languages, such as Persian or Turkish. Here are some common Muslim names, along with their English meanings:

Common Muslim Names	
girls' names	**boys' names**
Amal (hope)	Adil (fair, honest)
Anisah (friendly)	Akram (noble)
Hanan (mercy)	Bassam (smiling)
Iman (faith)	Faris (knight)
Jamilah (beautiful)	Fuad (heart)
Manal (achievement)	Hassan (handsome)
Nasreen (white rose)	Imad (pillar of support)

continued on next page

Common Muslim Names (continued)	
girls' names	boys' names
Nawal (gift)	Mansoor (victorious)
Rana (elegant)	Nadir (rare, precious)
Salwa (solace)	Rashad (wisdom)
Widad (affection, love)	Tariq (morning star)

Sons and Daughters

All children are celebrated and welcomed in Islam, but this was not always so. Before Islam, the birth of a girl was usually met with sorrow and disappointment. Female infanticide was commonplace, and girls who did grow up did so as unwanted, unloved servants.

Preference for Boys

The Qur'an criticizes the attitude of parents who are disappointed at the birth of a daughter. "When news is brought to one of them of the birth of a female child, his face darkens and he is filled with inward grief! With shame he hides himself from people, because of the bad news he has had! Shall he retain it in suffering and contempt, or bury her in the dust? Ah! What an evil choice they make" (16:58–59). Love and affection for a newborn child should be the same, regardless of gender.

Muslims recognize that God is the One who creates, and God alone is the One who chooses whether a child will be a boy or a girl. It is not something for us to despair over, because that would be questioning God's wisdom. The Qur'an reminds: "To God belongs the dominion of the heavens and the earth. He creates what He wills. He bestows children, male or female, according to His will. Or He bestows both males and females. And He leaves barren whom He will, for He is full of knowledge and power" (42:49–50).

Rewards for Raising Girls

Not only should parents be delighted at the birth of a daughter, they should treat her well and raise her in mercy and kindness. Islam encourages this attitude, reminding Muslims of the rewards for this unconditional love and care.

Muhammad once said, "The one who raises a daughter properly, she shall be his pass into Heaven." Another time he said, "Whoever has a daughter, and he does not bury her alive, does not insult her, and does not favor his son over her, Allah will enter him into Paradise." Muhammad himself had four daughters who grew to adulthood, and he was an example to others of how to lovingly treat a little girl.

The Education of Children

One of the primary responsibilities that parents have toward their children is to share knowledge with them and allow them the opportunity to reach their full potential. Very early on, Muslim parents guide and train their children to develop good character, manners, and a strong faith.

Muslims believe that children are born with *fitrah,* an inborn, natural predisposition toward God that exists at birth in all human beings. As a child grows, parents mold and shape him or her into their dominant beliefs and culture.

Islam orders all believers to seek knowledge, so parents have an obligation to educate their children, both boys and girls. Muhammad once said, "Seeking knowledge is mandatory on every Muslim, male and female." Unfortunately, some people stray from this clear advice, due to local culture and circumstances.

Religious education takes primary importance during a child's early years, because it serves as the foundation for the building of all future knowledge. However, secular or practical education is also encouraged, particularly in areas where one can make a positive contribution to society.

Love and Discipline

Muslim children learn that each Muslim has his or her duties and responsibilities. Even parents have rules that they must follow. It is the children's responsibility to listen to and obey their parents. It is worth noting the origin of the word "discipline" in English. Stemming from the word "disciple," it means a follower, or a devoted learner. An equivalent word in Arabic would be *tarbiyyah,* which means "cultivation" or "growth." The goal for Muslim parents, as indeed for most parents, is to cultivate their children, so that they grow into self-disciplined, independent people one day.

ALERT!

It is expected that Muslim children treat their parents with kindness and respect their authority. Muslim families are not loose disciplinarians, but are advised to treat children according to their nature and in accordance with their level of understanding.

The Prophet Muhammad serves as a role model to Muslims in this regard as well. It is well documented that he was never harsh with anyone, especially children. He would give children responsibilities within their limits, encourage them, and overlook their shortcomings. When giving advice, he would ask a child, "What do you think of this?" and allow the child to come up with possible solutions to his or her own problems. Most important, he never ridiculed, humiliated, yelled at, or struck a child, whether in private or in public.

Islamic Schooling in the West

Muslim parents prefer to raise their children in an environment where religious principles are adhered to and respected. Many Muslims in the West are uncomfortable with many school practices, such as the celebration of holidays, mixed-gender sports, and sex education (which Muslims believe should be done by parents).

As a minority community, Muslims strive to retain their own traditions and heritage in an environment where such things are considered old-fashioned or even backward. For this reason, many Muslim parents have organized to form private Islamic schools where children can pursue both their religious and practical education in a familiar environment, and where Islamic practices are the norm rather than the exception. There are over 200 private Islamic schools in the United States today, including nearly ten in the Detroit area alone.

From a Child to an Adult

When children reach puberty, they become responsible for all aspects of Islam, including worship, fasting, modest dress, and other duties. However, children don't just wake up one day as adults. A gradual process is observed to get children used to the responsibilities that come with adulthood.

For example, Muslim children first begin praying as toddlers, imitating their parents. At the age of seven, parents begin more formal instruction on how to perform the prayers, and by age ten require the children to participate. The same holds true for fasting. As youngsters, many Muslim children participate in fasting because they want to feel part of the family and community. It starts out as perhaps a half day, or one day during the week, then builds up from there. Only at puberty is a Muslim child obligated to perform the entire fast. This gradual process is observed in all aspects of Islamic teaching.

In Islam, the education of children is not only to prepare them for good jobs and successful careers, but for them to learn how to function properly in life. As children reach puberty, Muslim parents are responsible for making sure their children know about the responsibilities of adulthood, running a household, being a good husband or wife, and contributing in a positive way to society.

The Practice of Adoption

Islam encourages the tender care of children who do not have natural parents or whose natural parents are otherwise unable to meet their needs. However, certain stipulations must be adhered to in order to ensure that the adoptive child knows and respects his or her true family heritage and genealogy. The adoption laws in Islam are very similar to what is now known as "open adoption."

Care of Orphans

Muhammad once said: "I will be like this [showing his middle and forefingers together] in Paradise with the person who takes care of an orphan." Muhammad himself was orphaned at a young age, and the Qur'an repeats several times the blessings of those people who care for orphans. The care of orphaned children includes both material and emotional support.

In giving material support, a Muslim adult needs to be careful about keeping the child's financial records and deposits separate from his or her own. This property is to be returned to the child when he or she reaches adulthood. "To orphans, restore their property when they reach of age. Do not substitute your worthless things for their good ones, and do not devour their belongings by mixing them up with your own. This is indeed a great sin" (4:2).

Orphaned children can feel lonely and abandoned. The Qur'an encourages the Muslim adult to provide emotional comfort, and be kind and caring to them. "Let them [those who care for orphans] fear Allah, and speak words of appropriate comfort and kindness" (4:9–10). When raising adopted children, Muslim parents are encouraged to treat them well, the same as their other children.

FACT

Muhammad once said, "The one who strokes the head of an orphan, doing so only for the sake of Allah, will have blessings for every hair over which his hand passes. And if anyone treats well an orphaned boy or girl under his care, he and I will be like these two in Paradise," and he put two of his fingers together to illustrate.

Carrying the Father's Name

In today's world, many adopted children grow up wanting to learn about their birth mothers and fathers, and many suffer years of anguish when that information is kept secret from them. In Islam, one stipulation when adopting a child is that the child must carry his or her own family name. This is done in honor and respect for the child's true parentage, and so that children feel connected to their birth families. The Qur'an is clear:

Nor has Allah made your adopted sons your real sons. Such is only your way of speech by your mouths, but Allah tells you the truth and Allah shows you the right way. Call them by the names of their fathers; that is more just in the sight of Allah. But if you do not know their father's name, then call them your brothers in faith, or your associate. There is no blame upon you if you make mistakes; what counts is the intention in your heart. (33:4–5)

Muslims are to recognize that no matter their feelings and desires, adoptive children are not their real blood relations. Thus, adopted children do not inherit from their adoptive parents; they inherit from their natural parents. Likewise, adopted children carry their own family name, not the family name of their adoptive parents.

Chapter 21

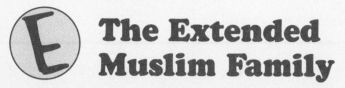

The Extended Muslim Family

According to Islamic teachings, the family is the foundation of society. But the family is not limited only to one's parents, brothers, and sisters. The Muslim family is a network of relatives near and far, all of whom have rights and responsibilities in the family structure.

Respect for Parents and Elders

A Muslim's duties to his or her parents are secondary only to duties toward Allah, their Lord and Creator. The Prophet Muhammad once asked his companions, "Shall I inform you of the biggest of the major sins?" He repeated the question three times, until the people answered, "Yes, please inform us." Then, he said, "Ascribing partners to Allah, and being undutiful to your parents."

> Muhammad once said that cursing one's parents is one of the greatest of sins. It is forbidden for Muslims to ridicule, abuse, or call names the father or mother of another person, even in jest.

Our life would not be possible without the sacrifice and hard work of our parents, who cared for us and met all our needs when we were young. The Qur'an addresses this point in one touching verse:

> And your Lord has decreed that you worship none but Him, and that you be kind to parents. If one or both of them attain old age during your life, say not to them a word of disrespect, nor repel them. But address them in terms of honor, and lower to them the wing of humility, out of mercy, and say, "My Lord! Bestow on them Your Mercy, as they did bring me up when I was young." (17:23–24)

Duties to Parents

Muslims are advised to treat their parents gently and respectfully. They should always strive to please them, and never become impatient or rude with them. Muslims consider it an honor and a blessing to be able to care for their parents in old age. After all, it's the least we can do to repay them for all of their hard work and sacrifice. Nursing homes and hospice care are virtually unheard of in the Muslim world. Elderly and ill family members almost always remain in the home of children or relatives, cared for and respected, until death.

Muhammad encouraged his followers to treat their parents well and to be mindful of their needs. Once, a young man came to him and wanted to join the Muslim army on the battlefield to defend the community from attack. Muhammad asked him if his parents were living. When the young man said they were, he told him: "Then go back to your parents, serve them, and deal with them kindly. This is as good as fighting for God's sake."

In another case, a young man traveled from Yemen to be with Muhammad. When he arrived, Muhammad asked him if he had asked his parents' permission before coming. He hadn't. So Muhammad sent him home, with these instructions: "If they permit you, then come back. Otherwise, be devoted to them."

Muslims consider their parents' opinions about important matters, such as choosing a career path, marriage, or relocating. As a Muslim gets older, any income he or she earns is partially used to support his parents and meet their needs. After their death, a Muslim prays that God will forgive his or her parents and show mercy toward them.

It is important to note, however, that a Muslim's duty toward his or her parents is not blind obedience. No Muslim should obey his or her parents if they order their child to do something that is in violation of Islamic law. In this situation, a Muslim strives to advise the parents, educate them about Islamic teachings in the matter, and ultimately serve God first and foremost.

Mother First

Among parents, it is usually the mother who makes the most sacrifice and endures the most hardship in the care of her children. Islam recognizes this fact, offering more honor to the mother as a parent. Muhammad once said, "Paradise is placed at the mothers' feet," so high is their status and regard.

The Qur'an reminds people of the sacrifices and hardships that mothers face on behalf of their children. "And we enjoined upon mankind concerning parents: his mother carried him in weakness upon weakness, and his weaning is two years. Therefore show gratitude to Allah and to your parents" (31:14).

On another occasion, some people asked the Prophet Muhammad, "To whom should we show kindness first?" He answered, "Your mother." Then he was asked again, "And after that, then whom?" Muhammad again replied, "Your mother." He was asked yet again, and he gave the same reply again, "Your mother." Only after that, when he was asked one more time, did he answer, "Then, your father."

Muhammad once said, "Let his nose be rubbed in the dust; let his nose be rubbed in the dust; let his nose be rubbed in the dust." When asked, "Who is it that should be humiliated in such a way?" he answered, "That person who finds his parents, one or both of them, attaining old age in his life, but does not enter Paradise by serving them."

Non-Muslim Parents

If a Muslim's parents do not believe in Islam, he or she is guided to treat them with kindness and mercy out of respect for their sacrifices and unconditional love. However, just as with Muslim parents, if a non-Muslim parent orders something that goes against the faith, the Muslim is not to obey: "But if they strive to make you join other gods in worship with Me, of which you have no knowledge, obey them not. Yet accompany them in this life with gentleness" (31:15). All other duties that a Muslim must show his or her parents hold true, regardless of their faith.

Family Relationships

The family in Islam is not restricted to immediate relatives of the "nuclear" family. Aunts, uncles, cousins, grandparents, second cousins, and even neighbors form a complex web of relationships that are tied through mutual rights and responsibilities.

In Arabic, any adult woman is called Auntie (*Khala*) and any adult male is called Uncle (*Amo*). One's uncles are as close as one's father, and one's aunts are as close as one's mother. A "cousin" could be any number of relations: first cousin, second cousin, cousins related through birth as well as through marriage.

If something happens to a member of the family, the entire clan pitches in to offer assistance. If a woman is widowed, her father and brothers help her. If she has no immediate family, then uncles and cousins are obliged to pitch in. The elders are cared for by their children or by their nieces, nephews, or great-grandchildren. In this way, nobody is left to suffer in loneliness or poverty; there is always someone to look out for them.

While the culture of each individual family may vary, it is generally understood that one person's business is open to the entire group. It is not considered rude for a distant cousin to ask about a relative's income, or for a grandmother to ask about a new couple's plans to have children. The personal boundaries can sometimes be blurred, because people consider "family business" to be everyone's concern. This is not done out of nosiness or to simply gossip. Within the family, there is generally a true desire to share, strengthen the bonds of trust, and offer sincere advice.

Duties to Kin

If Muslims are commanded to be respectful and caring toward their parents, elders, and other family members, how does one go about showing that respect? What duties does a Muslim have toward his or her family?

Emotional Ties

The Qur'an has strong words against those who "do not respect the ties of kinship," calling them people who "transgress all bounds" (9:10). The Prophet Muhammad once said, "The person who severs the bond of kinship will not enter Paradise." On another occasion, he said, "He who believes in Allah and the Last Day, let him be hospitable to his guest; and he who believes in Allah and the Last Day, let him maintain well the ties of kinship; and he who believes in Allah and the Last Day, must speak good or remain silent."

Cutting off ties with one's family is considered a serious sin, a violation of the sacred family unit. The first responsibility a Muslim has toward family is to keep in touch with them, inquire about them, and visit them in sickness and in health. When making life choices, a Muslim considers the opinions of family members and heeds the advice of elders.

Financial Obligations

In addition to the emotional connection, a Muslim has a financial obligation toward relatives. "And render to relatives their due rights, as also to those in need and to the wayfarer, and do not squander your wealth in the manner of a spendthrift" (17:26). In another verse, the Qur'an commands Muslims to spend in charity "for your kin, for orphans, for the needy, for the wayfarer, for those who ask, and for the ransom of slaves" (2:177).

When distributing money in charity, it is advisable to look in one's own backyard first. When Muslims give gifts to their family members, it is still considered charity and they gain the reward for every dime or dollar spent.

FACT

In Islam, female family members are entitled to financial support from their nearest relatives. If a woman has no father or brothers, this responsibility extends to uncles, cousins, or even the community at large. Female relatives have no such responsibilities.

Benefits of Extended Family

In today's world, it is often difficult for families beyond the nuclear family unit to remain together. Due to distance and time constraints, many families gather only on annual holidays, graduations, or weddings. Some relatives may practically be strangers to one another. This leaves individuals floating without an anchor, without a sense of community.

Support and Assistance

When a larger network of relatives is close with each other physically and emotionally, any individual member can count on the entire family for support. Grandma can watch the children, uncles can help with household chores, aunts share cooking responsibilities, and every adult contributes to the larger family unit. If one member needs help, the others pitch in. If someone is ill, someone else is there to nurse him or her back to health. Such was the lifestyle of countless generations, but it has been lost to many of us in the past fifty years.

Companionship for Young and Old

When there are more adults working together in the family, the children have more role models and advisors. The children can hear their grandparents' childhood stories and feel connected to the history of the family. In return, the elders feel needed and loved. Since these relationships are lacking in today's society, some people are trying to create them artificially. Schools and retirement homes have begun partnering up in some areas, bringing the young and the old together for companionship and education.

Friends and Neighbors

Beyond our own families, there are others who are deserving of our respect and attention. Part of being a good Muslim is paying particular attention to one's neighbors. When sharing a common area with someone, regardless of their religious affiliation, Muslims strive to be friendly and kind. Robert Frost's expression, "Good fences make good neighbors," does not apply in Islam. Rather, Islam subscribes to the "neighborhood watch" kind of attitude toward neighborly relations.

Muhammad once had a non-Muslim neighbor who would dump trash on his doorstep every single day. One morning, he left his home to find that there was no trash there. Concerned, he visited the woman's home to inquire about her health. Sure enough, she was very ill. She was moved by his concern, and later embraced Islam.

In Islam, neighbors should be attentive to each other and protect each other. Our close proximity to our neighbors can either result in friendship or conflict. The Prophet Muhammad once said, "He is not a believer, who eats his fill while his neighbor beside him is hungry." Neighbors should check on each other, and assist each other. Another time, the Prophet Muhammad forcefully said, "He is not a believer! He is not a believer! He is not a believer!" When the people asked him what he meant, he said that he was speaking of "the one whose neighbor does not feel safe from his evil."

Islamic Inheritance Laws

The Qur'an outlined Islamic inheritance laws to ensure that no person is denied what is rightfully due to him or her. The formulas for calculating inheritance are rather complicated. In all cases, the Qur'an makes clear that distribution of inheritance is done "after the payment of legacies and debts" (4:11). The rights of a lender have priority over the rights of the heirs, unless the debt is forgiven.

Half for Girls?

There is much debate over one aspect of Islamic inheritance law: the erroneous claim that boys are "worth" twice as much as girls. The verse in question is: "Allah thus directs you as regards your children's inheritance: to the male, a portion equal to that of two females" (4:11).

When considering this law, one must keep in mind the whole Islamic economic system, of which inheritance law is just one part. Women have the freedom and right to work and receive earnings. However, they are not obligated to spend their money on the family's needs. Men bear the sole burden of financially supporting every member of the family. So in essence, the money he earns is not his alone, but the whole family's.

The same is true of inheritance. The men of the family are obligated to use any income, including inheritance, to provide financial support to the entire family. Women receive their inheritance with no strings attached, no financial obligations to fulfill. Therefore, Muslims see it as only fair that the amounts be adjusted to reflect this reality. Among Muslims, this rule is not considered derogatory to women, but rather is an affirmation of their rights and freedoms.

In addition, this ruling applies only when children (brothers and sisters) are inheriting from their parents. When parents are heirs to their deceased children's estate, the male and female divisions (for mother and father) are equal. This indicates that the legal ruling is not a matter of men being better or worth twice as much as women. Rather, it has to do with a young man's financial obligations to his other family members after his parents are gone.

Before the coming of Islam, women themselves were objects of inheritance, part of the estate to be divvied up. The Qur'an abolished this practice: "From what is left by parents and near relatives, there is a share for men and a share for women—whether the property be small or large—a determinate share" (4:7). This was a revolutionary idea at the time; indeed, in many parts of the world women gained inheritance rights only in recent times.

In financial dealings, women are generally on an equal footing with men. There is equal pay for equal work, equal rights to own and dispose of property, and so forth. It is only in specific circumstances of inheritance that a man might be given more than a woman, to compensate for greater financial obligations in the future.

Life Insurance

As a concept, life insurance is forbidden in Islam. There are two reasons for this. First of all, only God knows the date and place of our impending death, and to seek some sort of protection in matters of death is considered "gambling" on God. This is unsavory, particularly if the contract involves the collection or payment of interest funds. Secondly, in the Islamic social system, there is no need for this extra protection. Individuals are cared for and protected by the circle of family, and in the absence of family, the wider community. If all else fails, zakat (alms) may be used by the state to assist people in need.

Nevertheless, Muslims are advised to put away money for their family's care in the event of their death, and some have organized Islamically acceptable insurance programs that involve mutual investment and cooperative risk.

Complicated Calculations

As a system of law, inheritance in Islam is a complex financial calculation. As the Qur'an stipulates, there is a "determinate share" for each member of the family. The estate of the deceased is divided, according to formula, among his or her parents, children, spouse, and siblings. Depending on the number of children and siblings, and what surviving relatives are to be included, the shares of inheritance may vary from situation to situation.

FACT

According to a tradition of the Prophet Muhammad, Muslims may bequeath up to one-third of their estate in a written will to any person or organization of their choosing. In addition, transfers of estate may be done at any time during a person's lifetime.

The Qur'an specifies: ". . . if only daughters, two or more, their share is two thirds of the inheritance; if only one, her share is a half. For parents, a sixth share of the inheritance to each, if the deceased left children; if no children, and the parents are the only heirs, the mother has a third. If the deceased left brothers or sisters, the mother has a sixth" (4:11). In a large family, the calculation can get very complicated. However, Muslims attempt to be fair and distribute the estate according to the law and the wishes of the deceased.

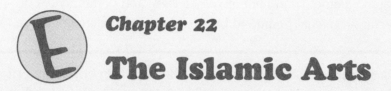

Chapter 22

The Islamic Arts

Many faiths use art to express religious ideas, from paintings of biblical scenes to sculptures of Buddha and beautiful Shinto temples. Islam's restriction on the use of religious imagery has led to the development of a unique approach to the arts. Some of the most beautiful calligraphy, architecture, tile work, and tapestries have come from the Muslim world.

Islamic Restrictions in the Arts

Islam takes a firm stand against idolatry in any form. As a result, Islamic artisans moved away from the portrayal of people through painting and sculpture, and developed their skills in other, more acceptable areas and mediums. The alternative art forms that developed in the Muslim world—calligraphy, geometric and arabesque design, and certain types of architecture—eventually came to be associated with Islamic culture.

ALERT!

Islam prohibits "image-making"—the sculpting or painting of figures such as people or animals. Muhammad once said that people who make such images will be punished on the Day of Resurrection, and that they will be asked to "make alive what you have created." Of course, they will be unable to do so.

For the most part, Islamic art is the work of anonymous artists. Religious humility and a focus on the art (rather than the artist) meant that artisans rarely signed their work.

Forbidden Arts

To avoid any perception of idolatry, certain art forms and styles are forbidden in Islam. Any use of figurative art is forbidden, particularly statues, paintings, or other representations of living things. Islam takes the position that such objects have often been used to glorify or idolize people or creatures, in violation of God's law against idolatry. Thus, anything that can be construed as an idol is forbidden. In addition, an artist takes pride in his "creation," while Muslims recognize that God Alone is the One Who creates all things. The conventions of Islamic art developed and flourished around these restrictions.

Encouraged Arts

The Qur'an warns against people becoming consumed by or passionate about the arts at the expense of their spiritual study. Those who are gifted in music are often advised to study the precise recitation techniques of the Qur'an. Those with an interest in poetry are encouraged to study the Qur'an as the supreme example of the classical Arabic language. Arts that have a direct relation to faith—calligraphic writing of the Qur'an, architectural design of mosques—are also encouraged. As with all things, Islam recommends moderation and the use of talent toward spiritual pursuits.

The Art of Calligraphy

Calligraphy is a highly respected and important art form in Islamic culture because of its role in recording the Word of God in the Qur'an. The very first words revealed of the Qur'an itself encouraged people to read and indicated that God teaches human beings "by the pen." As the Qur'an is so central to the faith of Islam, it was only natural that the highest art forms would develop around its preservation and beautification.

Arabic calligraphy developed as a way of beautifying the holy words of the Qur'an, but later came to be used for more mundane and secular purposes as well. While most early calligraphy was done in Arabic, the intricate script came to be applied to other languages that were part of the Islamic empire, including Persian, Turkish, and Urdu.

This application of beautiful writing also extended to other arts, including inscriptions on pottery, textiles, and architectural monuments. These inscriptions may include verses of the Qur'an, traditions of Muhammad, or other words of God's praise. Nearly all Islamic buildings have some inscription, often as a frame around doorways or ceilings, and a number of different writing styles may appear in different places. This gives variety and texture while attesting to the religious purposes of the building.

FACT

Muhammad Zakariya is known throughout the world for his beautiful calligraphy works. A California native, Zakariya developed his art through decades of study in Morocco, England, and Turkey. In 2001, his work was featured on the U.S. Postal Service's first Eid (Islamic festival) stamp celebrating Eid al-Adha and Eid al-Fitr.

Calligraphy Styles

Arabic is a purely cursive script, written from right to left. The letters flow through angles and curves, and can be shaped in a variety of ways and still be legible. Thus, Arabic script calligraphy can take on many styles, each developed to meet the demands of different occasions.

Each calligraphic style relies on geometic principles to make the words symmetrical and easy to read. The more rigid and angular scripts, such as the Kufi, were popular in the early Islamic world. The more cursive and rounded scripts, such as the Thuluth and Deewani, are considered more ornamental and beautiful. The most popular style for writing the Qur'an is known as the Naskh script, because the words are well spaced and easy to read. This style was developed into an art form in sixteenth-century Turkey.

Illumination Techniques

As the various scripts developed, so too did additional techniques used to adorn the pages of the Qur'an and other important manuscripts. Gilded gold leaf and colored inks provided texture and visually enhanced the calligraphy of the Qur'an. Producing a fully illuminated, calligraphic manuscript was a time-consuming project. Such effort would usually be exerted to produce only the most holy religious texts.

Illumination of the Qur'an was done in moderation, so that it did not distract the reader or detract from the meaning of the words. The most brilliant illumination was used sparingly, to mark the divisions between verses, to highlight chapter headings, or to frame an entire page or book cover.

Geometric and Arabesque Design

Decoration is a major factor in Islamic architecture and design. Islamic artists developed complex geometric designs to cover surfaces, using symmetry and repetition to extend the intricate patterns. Islamic artisans used mathematical precision to produce decorative tile work, architecture, tapestries, and even the page borders of books. Geometric designers made use of circles, squares, and triangles of various sizes and colors, to create sophisticated patterns of mosaics.

Muslim artisans also perfected the technique of creating decorative motifs of flowers, vines, and other graphics in precise geometric patterns. These "arabesque" motifs often cover walls, pottery, and other decorative objects. The floral designs were not just scribbled down; they were often very precise botanical drawings of flowering plants and vines. Again, these patterns and designs are governed by geometric and mathematical principles. The vines curve around and split off at very precise angles.

Muslim artisans rarely use just one technique or medium to decorate an object or building. One will find inscriptions in calligraphy, framed in arabesque designs, above a doorway decorated with mosaic tiles, leading to a hallway covered in Oriental carpets. While this may seem like it would be an overwhelming visual clash, Muslim artists and architects have been careful to reproduce patterns, follow decorative schemes, and create fluidity of space. The designs are multifaceted and multilayered, resulting in a sophisticated weave of connecting patterns.

Zillij (Slippery Tile)

A stroll through central Fez, Morocco, will delight the eye with shimmering patterns of color and texture, called *zillij*. The word "zillij" comes from the Arabic word for "slippery tile," which describes the smooth (or slippery) ceramic tile pieces that create the colorful patterns. Zillij uses intricate tile patterns to decorate a surface, often a wall, floor, or fountain. In Fez, these geometric tile works decorate mosques, homes, schools, and city streets.

To make a zillij tile work, a craftsman first bakes clay tile squares, mixing natural pigment to glaze them in various colors. Then the tiles are hand-cut into the many shapes needed for the pattern: stars, triangles, chevrons, hexagons, octagons, diamonds, and so on—zillij makes use of as many as 360 different geometric shapes, in dozens of different colors.

After cutting all the tile pieces, a layout artist spends days, or even weeks, arranging the thousands of tiny pieces on the floor, upside-down. Then concrete is poured over the whole thing. When the concrete dries, the panel can be lifted to expose the pattern on the other side. The panel is then installed in a floor, wall, or fountain.

FACT

By the thirteenth century, there were almost 200 ceramic workshops in Fez. The craft of zillij reached its peak during the fifteenth and sixteenth centuries, but is still being done today.

Other Visual Arts

The other visual arts in Islamic culture are generally abstracts or landscapes. Muslims generally frown on the painting or sculpture of living beings, even if the motives of the artist are pure. Any images of living things are considered "graven images" in religious terms. Historically, however, miniatures and portraits have been done in the Muslim world, particularly in Persia and Turkey.

Today, there is some debate in Islamic circles about whether even photography is permitted, and scholars debate over whether the photographer is creating an image, or merely a "shadow" of an image. As with all things, most Muslims choose a path of moderation and stick to what they know for sure is acceptable. Most Muslims will not hang photos or portraits on the walls of their home, but may keep personal photos in a private album.

Tapestries and Carpets

One of the best-known art forms in the Muslim world is the "oriental" carpet. The most famous of these carpets, known as "Persian" carpets, come from Iran. Ancient carpets are difficult to preserve, but examples have been saved of tapestries dating back to the sixteenth century. They are part of the artistic heritage of Persia, Turkey, Central Asia, Afghanistan, India, and China.

The carpets are traditionally decorated with arabesque and geometic design, figures, and bright colors. They are made by stretching the wool or silk threads on a loom, and then knotting them in rows and shearing the pile. The value of the carpet depends on how tightly the rug has been knotted, the more knots the better. A valuable oriental rug could contain more than 500 to 1,000 knots per square inch.

While these carpets are typically considered luxurious in the Western world, they are very commonplace in many Muslim countries. They cover the floors of many mosques, libraries, homes, and even city streets. One of the most famous historical carpets is the Ardabil Carpet, which has been preserved in London's Victoria and Albert Museum. This carpet dates back to 1539–1540, and was designed and commissioned by Maqsud of Kashan. Their design is typical of many oriental carpets, with flowers, pendants, medallions, leafy vines, and vibrant colors.

Mosques and Palaces

Examples of Islamic architecture can be found throughout the ancient and modern Muslim world, from Spain and Africa to Indonesia and China. Islamic architecture really began to flourish during the Umayyad dynasty (661–750 C.E.), a time that saw the construction of the Dome of the Rock in Jerusalem and the Great Mosque of Damascus.

Later designers were commissioned to build huge and luxurious palaces. These were often embellished and decorated with mosaic tile work, wood lattice carvings, and beautiful tapestries. The Alhambra in Granada, Spain, is the best-known example of the beautiful architecture and landscaping of the period.

Elements of Islamic Architecture

Islamic architecture developed as a combination of styles and techniques that were borrowed from throughout the Muslim lands and combined in a unique artistic approach. There are some common techniques and styles that distinguish Islamic architecture from other types. Many of these developed around mosque architecture due to a combination of spiritual, practical, and aesthetic needs.

Inner space is more important in Islamic architecture than exterior space. Courtyards surrounded by outer walls are common, both for large congregational open-air gatherings, and in homes to allow an area of privacy for the residents. Mosque prayer halls were large and bare, but lavishly decorated with tile work, ornamental pillars, and beautiful oriental rugs. *Muqarnas,* a honeycomblike architectural feature, helped to reflect light and open the space. The minaret, a slender tower reaching from a corner of the building, initially functioned as a high place from which to call the people to prayer. In modern times, speakers and stereo systems assist the mu'adhin in amplifying his voice; the minaret retains this function in merely a symbolic and traditional sense.

Masterpieces of Islamic Architecture

The Muslim world has produced many ancient and modern examples of beautiful architectural design and function. Among them are:

- The Dome of the Rock, Jerusalem, 692 C.E.
- The Alhambra, Granada, Spain, 1238 C.E.
- The Selimiye Mosque, Edirne, Turkey, 1574 C.E.
- The Taj Mahal, India, 1647 C.E.

Islamic Music

Islamic music is traditionally based on the human voice, sometimes accompanied by a simple drum. According to several traditions, Muhammad forbade the Muslims from playing or listening to musical instruments, such as wind or string instruments. He reportedly said, "From among my followers there will be some people who will consider illegal sexual intercourse, the wearing of silk, the drinking of alcoholic drinks, and the use of musical instruments as lawful."

Muslim scholars vary in their disapproval of music. Some say that it is outright forbidden, and others say that it is merely disapproved of. The reason for the disapproval of music is the effect it has on the listener. Music is designed to appeal to a person's soul and emotions, and a person can become "lost" or waste hours of time that could be spent on more productive pursuits (not to mention the money saved on tapes and CDs). Instead of music, Muslims are encouraged to fill their hearts and minds with recitation of the Qur'an and the remembrance of God.

ALERT!

When reciting the Qur'an, Muslims beautify the words with their voice, according to the instruction in the Qur'an: ". . . and recite the Qur'an in slow, measured, rhythmic tones" (73:4). To the untrained ear, this often sounds like singing, but is actually a very careful and precise method of recitation.

However, it is universally accepted for Muslims to sing and use an open drum known as the *daff* at appropriate times and with appropriate decorum. The traditional daff is similar to a tambourine, with the skin drawn tight on one side, but without the rattles. Muslims often sing at celebrations such as weddings or religious holidays, using words that promote virtues of faith, family, and other innocent themes. Muhammad himself approved of this practice.

Islamic songs must keep within the moral bounds of Islam; no licentious or suggestive lyrics are allowed. Songs with an Islamic theme are known as *nasheed,* a word that means "to seek," but also "to sing." Generally, nasheed carry themes about God, the natural world, and the seeking of God's guidance.

Faith in Literature

Books and literature have always flourished in Muslim countries. Written texts became widely available after paper was introduced from China in 751 C.E.—much earlier than in other parts of the world. Private and public libraries thrived, as did institutions of scholarship and study. Of course, the Qur'an is considered the most eloquent work in the Arabic language and the most profound piece of Islamic literature.

Islamic Poetry

Prior to Islam, the Arab people were known to be articulate and moving storytellers and poets. The art of verbal expression was very popular; people would gather to hear folktales, recite humor and proverbs, and share oral history. In pre-Islamic Mecca, annual fairs would be held in which poetry contests and storytelling were the main attraction. Arabic is a naturally poetic language with a wealth of expressive power, and those who master the art of fine poetry are often highly regarded.

Omar Al-Khayyam

It is rare for a person to excel in science as well as in poetry. Omar Al-Khayyam (1044–1123 C.E.), a Persian, is well known for both. Al-Khayyam means "tent-maker." He may have practiced that trade at one time, but he went on to make remarkable contributions in the fields of mathematics, astronomy, and physics. Omar Al-Khayyam was also a philosopher and poet. His most known poetic work, the *Rubaiyat,* is an extensive collection of four-line stanzas. Edward Fitzgerald rendered this work into English in 1859.

FACT

In one of his poems, Al-Khayyam wrote:

When events unfold with calm and ease;
When the winds that blow are merely breeze;
Learn from nature, from birds and bees;
Live your life in love, and let joy not cease.

Mahmoud Darwish

In more modern times, one of the best-known Muslim poets comes from the Arab world. Mahmoud Darwish, a native of Palestine, later lived in Egypt, Lebanon, Cyprus, and Paris. He returned to the West Bank in 1996, and has become known as a leading contemporary poet of the region. His poems generally express the plight of his people, search for identity, and lamentations of loss.

Mahmoud Darwish's poetry has filled over two dozen books, and has won several international writing awards: the Lotus Prize (1969), the Ibn Sina Prize (1982), the Lenin Peace Prize (1983), and the Lannan Foundation Prize for Cultural Freedom (2001). While his work has been translated into over twenty languages, his work has just begun to gain acceptance in the English-speaking world.

Mahmoud Darwish's twenty books of poetry include: *The Adam of Two Edens, Diwan, A Bed for the Stranger,* and *Eleven Planets.* Another book, *Memory for Forgetfulness*, is a collection of prose poems recounting the 1982 Israeli invasion of Lebanon.

Arabic Proverbs

Early Arab and Muslim orators would recite or write traditional proverbs, poetic sayings, and similes. These clever expressions are used in all cultures to impart some wisdom or human truth in a witty and clever way. While many are expressed similarly in all cultures, some are unique:

- An army of sheep led by a lion would defeat an army of lions led by a sheep.
- All sunshine makes a desert.
- When your son is young, discipline him; when he grows older, be a brother to him.
- Live together as brothers, and do business as strangers.
- The eye cannot go any higher than the brow.
- If your friend is like honey, then don't lick all of it (don't take advantage of it).
- One hand doesn't clap.

Chapter 23

A Faith of Exploration and Discovery

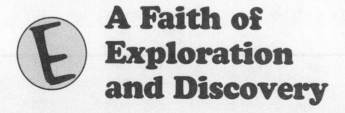

From the beginning, Islam has encouraged its followers to engage in intellectual pursuits and scientific exploration. Throughout its history, the Muslim world made vital contributions to science and medicine, philosophy and the arts. This was possible because of a natural harmony between faith and science.

Islam's Intellectual Tradition

People are never asked to blindly follow the teachings of Islam without contemplating and analyzing their validity. The Qur'an is repeatedly addressed to "people of knowledge" and "those endued with understanding." The Qur'an challenges all people to listen to and evaluate the message of Islam based on sound evidence and reasoning.

FACT

In Islam, education is mandatory for all people. Muhammad encouraged his followers to "seek knowledge, even unto China," meaning that one should travel as far as necessary to attain learning. Over time, the Muslim world did just that.

The Signs of Allah

The Qur'an encourages Muslims to seek out an understanding of the universe so that they might come to see the "Signs of Allah" in the natural world. The Qur'an asks people to contemplate the laws of nature, the intricate balance in which the universe exists, down to the minutest detail. This is cited as evidence of Allah's power and wisdom in His creation:

> Behold! In the creation of the heavens and the earth; in the alternation of the night and the day; in the sailing of ships through the ocean for the profit of mankind; in the rain which Allah sends down from the skies; and the life which He gives therewith to an earth that is dead; in the beasts of all kinds that He scatters through the earth; in the change of the winds, and the clouds which they trail like their slaves between the sky and the earth— Here indeed are Signs for a people that are wise. (Qur'an 2:164)

Questioning Is Encouraged

Muslims are encouraged to discuss Islam's teachings, seek answers, defend their opinions, and reason out questions in their minds. Muslims honor differences of opinion and respect disagreements as necessary in the pursuit of knowledge. The Prophet Muhammad once remarked,

"Differences [of opinion] in my ummah are a blessing." Entire books are written for Muslims about how to disagree with each other, and how to respect intellectual tradition.

One of the most renowned is *The Ethics of Disagreement in Islam,* by Taha al-Alwani, a work that explores the history of Islamic analytical debate and discussion. Al-Alwani emphasizes that the early Muslims did not depend on blind imitation—they questioned, presented evidence, and evaluated positions, always in an air of respect and humility.

At the same time, Muslims are warned against asking too many questions about things that are not meant to be part of human knowledge. Muhammad once told his companions that Allah hates the "asking of too many questions" in regards to religious matters, such as the nature of Allah, or the secrets of the unseen world. When it comes to Allah, there are some things that are beyond the reaches of human comprehension.

Scientific Knowledge in the Qur'an

Muslims find that the Qur'an itself contains references to scientific processes and natural laws, many of which were unknown to the world at the time of its revelation. Muslims do not therefore find a conflict between their holy text and the findings of modern science. The Qur'an itself testifies to this harmony of faith and knowledge: "Do they not consider the Qur'an? Had it been from any other than God, they would surely have found therein much discrepancy" (4:82).

The Universe

According to the Qur'an, Allah created the universe in an explosion that caused Earth and the heavenly bodies to form in perfect harmony and order: "Do the unbelievers not see that the heavens and earth were joined together [as one unit of creation], before We ripped them asunder? And We made from water every living thing. Will they not then believe?" (21:30).

In another verse, the universe is described as having been "smoke" that came together before being "ripped asunder" in an explosion (41:11). In verse 51:47, there is reference to Allah continuing to "expand" the sky.

These descriptions are found to be in accordance with modern theories regarding the Big Bang, the continued expansion of the universe, and the origins of life in water.

The following Qur'anic description of the sun and Earth's orbits was later found to be in agreement with scientific studies: "It is He Who created the night and the day, and the sun and the moon. All of the celestial bodies swim along, each in its rounded course" (21:33).

Development of Life

In the Qur'an, Allah is described as the Creator who developed life in "stages." These stages are not specified, but are described as being thousands upon thousands of years of time as we know it. While Islam teaches that Adam and Eve were the first humans, it leaves open the idea of the development of life in general over time. "And Allah has created every living thing from water. Of them are some that creep on their bellies; some that walk on two legs; and some that walk on four. Allah creates what He wills, for verily Allah has power over all things" (24:45).

The Qur'an also gives specific descriptions of the development of human beings in their mothers' wombs. "We reproduced him [humans] from a tiny drop, that is placed into a place of rest, firmly fixed. Then We made the drop into a hanging clot [embryo], then developed the hanging clot [embryo] into a lump [fetus]. Then We made the lump [fetus] into bones, and covered the bones with flesh. We thus developed out of it a new creature. So blessed be Allah, the best to create!" (23:12–14). Another verse describes the fetus as being developed "in stages, one after another, in three veils of darkness" (39:6). Some scholars now interpret this as referring to the abdominal wall, the uterine wall, and the placenta.

Other verses of the Qur'an describe the formation of mountains, or make reference to the nature of air and water currents. Some might argue that these verses are vague enough to be open to interpretation. Indeed, interpretation of these verses has changed over time, as new scientific discoveries have been made. However, Muslims believe that it is highly improbable that the Qur'an should use these terms and language based on the level of scientific knowledge of the time. Most important, none of the verses has been found to be in direct contradiction with current scientific knowledge.

These references to the "signs" of God have served as inspiration and a challenge for generations of Muslims to learn more about the natural world and the laws that govern it. Muslims study not just for the sake of knowledge, but to better understand Allah's order so that humans can maintain the intricate balance that Allah has set in place.

Islamic Education

In the early centuries of Islam, Muslims set out to establish a society based on justice and the pursuit of knowledge. At the height of the Islamic empire, the Muslim world was the center for learning. From all over the world, scholars of many faiths traveled to the large Muslim cities to participate in the research and scholarly exchanges that were taking place. Indeed, several centers of learning developed that gathered students, teachers, and researchers to live and study together. They were the first organized schools in the Muslim world.

The Early Madrasah

In the early years of Islam, those with religious knowledge would informally tutor a group of students. Over time, more formal institutions of education were founded. The *madrasahs,* or schools for the training of religious and societal leaders, still exist today.

ALERT!

Islam places a very high value on literacy. Even during the early years, when Muslims were engaged in wars of defense, enemy prisoners of war could earn their freedom by teaching ten young Muslims how to read and write.

Madrasahs brought together young students to study, live, and learn from resident scholars. The Qur'an was the foundation of the curriculum. While learning to read and write the classical Arabic language, students were also instructed in Islamic beliefs, law, and behavior. This served as a foundation for all future studies.

There were several fundamental principles of the madrasah. First was the idea that all knowledge must be based on a strong spiritual foundation. Secondly, education was to be open to all, including both boys and girls, on equal terms. Students were not required to pay tuition; all costs (including room and board) were subsidized by the Islamic government and local rulers. Finally, while religious studies served as a foundation, the curriculum also included many other disciplines, including literature and poetry, mathematics and astronomy, chemistry and the natural sciences.

Bayt al-Hikmah

For adult education, one of the most remarkable assemblies of scholars took place in Baghdad, at the Bayt al-Hikmah ("House of Wisdom"), organized by Caliph al-Mamun, the son of Harun al-Rashid. In the eighth century, he received permission from the Byzantine emperor to access the libraries of Constantinople and other cities. Scholars were dispatched to collect the scientific and philosophical manuscripts of the Ancient Greeks, which were brought back to Baghdad for translation and study.

At Bayt al-Hikmah, scholars from around the world gathered to translate the Greek manuscripts and conduct their own independent research in the free academic environment. These scholars made incredible achievements in mathematics, geometry, astronomy, and medicine. Most of them were generalists, not specializing in a particular field of study. It was not uncommon for one person to write treatises on subjects as diverse as rainfall, animal husbandry, and human anatomy.

FACT

The Quarouiyine (Karouine) University in Fez, Morocco, has the distinction of being the oldest university in the Western world that still remains in use today. This center of learning was founded by a Muslim woman, Fatima El-Fihria, in 859 C.E.

Famous Muslim Scientists

The Muslim world did more than just translate ancient works and pass them on to Europe at the end of the Dark Ages. Over the centuries, these works were studied, incorporated into the current framework of knowledge, and then expounded. The scholars of Bayt al-Hikmah and other centers of learning were heavily involved in original research and discoveries. Among the most notable were the introduction of Arabic numerals, the study of algebra, medical anatomical drawings, advances in optics, geographical maps, and the production of several scientific instruments, such as the astrolabe (used in ancient times to determine the position of the sun and stars).

Medicine

Islamic scholars took up the study of Greek medicine very early on. Translators at Bayt al-Hikmah worked diligently to translate the works of Hippocrates, Dioscorides, Galen, and others into Arabic. At the same time, the first modern hospitals were established throughout the Islamic world. Harun al-Rashid (founder of Bayt al-Hikmah) created the first modern hospital in Baghdad in 805 C.E. Libraries and medical schools were connected to the larger hospitals, and medical students put into direct practice what they had been learning from master physicians.

Abu Bakr Al-Razi is one of the best-known contributors to medical knowledge. A native of Persia, Al-Razi traveled to Baghdad to study medicine and later became director of a large hospital there. He wrote over 200 books, and was a master of observation and experimental medicine. He is attributed with great discoveries and treatises on subjects as diverse as pediatrics, oral hygiene, smallpox, measles, allergies, scabies, and kidney stones.

Another great Muslim medical scholar is known in the West as Avicenna. Abu Ali ibn Sina was born in tenth-century Bukhara, Persia (present-day Uzbekistan). Ibn Sina was a young prodigy, engaging in studies of medicine, philosophy, and poetry. By the age of eighteen, he was well known as a great physician, and was summoned to treat the Samanid royal family.

Ibn Sina's masterpiece work was titled *The Canon of Medicine*. This encyclopedia of all medical knowledge of the time consisted of over a million words, and included summaries of Greek medicine, anatomical drawings, descriptions of diseases and their cures, and an outline of 760 medicinal plants and the drugs that could be derived from them. This monumental work was translated into many languages and served as the main medical textbook and teaching guide until the mid-nineteenth century.

In addition to the works of these two great medical authorities, the works of over 400 other physicians and authors were translated into European languages. All had a great impact on the future of medicine.

Astronomy

The study of astronomy developed in Islamic society because of a religious need. Scholars needed to observe and study the sun and moon in order to determine the months of the lunar calendar, to figure out the prayer and fasting times, and to find the direction of the qiblah (direction of Mecca for prayer). Islamic scholars mapped the celestial sky, figured celestial orbits, and questioned the accuracy of Ptolemy's theories.

FACT

The Muslim physicist Ibn Al-Haytham (965–1040 C.E.) calculated the height of Earth's atmosphere at 52,000 paces, which is equivalent to about thirty-two miles. His calculations were very accurate for the time; modern scholarship has concluded that the atmosphere extends thirty-one miles from Earth.

Muslim scientists built observatories all over the Islamic world, and took to refining and revising Ptolemy's catalog and coordinates for the stars. Muslim scholars also excelled in making astronomical instruments. In the eleventh century, Nasir Al-Tusi of Baghdad invented the Azimuth Quadrant and the Torquetum, early instruments used to compute and measure star positions. Indeed, the word "azimuth" comes from the Arabic word *as-sumut,* which means "compass bearings."

Mathematics

The study of mathematics was closely connected to working out astronomical problems and calculations of physics. Mathematics was a specialty of the early Islamic scholars, and the Muslim world developed many well-known mathematicians.

QUESTION?

Why are modern numerals called "Arabic numerals"?
The numerals we use today originated in India, but were transmitted to the Western world by Arab Muslim scholars in the eighth century. Muslim mathematicians improved on the system by developing the cipher (*sifr*), or zero.

One of the greatest mathematicians that ever lived was Abu Abdullah al-Khawarizmi. Born in modern-day Uzbekistan, he was raised near Baghdad and was associated with the great institutions of learning there. Al-Khawarizmi is known as the founder of algebra, a word that comes from the title of a book that he wrote on the subject, *Al-Jabr wa al-Muqabilah* (The Book of Integration and Equation), and for introducing the concept of an algorithm (the term "algorithm" comes from his last name).

Al-Khawarizmi brought together the prevailing knowledge of the time, and enriched it with his unique contributions. He developed solutions for linear and quadratic equations, detailed trigonometric tables, and many geometric and arithmetical concepts.

Another famous mathematician, Abu Raihan Al-Biruni, was born in modern-day Uzbekistan in 973 C.E. He studied several languages (Greek, Syriac, Sanskrit) and was a contemporary of the famous physician Ibn Sina. Al-Biruni made such extensive contributions to science that an index of his written works would cover more than sixty pages! He wrote about Earth's rotation, made calculations of latitude and longitude, and used mathematical techniques to determine the seasons.

Al-Biruni wrote about the speed of light versus the speed of sound, and accurately determined the weights of over a dozen elements and compounds. He studied angles, trigonometry, and the Indian numeral system. Like all other Muslim scholars of the time, his interests were diverse. He also wrote about botany, ancient history, and geography.

Geography

Many Muslim scientists were involved in the development of geographical knowledge. Muslims were among the first to calculate Earth's circumference, publish detailed world maps, and study elements and minerals. Muslim geographers traveled all over the world to gather data.

Mathematician al-Khawarizmi also contributed to the field of geography. Under his leadership, seventy geographers worked together to produce the first map of the globe, in 830 C.E. One of the better-known geographers was Al-Idrisi, who grew up in Muslim Spain in the early twelfth century. Al-Idrisi was educated in Cordoba, and was hired to produce a world map for the Norman King of Sicily, Roger II. Several of Al-Idrisi's books were translated into Latin, and his work spread rapidly through Europe. Christopher Columbus used a map that was derived from Al-Idrisi's work in his explorations of the New World.

English Words of Arabic Origin

The Muslim world had an incredible influence on the discovery and development of modern scientific ideas. This influence is reflected in the many English words that originated from the Arabic language.

Words of Arabic Origin	
English	**Arabic**
admiral	*amir*
alchemy	*al-kimiya*
alcohol	*al-kohl*
alcove	*al-qubba*
algebra	*al-Jabr* (from a book title by al-Khawarizmi)
algorithm	al-Khawarizmi (mathematician who introduced the concept)
almanac	*al-manaakh*
atlas	*atlas*
camphor	*kafur*
cipher/zero	*sifr*
cornea	*al-qarniya*
cotton	*al-qutn*
elixir	*al-aksir*
gauze	*al-gazz*
monsoon	*mawsim*
safari	*safara*
sofa	*suffa*
talc	*talq*
typhoon	*tufaan*
vizier	*waxir*
zenith	*semit*

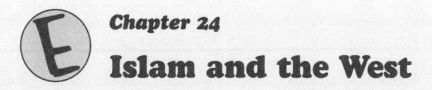

Chapter 24

Islam and the West

Throughout history, Islam has had a tenuous relationship with the Western, non-Muslim world. Centuries of conflict have left slow-healing wounds and have deepened the misunderstanding and mistrust. However, recent years have brought about a reassessment of Islam from within the Muslim community, and with it the hope that Muslims can improve their relationship with other communities of the world.

Centuries of Conflict

Conflict stems from fear and mistrust. In the early years, the message of Islam spread rapidly throughout the world, catching everyone off guard. Leaders of the Roman and Byzantine Empires were astounded by the fast expansion of Islamic civilization. Unwilling to relinquish power to this "infidel" force, the Christian world braced for conflict. Legends were born about unspeakable horrors that the Christians were suffering at the hands of Muslims. Fears and prejudices falsified history, and planted seeds of mistrust that persist to this day. Collective memories of the Crusades and colonial campaigns, their bitter betrayals and their unspeakable losses, linger in the hearts of many.

Early Expansion of Islam

In the early years, the message of Islam spread quickly through the world. The growing Muslim nation needed to absorb a diverse population while forging relationships and treaties with existing communities. Many of the societies that came into the fold of the Islamic empire were previously suffering from great oppression, primarily at the hands of the Persian and Roman empires.

As the Islamic armies traveled through the land, they largely met no resistance from the local people. Many of the common people accepted Islam, or at the very least accepted the rule of the Islamic leaders. They were simply happy to be liberated from the tyranny of their previous rulers. In a few cases, the Muslims were invited by local villagers to liberate land from kings and warlords. In Byzantine Egypt and in Spain, the Muslims were welcomed with open arms as liberators.

The Muslim world has always been multireligious, and the Muslim state offered people freedom of worship and protection of their personal rights. This was seen most clearly in places such as Damascus, Istanbul, Muslim Spain, and the Balkans, where Muslims lived peacefully side by side with their Christian and Jewish neighbors for centuries. Exceptions to this reality were few and far between.

The Crusades

Christian leaders first decided to invade the Muslim empire in the eleventh century. Their decision was backed by an intense propaganda campaign aimed at discrediting Islam, Muhammad, and the Muslim way of life. The rallying cry was to destroy the evil Islamic empire, and the fervor with which it was carried out gave rise to numerous atrocities.

FACT

In one notable event, the Crusaders ransacked the city of Jerusalem in 1099, pillaging the Dome of the Rock and massacring thousands of civilians. While the Crusades did not achieve any lasting military results, their cultural and historical legacy remains.

Muslims Lose Spain

The Crusades were barely over when Ferdinand and Isabella embarked on an ethnic-cleansing campaign to rid Spain of Muslim influence. The model of tolerant Islamic civilization for over 800 years, the Muslims of Andalusia were exiled or wiped out in a matter of months.

In 1492, the last Muslim king left Granada. It is reported that he stopped at a hilltop and looked back for a last glimpse of the Alhambra in the distance. His mother then said to him, bitterly, "Weep like a woman for the city you could not defend like a man!"

The Era of Colonialism

The move of European powers into Muslim lands continued as Napoleon invaded Egypt, Britain entered the Arabian Peninsula, and Ferdinand de Lesseps constructed the Suez Canal. As European colonial powers continued to carve up North Africa and the Middle East, many Muslims came to feel that the Crusades never quite ended.

Bitterness continued to grow in response to the interference of European colonial nations in Muslim-dominated areas. From Egypt to Syria, Iran to Palestine, Muslims around the world began to feel that their rights to independently develop their nations had been hindered by outside forces. The perception developed that "democracy" and "self-determination" are valid for all people, except those who support Islam.

Politics of the Muslim World

In Islam, religion and politics are closely intertwined. Islam is a complete way of life, and politics is just another aspect of it on a community level. Just as it does for other areas of life, Islam provides guidance for governmental organization.

In Islam, the political system is based on several principles: sovereignty of God, accountability of government, and consultation. Muslims today find it intolerable that these principles are not being adhered to in most Muslim countries. Politics in the Muslim world are dominated by corruption, exploitation, and lack of popular support.

The Ideal: Shura

An ideal Islamic political system is based on the principle of *shura,* or mutual consultation. "Shura" comes from an Arabic word that originally meant to "extract honey from beehives," and it is also used to mean "legislative assembly." Just like obtaining honey from a hive, the process of reflection and consultation extracts new ideas from people's minds and puts them out on the table. Those ideas and opinions are as sweet as honey!

In essence, shura is simply a procedure for making decisions by consulting with others. This process can be used by any group of people, making any sort of decision. Shura is mentioned in the Qur'an, in a chapter named after this process:

> . . . those who believe and put their trust in their Lord; those who avoid the greater sins and indecencies, and when they are angry, even then forgive; those who respond to their Lord, and establish regular prayer; who conduct their affairs by mutual consultation [shura]; who spend out of what We have bestowed on them for sustenance . . . (42:36–38)

ALERT!

The process of shura can be used at the national level, for political decisions, or by any other group of people. In Islam, the family unit is also to be governed through shura, with all members of the family consulting with each other before a decision is made.

Islam agrees with the concept that people have the right to choose their rulers. This was evident in the example of Muhammad, who left it to his companions to choose his successor. Subsequently, the Sunni community continued to choose their leaders from among themselves. The exact process for this selection is not spelled out in Islamic law; it has been done differently by various groups of people in different times and places. While the structural details may vary between countries, depending on local needs, the guiding principle remains: Leaders should be chosen by the people.

God Is Supreme

To rule strictly "by the people, for the people" removes God's law and legislation, rendering it irrelevant. This places human beings in the position of God, drawing up whatever laws and regulations they deem fit and valuable. This idea is not compatible with Islam—any system accepted by Islam must recognize first and foremost the authority of God over all of humanity. Any human system that enacts law that is contrary to God's law is wholeheartedly rejected in Islam.

Central to this understanding is the recognition that Muslims do not view religion as something detached from the rest of life; religion is a way of life, encompassing every aspect of human activity. Everything is subservient to God—individuals as well as personal, social, international, and political institutions. This does not mean that every citizen within the state must be a Muslim; legislation at the heart of the Islamic system safeguards those of other faiths who live within and under the protection of the Islamic government.

Islam and Democracy

The question of whether Islam is compatible with modern ideas of democracy is hotly debated within Islamic circles. Among Muslims, there are many different theories and interpretations of the relationship between the state, democracy, and Islam. There is no consensus.

FACT

Women have held high positions of leadership in several Muslim countries: Benazir Bhutto (Prime Minister of Pakistan, 1988–1990, 1993–1996), Begum Khalida Zia (Prime Minister of Bangladesh, 1991–1996), Sheikh Hasina (Prime Minister of Bangladesh, 1996– present), Megawati Sukarnoputri (President of Indonesia, 2001– present), Massumeh Ebtekar (Vice President of Iran, 1997–present), and Tansu Ciller (Prime Minister of Turkey, 1993–1996).

On the surface, one might think that the process of mutual consultation is strikingly similar to the ideas of "by the people, for the people." However, in most modern democracies, it is believed that religion should be entirely separated from public policy, and should have no weight in the decision-making or legislative process. This is the fundamental difference between Islamic ideals of government and modern democratic ones. In an Islamic state, matters of faith are not only a private matter, they are the foundation of the entire system.

However, a system might be called an "Islamic democracy" if a group of Muslims mutually agree to run their society by mutual consultation, recognizing God's supremacy, and agreeing that their government will enact legislation within the limits of His guidance.

A Sample Islamic System

Many Islamic reformers envision the following structure of an "Islamic democracy": A head of state would be elected through free and open elections to serve for a fixed term of office. The shura (consulting legislative assembly) would also be freely elected. The judiciary would independently interpret Islamic law, so that there is distribution of power among the three branches of government. Human rights and civil liberties would be guaranteed, including the rights of non-Muslim religious minorities within the state.

The importance of God's law in the Islamic state places a balance between the executive, legislative, and judicial branches of modern government. As long as there is emphasis on the judicial system, the scholars of which interpret Islamic religious law, no other person can single-handedly make sweeping changes. These principles have been accepted and adopted in varying degrees by Islamic reform movements all over the world—in Tunisia, Malaysia, Bangladesh, and Morocco, to name a few.

Affecting Change

The vast majority of Muslims attempt to make change in their societies through peaceful and democratic means: establishing political parties, voting for reform, educating the public, and mobilizing campaigns. They renounce any attempts to affect change through instability, including revolutions, coup d'etats, political assassinations, or terrorism.

Lashing Out at the West

Islam looks very disapprovingly at hypocrites. Indeed, hypocrisy will earn a person the lowest depths of Hellfire. When a Muslim perceives hypocrisy, the reaction is disgust and contempt. This is the source of much of the Muslim world's disdain for the politics of many Western nations, particularly the United States. The perception is that the hypocrisy of these governments is astounding; their stance on issues depends on whether it serves their own best interests.

So what do people in the Muslim world want? For the most part, they want what everyone else does: to reclaim their independence, preserve their cultural traditions, and build their future free of any outside influences. In their frustration, some people lash out at the European and Western powers that they feel have led them to the state they are in today.

QUESTION?

Why do Muslims hate Westerners?
Muslims do not "hate" all Westerners, Americans, Christians, or Jews. Some Muslims take issue with the politics of certain countries, and direct their protest against those policies. However, good Muslims should be able to separate politics from their relationships with others on a personal level.

Islam Today

Muslims are constantly asking themselves how they can create a unified and strong community, setting an example of enlightenment to the world. They have a theoretical model to work from, as well as historical evidence that such a system was successfully achieved in Islamic history. However, outsiders seem to feel that Islam has become stuck in the past, unable to change with the times—an ancient religion that needs to be updated for the modern world. Are Muslims blindly stuck in their glorious past?

Recognizing the Need for Reform

Today, most Muslims recognize that reform is needed within the Muslim community. Throughout Islamic history, there have frequently been movements to purify and reform society and religious practice. Such an Islamic revival is beginning to take place again, as people rediscover the true Islamic basis upon which to build life, a system for rebuilding and molding their societies.

Muslims throughout the world have become more critical of their own communities, government systems, and societal structures. The rumbling that was once heard only on the street, or behind closed doors, is now entering public discourse. Muslims in the West, in particular, are raising questions about the key issues Muslims face in the world today and how to define the community in relation to those outside the faith. These issues are addressed by looking at the core teachings of the faith. There is an attempt, by civic and religious leaders around the world, to filter through cultural traditions and extreme interpretations, to focus in on what is true religious practice.

However, rather than rejecting their faith or substantially trying to change it, most Muslims see a return to the fundamentals of their faith as the path to this change. The belief is that Muslims are downtrodden in today's world because they have departed from the spirit and letter of Islamic teachings. God has not blessed them because they have abandoned their faith in Him. The answer, then, is to return to and strengthen Islam, not discard it or try to "modernize" it.

This should not be a frightening proposition for the rest of the world.

If the Muslim nations are able to get their own houses in order, then they will be able to more honestly and adequately address their relationships with the rest of the world community. If the principles of Islam are adhered to, this will be approached as a search for common ground in peace, cooperation, and justice.

ALERT!

There are several valuable and fundamental principles that shape Muslim society. They include the concepts of *tawhid* (unity), *khilafa* (trusteeship), *ijtihad* (reasoning), *ijmah* (consensus), *shura* (consultation), and *istislah* (public interest).

Self-Reflection

Islam calls upon people to engage in self-evaluation, critically looking at each of the choices we make in life. The Islamic-reform dialogue is considering the needs of the community on several levels:

How do we, as Muslims, reduce internal divisions and bickering?

How can we strengthen our social and educational institutions?

What can we, as a community, do to regain our lost sense of identity and unity?

How do we overcome apathy, pessimism, and anger?

How is Islam compatible with democracy? How can an Islamic environment be established on the basis of shura?

How should Muslims approach their grievances without resorting to violence?

All of these concerns are internal; they have nothing to do with trying to take over or destroy the Western world. On the contrary, modern reform movements have grown in reaction to internal social and economic problems. Basically, it is a reaction to the powerlessness that people feel as they are pressured toward modernity. This is compounded by the frustrating lack of a political voice, whether in their own countries or on the world political stage.

The reform that is taking place within the Muslim community must be done by and for Muslims themselves, without outside interference or criticism. The faithful must come to reform themselves in accordance with Islamic teaching. Muslims see education as the first step in combating ignorance and developing a sense of unity and identity among the faithful. This education must be established in the fundamentals of faith, manners, and rights that were followed by earlier generations of Muslims.

Certainly there is still much to be done on the political front, but the needs and desires of the masses are beginning to be heard. We can begin to look toward a brighter future, where Muslims can be free and independent of foreign domination, where Muslims live in peace with their neighbors, and where the true values of Islam are finally realized.

Coming to an Understanding

The modern world is filled with examples that seem to confirm that Islam is in a state of violent conflict with the West. Airplane hijackings, hostage taking, suicide bombings, attacks on tourists—all have come to be identified with the faith of Islam. Such incidents certainly affect the relations between the larger Muslim community and the rest of the world.

In embracing ignorant stereotypes, people fall into the trap of judging the entire faith of Islam by the conduct of a tiny fraction of its people. This is neither an objective nor truthful analysis, and cuts off the parties from future dialogue and discussion. The only way out of this trap is for everyone, Muslims and non-Muslims alike, to critically evaluate the true belief system of Islam. Look at its sources; talk to the people who practice the faith.

Finding Common Ground

Muslims may differ in their views regarding salvation, the role of prophets, original sin, and the nature of God. But like other monotheists around the world, Muslims agree that God alone is the Creator and Sustainer, and that we all depend on His mercy and guidance. Like other people of conscience, Muslims strive to do good in the world.

You have taken the first step toward understanding by reading this book. Hopefully, it has helped you realize that Islam, as a faith, has many virtuous elements and shares much in common with the other great monotheistic faiths.

Islam is in accordance with the rest of the world community in that there are certain human rights that must be guaranteed to all people:

- The security of life and property: "Your lives and properties are forbidden to one another until you meet your Lord on the Day of Resurrection" (Muhammad).
- The protection of honor: "O you who believe! Let not some men among you laugh at others . . . nor defame, nor be sarcastic to each other, nor call each other by offensive nicknames" (Qur'an 49:11).
- The sanctity and security of private life: "O you who believe! Avoid suspicion as much as possible . . . and spy not on each other, nor speak ill of each other behind their backs" (Qur'an 49:12). "O you who believe! Do not enter houses other than your own, until you have asked permission and saluted those within them" (Qur'an 24:27).
- The security of personal freedom: According to the teachings of Islam, no citizen can be imprisoned unless his or her guilt has been proved in an open court of law.
- The right to protest against tyranny: "God loves not the shouting of evil words in public speech, except by one who has been wronged" (Qur'an 4:148). "The greatest jihad is to speak the truth in the face of a tyrannical ruler" (Muhammad).
- Freedom of expression: Islam grants freedom of thought and expression to all citizens equally, on the condition that this freedom is not used for evil or wicked purposes (slander, hate speech, blasphemy, and so on).
- Freedom of association: Islam has also established the freedom to gather in assemblies or organizations, subject to certain general rules against evil or wrongdoing.
- Freedom of conscience and conviction: "Let there be no compulsion in religion" (Qur'an 2:256).

- The right to basic necessities of life: "And in their wealth there is a due share for the beggar and the deprived" (Qur'an 51:19).
- Equality before the law: In Islam, all citizens are equal before the law. "The nations that lived before you were destroyed by God because they punished the common man for their offenses, and let their dignitaries go unpunished for their crimes" (Muhammad).
- The right to participate in affairs of the state: "Those who . . . conduct their affairs by mutual consultation" (Qur'an 42:38).

A Look Within

Muslim reformers acknowledge that the Muslim world needs to make more of an effort to understand the Western world, and not blindly strike out in anger and hatred against perceived injustices. We can all benefit from looking at ourselves with a critical eye and asking these questions:

- Is there such a thing as absolute freedom? Where does one find the balance between freedom and responsibility?
- Are some cultures more "advanced" than others?
- What brings people happiness in the modern world? How has this changed over time, in all cultures?
- As civilization has progressed, have we moved too quickly, or not quickly enough? How do we feel about others who take a different pace toward change?

The first step to understanding is to get to know other people, their viewpoints, and their beliefs. By building bridges rather than erecting walls, we can foster respect and trust among all people. From that foundation, we may engage in respectful dialogue and move toward peaceful resolutions to the problems we face together in the world. Ⓔ

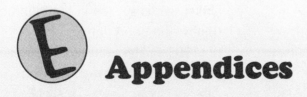

Appendices

Appendix A
Glossary of Islamic Terms

Appendix B
Islamic Organizations

Glossary of Islamic Terms

abaya: a style of overgarment often worn in the Gulf States

adhan: the Islamic call to prayer

Ahl-al-Bayt: "People of the House [of Muhammad]"; **Shi'a** Muslims

akhirah: the life of the Hereafter, as opposed to the life of this world

Al-Lat: idol worshipped by pre-Islamic Arabs

Allah: the name of Almighty God; it connotes neither gender nor plurality

Allahu Akbar: "God is Great"

aqiqah: the celebration marking the birth of a new baby

Ashura: tenth day of the Islamic month of Muharram; observed by **Shi'a** Muslims as a day of mourning

'Asr: the mid-afternoon prayer

Assalaamu 'alaykum: "peace be upon you"

Badr: a famous battle of early Islamic history in which the small Muslim army successfully defended itself against an attacking force several times its size

Bayt al-Hikmah: "The House of Wisdom," a center of learning in eighth-century Baghdad

bint: "daughter of"; used in the Arabic naming system to denote relationships between father and daughter

bismillah: "in the name of Allah"

chador: a style of overgarment that extends from the top of the head to the floor; it is often worn by women in Iran

daff: a simple open-air drum; the only musical instrument universally accepted among Muslims

da'wah: calling others to Islam

deen: living in accordance with one's faith

dhikr: words spoken in remembrance of God

Dhuhr: the noon prayer

Dhul-Hijjah: the month of pilgrimage, the twelfth month in the Islamic calendar

du'a: personal prayers or supplications

dunya: the life of this world

Eid al-Adha: the Festival of Sacrifice, which marks the end of the **Hajj**

Eid al-Fitr: the Festival of Fast-Breaking, which marks the end of **Ramadan**

Fajr: the predawn prayer

fatwa: a formal legal opinion issued by a qualified Muslim scholar

fiqh: Islamic jurisprudence

fitoor: the evening meal during **Ramadan**

fitrah: an inborn, natural predisposition toward God, which exists at birth in all human beings

ghusl: a full bath ablution

hadith: the recorded words and actions of Muhammad, compiled and authenticated by early scholars

Hajj: the Islamic pilgrimage to Mecca that a Muslim is required to perform once in a lifetime

halal: the permitted actions or foods in Islam

haram: the forbidden actions or foods in Islam

hijab: a common term for the headcovering worn by Muslim women

Hijrah: the migration from Mecca to Madinah, which marks the beginning of the Muslim calendar; also the Muslim calendar itself

Hira': the cave near Mecca where Muhammad received his first revelation

Hudaibiyah: a suburb area of Mecca where a treaty was negotiated for the Muslims to return to Mecca after having been forced out

Iblis: Satan; also called **Shaytan**

ibn: "son of"; used in the Arabic naming system to denote relationships between father and son

iddah: a waiting period that a woman observes when widowed or divorced before remarrying

ihram: the simple white clothes that Muslims wear during the **Hajj**

ijmah: legal judgments made by agreement of the companions of the Prophet, for issues that came up shortly after Muhammad's death

imam: the leader of Muslim prayers

Injeel: the revelations of Jesus

iqra': "read"; the first word of revelation given to Muhammad, and the origin of the word **Qur'an**

'Isha: the late-evening prayer

Islam: Muslim faith; term is derived from a root word meaning "peace" and "submission" to God

isra': the night journey that Muhammad made to Jerusalem

Jahannam: the punishment of Hell

Jahiliyyah: "the days of ignorance"; this term is often used to describe pre-Islamic Arabia

Jannah: the Garden of Paradise

jihad: the "struggle" to defend one's faith in the face of opposition

jilbab: the overgarment worn by Muslim women

jinn: a community of unseen beings that Allah created from fire; Satan is one of them

jizyah: a tax that non-Muslims pay to the Muslim state to compensate for their exemption from military duty and religious alms

jumu'ah: "the gathering"—the prayer that Muslim men must attend on Friday afternoon

Ka'aba: the structure in the center of Mecca, toward which Muslims face when praying

kafir: "rejecter of faith"; a non-Muslim

khalifa: caliph, a leader of the Muslim community

khimar: another term used to describe the headcovering worn by Muslim women

kunya: an honorable nickname given to parents of a child; for example, Abu Mustafa is the father of Mustafa, and Um Mustafa is the mother of Mustafa

La ilaha illa Allah wa Muhammad ar-rasulullah: "There is no god worthy of worship except Allah, and Muhammad is His messenger" (a Muslim testimony of faith)

Madinah: the city north of Mecca to which the early Muslims immigrated and where they established a Muslim state

madrasah: Islamic school

Maghrib: the sunset prayer

mahr: the wedding gift that a husband gives to his wife at the time of marriage

makrooh: undesirable or doubtful things that are best to avoid

mala'ika: the angels

Mecca: the city in modern-day Saudi Arabia that is a focal point for Muslim pilgrimage and worship

mi'raj: the ascension to Heaven that Muhammad made during his night journey to Jerusalem

mosque: a Muslim house of worship

mu'adhin: person who calls the Muslims to prayer

Muhajireen: the early Muslims who emigrated from Mecca to **Madinah**

mushrikoon: pagan

Muslim: a person who willingly submits to Allah

qiblah: the direction in which Muslims face when they are praying

qiyass: legal judgments made by Islamic scholars based on the Qur'an, Sunnah, and the opinions of the first generation of Muslims

Qur'an: the sacred revelation given to Muhammad; the holy book of Muslims

raka'at: the cycles of Muslim prayer

Ramadan: the month of fasting

sadaqah: voluntary charity

salaat: the five formal daily prayers

salaat-l-janazah: the funeral prayer

shaheed: a martyr, literally "witness"

shalwar kameez: a long tunic and pants, the style of dress that is common among both men and women in the Indian subcontinent

Shari'ah: Islamic law derived from the Qur'an and Sunnah

Shaytan: Satan; also called **Iblis**

sheikh: a tribal leader or elder; the leader of a **Sufi** community

Shi'a: those who believe that leadership of the Muslim community should have remained in Muhammad's family; approximately 15 percent of Muslims worldwide today

shirk: the sin of associating others with Allah

shura: reflection and consultation as a tool for decision-making

Sufi: a mystic trend of Islam

suhoor: the predawn meal during **Ramadan**

Sunnah: the way of life as prescribed by the teachings of Muhammad; a secondary source of Islamic law

Sunni: those who believe that leadership of the Muslim community was properly transferred to the most qualified and trustworthy person; approximately 85 percent of Muslims today

tafsir: commentary, explanation, or exegesis of the Qur'an

tahaarah: purity or cleanliness

taqwa: to approach God with reverence and piety

taraweeh: the special evening prayers observed during **Ramadan**

tarbiyyah: the religious upbringing of children

tariqa: the "path"; a **Sufi** order

Tawhid: the "unity" of Allah, the cornerstone of the faith

Tawrah: the revelation given to Moses; the Torah

Uhud: a famous battle of early Islamic history that brought a painful defeat for the small Muslim community

ummah: "nation"; worldwide Muslim community

umrah: lesser pilgrimage to Mecca made during the year, outside of the dates of **Hajj**

Wali: "protector," a woman's representative in the marriage contract

walimah: the wedding banquet or celebration

wudu: ablutions that are done before prayer

Yathrib: the ancient name of **Madinah**

youm: day or era

Youm al-Qiyama: the Day of Judgment

zabihah: meat that has been slaughtered in accordance with Islamic requirements

Zabur: the "Psalms"

zakat: required alms, paid at the rate of 2.5 percent of accumulated wealth

Zamzam: a spring in Mecca that dates back to the time of Abraham

Islamic Organizations

American Muslim Alliance (AMA)
39675 Cedar Boulevard, Suite 220E
Newark, CA 94560
510-252-9858   *www.amaweb.org*

American Muslim Council (AMC)
1212 New York Avenue NW, Suite 400
Washington, DC 20005
202-789-2262   *www.amconline.org*

Council on American-Islamic Relations (CAIR)
453 Jersey Avenue SE
Washington, DC 20003
202-488-8787   *www.cair-net.org*

Council on Islamic Education (CIE)
P.O. Box 20186
Fountain Valley, CA 92728
714-839-2929   *www.cie.org*

Institute of Islamic Information and Education (III&E)
P.O. Box 41129
Chicago, IL 60641
773-777-7443   *www.iiie.net*

International Institute of Islamic Thought
P.O. Box 669
Herndon, VA 20172
703-471-1133   *www.iiit.org*

Islamic Art and Architecture Organization
5270 Timberline Road
Columbus, OH 43220   *www.islamicart.com*

Islamic Assembly of North America (IANA)
3588 Plymouth Road
Ann Arbor, MI 48105
734-528-0006   *www.iananet.org*

Islamic Circle of North America (ICNA)
166-26 89th Avenue
Jamaica, NY 11432
718-658-1199   *www.icna.com*

Islamic Food and Nutrition Council of America
5901 North Cicero Avenue, Suite 309
Chicago, IL 60646
773-283-3708   *www.ifanca.org*

Islamic Society of North America (ISNA)
P.O. Box 38
Plainfield, IN 46168
317-839-8157   *www.isna.net*

Islamic Training Foundation
2560 Howard Drive
Sparks, NV 89434
775-355-1461   *www.islamist.org*

Latino American Dawah Organization (LADO)
www.latinodawah.org

Muslim Public Affairs Council (MPAC)
994 National Press Building
529 14th Street NW
Washington, DC 20045
202-879-6726   *www.mpac.org*

Muslim Student Association (MSA)
P.O. Box 18612
Washington, DC 20036
703-820-7900   *www.msa-natl.org*

Muslim Women's League (MWL)
3010 Wilshire Boulevard, Suite 519
Los Angeles, CA 90010
626-358-0335   *www.mwlusa.org*

Index

THE EVERYTHING SERIES!

BUSINESS & PERSONAL FINANCE

Everything® Accounting Book
Everything® Budgeting Book, 2nd Ed.
Everything® Business Planning Book
Everything® Coaching and Mentoring Book, 2nd Ed.
Everything® Fundraising Book
Everything® Get Out of Debt Book
Everything® Grant Writing Book, 2nd Ed.
Everything® Guide to Buying Foreclosures
Everything® Guide to Mortgages
Everything® Guide to Personal Finance for Single Mothers
Everything® Home-Based Business Book, 2nd Ed.
Everything® Homebuying Book, 2nd Ed.
Everything® Homeselling Book, 2nd Ed.
Everything® Human Resource Management Book
Everything® Improve Your Credit Book
Everything® Investing Book, 2nd Ed.
Everything® Landlording Book
Everything® Leadership Book, 2nd Ed.
Everything® Managing People Book, 2nd Ed.
Everything® Negotiating Book
Everything® Online Auctions Book
Everything® Online Business Book
Everything® Personal Finance Book
Everything® Personal Finance in Your 20s & 30s Book, 2nd Ed.
Everything® Project Management Book, 2nd Ed.
Everything® Real Estate Investing Book
Everything® Retirement Planning Book
Everything® Robert's Rules Book, $7.95
Everything® Selling Book
Everything® Start Your Own Business Book, 2nd Ed.
Everything® Wills & Estate Planning Book

COOKING

Everything® Barbecue Cookbook
Everything® Bartender's Book, 2nd Ed., $9.95
Everything® Calorie Counting Cookbook
Everything® Cheese Book
Everything® Chinese Cookbook
Everything® Classic Recipes Book
Everything® Cocktail Parties & Drinks Book
Everything® College Cookbook
Everything® Cooking for Baby and Toddler Book
Everything® Cooking for Two Cookbook
Everything® Diabetes Cookbook
Everything® Easy Gourmet Cookbook
Everything® Fondue Cookbook
Everything® Fondue Party Book
Everything® Gluten-Free Cookbook
Everything® Glycemic Index Cookbook
Everything® Grilling Cookbook
Everything® Healthy Meals in Minutes Cookbook
Everything® Holiday Cookbook
Everything® Indian Cookbook
Everything® Italian Cookbook

Everything® Lactose-Free Cookbook
Everything® Low-Carb Cookbook
Everything® Low-Cholesterol Cookbook
Everything® Low-Fat High-Flavor Cookbook
Everything® Low-Salt Cookbook
Everything® Meals for a Month Cookbook
Everything® Meals on a Budget Cookbook
Everything® Mediterranean Cookbook
Everything® Mexican Cookbook
Everything® No Trans Fat Cookbook
Everything® One-Pot Cookbook
Everything® Pizza Cookbook
Everything® Quick and Easy 30-Minute, 5-Ingredient Cookbook
Everything® Quick Meals Cookbook
Everything® Slow Cooker Cookbook
Everything® Slow Cooking for a Crowd Cookbook
Everything® Soup Cookbook
Everything® Stir-Fry Cookbook
Everything® Sugar-Free Cookbook
Everything® Tapas and Small Plates Cookbook
Everything® Tex-Mex Cookbook
Everything® Thai Cookbook
Everything® Vegetarian Cookbook
Everything® Whole-Grain, High-Fiber Cookbook
Everything® Wild Game Cookbook
Everything® Wine Book, 2nd Ed.

GAMES

Everything® 15-Minute Sudoku Book, $9.95
Everything® 30-Minute Sudoku Book, $9.95
Everything® Bible Crosswords Book, $9.95
Everything® Blackjack Strategy Book
Everything® Brain Strain Book, $9.95
Everything® Bridge Book
Everything® Card Games Book
Everything® Card Tricks Book, $9.95
Everything® Casino Gambling Book, 2nd Ed.
Everything® Chess Basics Book
Everything® Craps Strategy Book
Everything® Crossword and Puzzle Book
Everything® Crossword Challenge Book
Everything® Crosswords for the Beach Book, $9.95
Everything® Cryptic Crosswords Book, $9.95
Everything® Cryptograms Book, $9.95
Everything® Easy Crosswords Book
Everything® Easy Kakuro Book, $9.95
Everything® Easy Large-Print Crosswords Book
Everything® Games Book, 2nd Ed.
Everything® Giant Sudoku Book, $9.95
Everything® Giant Word Search Book
Everything® Kakuro Challenge Book, $9.95
Everything® Large-Print Crossword Challenge Book
Everything® Large-Print Crosswords Book
Everything® Lateral Thinking Puzzles Book, $9.95
Everything® Literary Crosswords Book, $9.95
Everything® Mazes Book
Everything® Memory Booster Puzzles Book, $9.95
Everything® Movie Crosswords Book, $9.95

Everything® Music Crosswords Book, $9.95
Everything® Online Poker Book
Everything® Pencil Puzzles Book, $9.95
Everything® Poker Strategy Book
Everything® Pool & Billiards Book
Everything® Puzzles for Commuters Book, $9.95
Everything® Puzzles for Dog Lovers Book, $9.95
Everything® Sports Crosswords Book, $9.95
Everything® Test Your IQ Book, $9.95
Everything® Texas Hold 'Em Book, $9.95
Everything® Travel Crosswords Book, $9.95
Everything® TV Crosswords Book, $9.95
Everything® Word Games Challenge Book
Everything® Word Scramble Book
Everything® Word Search Book

HEALTH

Everything® Alzheimer's Book
Everything® Diabetes Book
Everything® First Aid Book, $9.95
Everything® Health Guide to Adult Bipolar Disorder
Everything® Health Guide to Arthritis
Everything® Health Guide to Controlling Anxiety
Everything® Health Guide to Depression
Everything® Health Guide to Fibromyalgia
Everything® Health Guide to Menopause, 2nd Ed.
Everything® Health Guide to Migraines
Everything® Health Guide to OCD
Everything® Health Guide to PMS
Everything® Health Guide to Postpartum Care
Everything® Health Guide to Thyroid Disease
Everything® Hypnosis Book
Everything® Low Cholesterol Book
Everything® Menopause Book
Everything® Nutrition Book
Everything® Reflexology Book
Everything® Stress Management Book

HISTORY

Everything® American Government Book
Everything® American History Book, 2nd Ed.
Everything® Civil War Book
Everything® Freemasons Book
Everything® Irish History & Heritage Book
Everything® Middle East Book
Everything® World War II Book, 2nd Ed.

HOBBIES

Everything® Candlemaking Book
Everything® Cartooning Book
Everything® Coin Collecting Book
Everything® Digital Photography Book, 2nd Ed.
Everything® Drawing Book
Everything® Family Tree Book, 2nd Ed.
Everything® Knitting Book
Everything® Knots Book
Everything® Photography Book
Everything® Quilting Book

Everything® Sewing Book
Everything® Soapmaking Book, 2nd Ed.
Everything® Woodworking Book

HOME IMPROVEMENT

Everything® Feng Shui Book
Everything® Feng Shui Decluttering Book, $9.95
Everything® Fix-It Book
Everything® Green Living Book
Everything® Home Decorating Book
Everything® Home Storage Solutions Book
Everything® Homebuilding Book
Everything® Organize Your Home Book, 2nd Ed.

KIDS' BOOKS

All titles are $7.95
Everything® Fairy Tales Book, $14.95
Everything® Kids' Animal Puzzle & Activity Book
Everything® Kids' Astronomy Book
Everything® Kids' Baseball Book, 5th Ed.
Everything® Kids' Bible Trivia Book
Everything® Kids' Bugs Book
Everything® Kids' Cars and Trucks Puzzle and Activity Book
Everything® Kids' Christmas Puzzle & Activity Book
**Everything® Kids' Connect the Dots
    Puzzle and Activity Book**
Everything® Kids' Cookbook
Everything® Kids' Crazy Puzzles Book
Everything® Kids' Dinosaurs Book
Everything® Kids' Environment Book
Everything® Kids' Fairies Puzzle and Activity Book
Everything® Kids' First Spanish Puzzle and Activity Book
Everything® Kids' Football Book
Everything® Kids' Gross Cookbook
Everything® Kids' Gross Hidden Pictures Book
Everything® Kids' Gross Jokes Book
Everything® Kids' Gross Mazes Book
Everything® Kids' Gross Puzzle & Activity Book
Everything® Kids' Halloween Puzzle & Activity Book
Everything® Kids' Hidden Pictures Book
Everything® Kids' Horses Book
Everything® Kids' Joke Book
Everything® Kids' Knock Knock Book
Everything® Kids' Learning French Book
Everything® Kids' Learning Spanish Book
Everything® Kids' Magical Science Experiments Book
Everything® Kids' Math Puzzles Book
Everything® Kids' Mazes Book
Everything® Kids' Money Book
Everything® Kids' Nature Book
Everything® Kids' Pirates Puzzle and Activity Book
Everything® Kids' Presidents Book
Everything® Kids' Princess Puzzle and Activity Book
Everything® Kids' Puzzle Book
Everything® Kids' Racecars Puzzle and Activity Book
Everything® Kids' Riddles & Brain Teasers Book
Everything® Kids' Science Experiments Book
Everything® Kids' Sharks Book
Everything® Kids' Soccer Book
Everything® Kids' Spies Puzzle and Activity Book
Everything® Kids' States Book
Everything® Kids' Travel Activity Book
Everything® Kids' Word Search Puzzle and Activity Book

LANGUAGE

Everything® Conversational Japanese Book with CD, $19.95
Everything® French Grammar Book
Everything® French Phrase Book, $9.95
Everything® French Verb Book, $9.95
Everything® German Practice Book with CD, $19.95
Everything® Inglés Book
Everything® Intermediate Spanish Book with CD, $19.95
Everything® Italian Practice Book with CD, $19.95
Everything® Learning Brazilian Portuguese Book with CD, $19.95
Everything® Learning French Book with CD, 2nd Ed., $19.95
Everything® Learning German Book
Everything® Learning Italian Book
Everything® Learning Latin Book
Everything® Learning Russian Book with CD, $19.95
Everything® Learning Spanish Book
Everything® Learning Spanish Book with CD, 2nd Ed., $19.95
Everything® Russian Practice Book with CD, $19.95
Everything® Sign Language Book
Everything® Spanish Grammar Book
Everything® Spanish Phrase Book, $9.95
Everything® Spanish Practice Book with CD, $19.95
Everything® Spanish Verb Book, $9.95
Everything® Speaking Mandarin Chinese Book with CD, $19.95

MUSIC

Everything® Bass Guitar Book with CD, $19.95
Everything® Drums Book with CD, $19.95
Everything® Guitar Book with CD, 2nd Ed., $19.95
Everything® Guitar Chords Book with CD, $19.95
Everything® Harmonica Book with CD, $15.95
Everything® Home Recording Book
Everything® Music Theory Book with CD, $19.95
Everything® Reading Music Book with CD, $19.95
Everything® Rock & Blues Guitar Book with CD, $19.95
Everything® Rock & Blues Piano Book with CD, $19.95
Everything® Songwriting Book

NEW AGE

Everything® Astrology Book, 2nd Ed.
Everything® Birthday Personology Book
Everything® Dreams Book, 2nd Ed.
Everything® Love Signs Book, $9.95
Everything® Love Spells Book, $9.95
Everything® Paganism Book
Everything® Palmistry Book
Everything® Psychic Book
Everything® Reiki Book
Everything® Sex Signs Book, $9.95
Everything® Spells & Charms Book, 2nd Ed.
Everything® Tarot Book, 2nd Ed.
Everything® Toltec Wisdom Book
Everything® Wicca & Witchcraft Book, 2nd Ed.

PARENTING

Everything® Baby Names Book, 2nd Ed.
Everything® Baby Shower Book, 2nd Ed.
Everything® Baby Sign Language Book with DVD
Everything® Baby's First Year Book
Everything® Birthing Book

Everything® Breastfeeding Book
Everything® Father-to-Be Book
Everything® Father's First Year Book
Everything® Get Ready for Baby Book, 2nd Ed.
Everything® Get Your Baby to Sleep Book, $9.95
Everything® Getting Pregnant Book
Everything® Guide to Pregnancy Over 35
Everything® Guide to Raising a One-Year-Old
Everything® Guide to Raising a Two-Year-Old
Everything® Guide to Raising Adolescent Boys
Everything® Guide to Raising Adolescent Girls
Everything® Mother's First Year Book
Everything® Parent's Guide to Childhood Illnesses
Everything® Parent's Guide to Children and Divorce
Everything® Parent's Guide to Children with ADD/ADHD
Everything® Parent's Guide to Children with Asperger's Syndrome
Everything® Parent's Guide to Children with Asthma
Everything® Parent's Guide to Children with Autism
Everything® Parent's Guide to Children with Bipolar Disorder
Everything® Parent's Guide to Children with Depression
Everything® Parent's Guide to Children with Dyslexia
Everything® Parent's Guide to Children with Juvenile Diabetes
Everything® Parent's Guide to Positive Discipline
Everything® Parent's Guide to Raising a Successful Child
Everything® Parent's Guide to Raising Boys
Everything® Parent's Guide to Raising Girls
Everything® Parent's Guide to Raising Siblings
Everything® Parent's Guide to Sensory Integration Disorder
Everything® Parent's Guide to Tantrums
Everything® Parent's Guide to the Strong-Willed Child
Everything® Parenting a Teenager Book
Everything® Potty Training Book, $9.95
Everything® Pregnancy Book, 3rd Ed.
Everything® Pregnancy Fitness Book
Everything® Pregnancy Nutrition Book
Everything® Pregnancy Organizer, 2nd Ed., $16.95
Everything® Toddler Activities Book
Everything® Toddler Book
Everything® Tween Book
Everything® Twins, Triplets, and More Book

PETS

Everything® Aquarium Book
Everything® Boxer Book
Everything® Cat Book, 2nd Ed.
Everything® Chihuahua Book
Everything® Cooking for Dogs Book
Everything® Dachshund Book
Everything® Dog Book, 2nd Ed.
Everything® Dog Grooming Book
Everything® Dog Health Book
Everything® Dog Obedience Book
Everything® Dog Owner's Organizer, $16.95
Everything® Dog Training and Tricks Book
Everything® German Shepherd Book
Everything® Golden Retriever Book
Everything® Horse Book
Everything® Horse Care Book
Everything® Horseback Riding Book
Everything® Labrador Retriever Book
Everything® Poodle Book
Everything® Pug Book

Everything® Puppy Book
Everything® Rottweiler Book
Everything® Small Dogs Book
Everything® Tropical Fish Book
Everything® Yorkshire Terrier Book

REFERENCE

Everything® American Presidents Book
Everything® Blogging Book
Everything® Build Your Vocabulary Book, $9.95
Everything® Car Care Book
Everything® Classical Mythology Book
Everything® Da Vinci Book
Everything® Divorce Book
Everything® Einstein Book
Everything® Enneagram Book
Everything® Etiquette Book, 2nd Ed.
Everything® Guide to C. S. Lewis & Narnia
Everything® Guide to Edgar Allan Poe
Everything® Guide to Understanding Philosophy
Everything® Inventions and Patents Book
Everything® Jacqueline Kennedy Onassis Book
Everything® John F. Kennedy Book
Everything® Mafia Book
Everything® Martin Luther King Jr. Book
Everything® Philosophy Book
Everything® Pirates Book
Everything® Private Investigation Book
Everything® Psychology Book
Everything® Public Speaking Book, $9.95
Everything® Shakespeare Book, 2nd Ed.

RELIGION

Everything® Angels Book
Everything® Bible Book
Everything® Bible Study Book with CD, $19.95
Everything® Buddhism Book
Everything® Catholicism Book
Everything® Christianity Book
Everything® Gnostic Gospels Book
Everything® History of the Bible Book
Everything® Jesus Book
Everything® Jewish History & Heritage Book
Everything® Judaism Book
Everything® Kabbalah Book
Everything® Koran Book
Everything® Mary Book
Everything® Mary Magdalene Book
Everything® Prayer Book
Everything® Saints Book, 2nd Ed.
Everything® Torah Book
Everything® Understanding Islam Book
Everything® Women of the Bible Book
Everything® World's Religions Book

SCHOOL & CAREERS

Everything® Career Tests Book
Everything® College Major Test Book
Everything® College Survival Book, 2nd Ed.
Everything® Cover Letter Book, 2nd Ed.
Everything® Filmmaking Book
Everything® Get-a-Job Book, 2nd Ed.
Everything® Guide to Being a Paralegal
Everything® Guide to Being a Personal Trainer
Everything® Guide to Being a Real Estate Agent
Everything® Guide to Being a Sales Rep
Everything® Guide to Being an Event Planner
Everything® Guide to Careers in Health Care
Everything® Guide to Careers in Law Enforcement
Everything® Guide to Government Jobs
Everything® Guide to Starting and Running a Catering Business
Everything® Guide to Starting and Running a Restaurant
Everything® Job Interview Book, 2nd Ed.
Everything® New Nurse Book
Everything® New Teacher Book
Everything® Paying for College Book
Everything® Practice Interview Book
Everything® Resume Book, 3rd Ed.
Everything® Study Book

SELF-HELP

Everything® Body Language Book
Everything® Dating Book, 2nd Ed.
Everything® Great Sex Book
Everything® Self-Esteem Book
Everything® Tantric Sex Book

SPORTS & FITNESS

Everything® Easy Fitness Book
Everything® Fishing Book
Everything® Krav Maga for Fitness Book
Everything® Running Book, 2nd Ed.

TRAVEL

Everything® Family Guide to Coastal Florida
Everything® Family Guide to Cruise Vacations
Everything® Family Guide to Hawaii
Everything® Family Guide to Las Vegas, 2nd Ed.
Everything® Family Guide to Mexico
Everything® Family Guide to New England, 2nd Ed.
Everything® Family Guide to New York City, 3rd Ed.
Everything® Family Guide to RV Travel & Campgrounds
Everything® Family Guide to the Caribbean
Everything® Family Guide to the Disneyland® Resort, California Adventure®, Universal Studios®, and the Anaheim Area, 2nd Ed.
Everything® Family Guide to the Walt Disney World Resort®, Universal Studios®, and Greater Orlando, 5th Ed.
Everything® Family Guide to Timeshares
Everything® Family Guide to Washington D.C., 2nd Ed.

WEDDINGS

Everything® Bachelorette Party Book, $9.95
Everything® Bridesmaid Book, $9.95
Everything® Destination Wedding Book
Everything® Father of the Bride Book, $9.95
Everything® Groom Book, $9.95
Everything® Mother of the Bride Book, $9.95
Everything® Outdoor Wedding Book
Everything® Wedding Book, 3rd Ed.
Everything® Wedding Checklist, $9.95
Everything® Wedding Etiquette Book, $9.95
Everything® Wedding Organizer, 2nd Ed., $16.95
Everything® Wedding Shower Book, $9.95
Everything® Wedding Vows Book, $9.95
Everything® Wedding Workout Book
Everything® Weddings on a Budget Book, 2nd Ed., $9.95

WRITING

Everything® Creative Writing Book
Everything® Get Published Book, 2nd Ed.
Everything® Grammar and Style Book, 2nd Ed.
Everything® Guide to Magazine Writing
Everything® Guide to Writing a Book Proposal
Everything® Guide to Writing a Novel
Everything® Guide to Writing Children's Books
Everything® Guide to Writing Copy
Everything® Guide to Writing Graphic Novels
Everything® Guide to Writing Research Papers
Everything® Improve Your Writing Book, 2nd Ed.
Everything® Writing Poetry Book